Anti-Social Policy

Anti-Social Policy
Welfare, Ideology and the Disciplinary State

Peter Squires
Lecturer in Social Policy, Brighton Polytechnic

HARVESTER WHEATSHEAF

New York   London   Toronto   Sydney   Tokyo   Singapore

First published 1990 by
Harvester Wheatsheaf
66 Wood Lane End, Hemel Hempstead
Hertfordshire HP2 4RG
A division of
Simon & Schuster International Group

Typeset in 10/12 pt Times
by Input Typesetting Ltd., London

Printed and bound in Great Britain by
BPCC Wheatons Ltd, Exeter

British Library Cataloguing in Publication Data

Squires, Peter, *1958–*
    Anti-social policy: welfare, ideology and the
    disciplinary state.
    1. Governments. Social policies
    I. Title
    361.61

    ISBN 0–7450–0476–8
    ISBN 0–7450–0810–0 pbk

1 2 3 4 5 94 93 92 91 90

For Kathy, with love

Contents

Preface and acknowledgements

We began to become aware . . . at the beginning of the sixties that,
having eliminated responsibility from the sphere of social relations,
the disposition of State and individuals is such that the former has
to make *allocations* to everyone as the price of the *promised*
progress for which it is responsible, while individuals settle for being
permanent *claimants* from the State as compensation for the grip
on their *evolution* of which it has dispossessed them. And it is that
between state and individuals, so it comes to be said, there is no
longer a society.
(From J. Donzelot, *L'invention du sociale*. Paris 1984. Translated
by G. Burchell in *Economy and Society* vol. 17, no. 3, 1988,
(emphasis in original).

'There is no such thing as society . . .'
(Margaret Thatcher, speech to Conservative Political Centre, 1988)

In 1989, whilst the final drafts of this book were being completed, Mrs
Thatcher's government still remained adamant in its refusal to accept
even a watered-down version of the European Community's Social
Charter. This rejection provides an important point of reference for a
number of the ideas developed later within the book. The Prime Minister was not alone amongst senior Conservatives in referring to the
European Social Charter as nothing but a form of 'socialism by the
back door'. Yet aside from what such remarks reveal about the extent
of the Thatcher government's commitment to European partnership –
only by the tradesman's entrance, thank you – my particular interest
centred upon Thatcherism's apparent attempt to erase every last trace

of 'socialism' and to subvert, transform, reorient or expunge everything hitherto prefaced by the adjective 'social'. It is as if the New Right had suddenly acquired the ability, and the will, to peer beyond what Hayek termed the 'mirage of social justice' and rediscover the foundations of an alternative political and economic order.

Yet the reconstruction of a political order steeped in liberal individualism raises fundamental questions for the analysis and development of 'social' policies – questions that the assorted disciplines making up the field of social policy have scarcely begun to tackle. Simply put, if the New Right rejects society and proposes the abandonment of 'social' justice and the stripping-down of 'social' policy, then just what kind of 'anti-social' culture might its members have in mind? How might we describe, other than by the designation 'anti-social policy', proposals which increase the distance between rich and poor in terms of health, housing and education; proposals which increase dependency upon inadequate means-tested benefits and increase the numbers of the homeless; policies which further imperil the environment; or legislation which systematically dismantles local democracy, centralises political power and undermines civil liberties?

Certainly such policies are 'anti-social'. Hayek advocated the abandonment of 'the social' in the mid–1970s and over a decade later New Right politicians have made their intentions quite plain. But in a paradoxical fashion, such policies are also part of 'the social', they are deeply implicated in its machinations. 'The social' hardly thwarted the revolutionary power of capitalist development, for a while it even became its most successful offspring. The divisions and disciplines, restrictions and regulations now exacerbated in an authoritarian political culture were always part and parcel of 'the social'. In a sense, 'the social' scarcely lived up to its promise but then, given the conditions of its emergence, this is hardly surprising. In one epoch 'the social' might be said to have represented the free spirits of civil society, a foundation for claims of right, freedom and citizenship, in later periods it has stood for a more mundane promise of welfare. While 'the social' has never been a true expression of consensus, more recently as the fortunes of consensus politics have appeared rather bleak, consensus politicians and academics have sought to claim it as their own. Of course, the underlying point is that 'the social' has changed. It is changing still and we ought to remain alert to its contemporary metamorphoses.

As the preceding remarks might suggest, the concerns of this book traverse a number of social science disciplines. Its central preoccupation is with what might be called an 'alternative' history of social policy. In this sense, social historians and those involved in the development of social policy might find Chapters 4 to 7 of most interest. Likewise, social administrators, most directly interested in the post-war Welfare State and the recent restructuring of social welfare, might find the introduction and the last two chapters of most relevance. Finally, people working on social and political theory might be most interested in the themes of the first three chapters and in Chapter 8. For myself, I should prefer the book to be taken as a whole. The historical sections, informed by new theoretical work, seek to elaborate a new approach to social policy analysis. In turn, the new analyses serve as the basis for a new critique and for new insights for the future development of social policies.

Consequently, in the course of the following chapters and through an historical review of an increasingly 'social' preoccupation at the centre of governmental activity, I have tried to illustrate something of the origins, transformations and tensions at the heart of 'the social'. Chapter 1 addresses what might be called the 'dilemma of the social' and seeks to expose the naïve, one-dimensional reformism implicit in many interpretations of social policy development. The chapter tries to take seriously Richard Titmuss's own observation that some 'welfare states' could be very 'anti-social' indeed. In Chapter 2 I try to explore this theme further by reference to some of the prominent dimensions of 'the social', in particular: its relation to an idea of civil society; its proximity to conceptions of the nation; its connection with the state; its interaction with conceptions of 'socialism'; and finally, its relationship to an ideal of 'welfare'.

One of the underlying themes of the opening chapters is the recognition that social policy operates very much as a double-edged sword, disseminating advantages and disadvantages, benefits and sanctions. These themes are further developed in order to outline an approach to a distinctly 'social' series of disciplinary policy mechanisms within the era of the Welfare State. Moral and judicial forms of control and coercion are displaced by more efficient and self-sustaining processes of security and advancement that are central to the operation of contemporary relations of welfare.

Chapters 3 to 6 chart the development of an increasingly state-centred discourse of 'social politics'. Beginning with early interventions into the lives of the poor by alms-givers, moralists, statisticians and reformers, the sequence of chapters traces the refinement and extension of techniques of 'social' disciplining associated with the appearance of a politics focusing on principles of liberal political order and capitalist competitive individualism. These developments are pursued through the implementation of the nineteenth-century Poor Law, the flowering of late nineteenth-century philanthropy, the emergence of collectivist forms of solidarity especially the introduction of insurantial techniques and fin-ally, after the Second World War, the simultaneous expansion and individualisation of forms of social security and personal incentive.

The final chapter deals with a number of tensions appearing within 'social' discourses in recent years. These tensions have taken two related forms, efforts to erase specific references to a social politics and to free the market of its erstwhile 'social' responsibilities, and attempts to 'socialise' institutions and processes hitherto considered quite antitheti-cal to a 'social' interest. In effect, 'the social' is being dismantled and reassembled around the celebrated landmarks of liberalism and monuments to the private sector. The 'social market', the family, the superstore, the leisure centre, the personal pension scheme and com-pany car all begin to acquire an increasingly explicit 'social' interest.

In achieving this dislocation of 'the social', the New Right govern-ments of the 1980s have begun to realise their own visionary sense that, 'there is no such thing as society'. They have effectively exploited the frustrated and dispossessed individualisms of the contemporary political culture. The constructed discourses of 'the social' wielded by the state's 'social' institutions and the 'social' professions bear precious little relation to the aspirations of civil society that the progressive and democratic socialist tradition has long embraced. Considering these issues, and endeavouring to discover some new life within 'the social', the book draws to a close.

At times the book and the research which preceded it, draws fairly heavily upon analysis of important documents in the history of social policy development. It is sometimes suggested that this is an inadequate approach to the study of policy development, that it implies conspiracy by privileging the intentions of the authors of such documents or, conversely, it is claimed that there are 'no people' in the story. At times I am inclined to agree with some of these contrasting criticisms. But I have maintained all along that the project has been an attempt to develop a new form of theoretical analysis and an alternative concep-tion of the subject matter of Social Policy. Perhaps when one endeav-ours to establish a new approach, one can be forgiven for sometimes understating the old. Even so, conspiracy theory is hardly my ambition. There are undoubtedly conspiracies but, more often than not, my objec-tive has been to elaborate and elucidate the discourses of 'the social' through which the conspirators (people) have sought to erect their programmes, policies and institutions, or within which the conspirators (people) have been caught. Throughout the book I have tried to avoid resorting to sexist language except where the point is specifically intended to refer to men.

Much of the groundwork for the book was done during the early 1980s, sponsored by what must have been one of the last Social Science Research Council (SSRC) quota awards. I should like to thank Professor Roy Parker and the staff of the Department of Social Administration, University of Bristol, for their confidence in my ability to take on the project. Above all, however, thanks must go to Paddy Hillyard, my supervisor during those years. Research that was primarily theoretical, involving not just Marxism but especially the work of Foucault, seemed to brush against the grain of much that went by the name of Social Policy and Administration. Paddy gave constant encouragement and provided support when it was most needed. Above all, he gave his commitment and a strong sense that the project was important. It goes without saying, however, that neither he nor any of the following people bear any responsibility for the final arguments or analysis.

At various points during the project, a number of other individuals contributed their time and their ideas. Roy Parker and Suzanne MacGregor read a rather overlengthy Ph.D. thesis. Max Krafchik, David Watson, Lyn Harrison, Robert Reiner, David Bull, Bob Skelton, Bill Jordan, Peter Craig, Noelle Whiteside, Martin Hewitt, Peter Taylor-Gooby, Nigel South and Bob Fine consented to read and discuss early drafts and extracts of my work at times when typing, punctuation, grammar and, on occasion, length were sufficient to deter all but the most enthusiastic. Finally, I should like to thank the editors at Harvester Wheatsheaf, especially Clare Grist and Richard Leigh, for their help, support and encouragement throughout the process of the book's production.

Peter Squires
Brighton 1990

1
Anti-social policy?

This is a book about the emergence of a disciplinary 'welfare state' and about the punitive and coercive forms of social policy frequently deployed under the mantle of 'welfare'. It suggests that where the repressive, exploitative or sectarian features of a 'welfare state' intensify and develop to a sufficient level they risk overwhelming the state's claims to welfare altogether. At this point, social policy becomes 'anti-social' policy. Following an analysis of the accumulation of coercive power within the embrace of the state's 'welfare' policies and of the intensification of a disciplinary politics of welfare, the book suggests that we may be nearer this point than some might think.

Although my central themes are undoubtedly welfare and social policy I focus upon these mainly in order to concentrate upon the ways in which social policies are constructed and employed. I am less interested in poverty and inequality than in the roles they are made to play and, ultimately, less preoccupied with particular concepts of welfare than with the way welfare is incorporated into social and political discourses and transformed into a power relation.

In the course of the book, I shall be using the concept 'social' in two related ways: first, to represent a site of political intervention (society) – the site where conflicts over questions of welfare are fought out, second, to represent a particular kind of political rationality, a rationality addressing itself to the relations between individual and collective well-being and notions of moral order. Both of these aspects of 'the social' are recognised as clearly constructed features, although the concept as a whole has a sufficiently clear history to allow us to establish its meaning and significance. Thus, a key theme of the book is an examination of how particular constructions of 'the social' come to utilise poverty and inequality in different ways or deploy differing ideas about welfare. As the book progresses, a paradox I begin to identify is the fact that constructions of 'the social' (and certain ideologies of welfare) are frequently disciplinary in practice and profoundly 'anti-social' in their consequences. I consider some of the implications of this towards the end of the book.

Liberalism and the 'anti-social' market

Between the late 1970s and the late 1980s we witnessed some of the most wide-ranging transformations in the shape and structure of society and in the Welfare State. We have seen, in both Britain and the United States, neo-liberal governments ideologically committed to economic growth, often at the expense of 'social' priorities. Indeed, these governments would undoubtedly claim that economic growth *was* the key social priority. Britain, in particular, has had a government which has perceived the public sector as a burden upon the workings of the free market and which has pursued vigorous campaigns promoting the privatisation of the economy, the domestication of social care, and the centralisation of political authority. It has sought the retrenchment of civil liberties and advanced the power of private property, whilst defending the privileges of rank and reasserting the merits of inequality, patriarchy and nationalism.

At the end of such a period it might not seem too unreasonable to argue for the validity and integrity of an idea such as 'anti-social policy'. The term would be no more than a description of the government's political output since 1979. Indeed, policies which have widened inequalities and exacerbated social tensions, restricted rights to welfare, increased the numbers suffering from poverty or homelessness, or undermined the aspirations of many whilst leading even more people to suspect that the overall quality of life is declining, might well merit the label 'anti-social'.

In fact, an entire book could be taken up describing the 'anti-social' characteristics displayed by Thatcherism and the 'anti-social' consequences that 'new-right' policies have wrought in the fabric of society; in the aspirations of young people; in the character of our towns and countryside and in the relative harmony of the nation, now so seemingly divided by geography, class, gender, generation and race.

However, this is not such a book. In any event, such a project would be fundamentally misconceived. Rather like attributing the height of the waves to the person on the surfboard, any such study of the allegedly 'anti-social' consequences of the Thatcher governments would risk privileging those same governments with the authorship of political and economic developments of which they were, if sometimes aware, less often able to control (although recent governments have undoubtedly initiated a good deal of anti-social policy). However, any book concentrating primarily upon the 'anti-social' characteristics of present government policy might seem to imply the existence of some benevolent, socially integrative and normative social order predating Thatcherism. The image of such a social order, sometimes hinted at, sometimes boldly stated, in a language derived from either 'consensus politics' (Crosland, 1964; Abel-Smith, 1980) or conservative sociology (Bell, 1960; Marshall, 1963; Nisbet 1967; Robson, 1976) is part of our problem.

The social fabric has never been unruffled, except perhaps in our historical memory. In modern societies, the aspirations of young people have often been perceived only in a problematic light, whilst the divisions and political interests of class, gender, geography, generation and race have frequently counted for more than some concept of the national interest – so much so that it has often taken quite exceptional events to drum up any such notion. Evidently, the idea of a national interest or the principle of national harmony are socially constructed entities. Nevertheless, it is often precisely such a normative principle, which has long stood as one of Social Policy's key ideological reference points (Myrdal, 1960; Boulding, 1967; Titmuss, 1970; Watson, 1980).

Yet despite Titmuss's own major contribution to this tradition in the study of social welfare, he recognised that it could work in two opposing ways. The same policies which harmonised and integrated some social groups could divide and rule others; benefits to some could become barriers for others. In this light, social policy seems very much a double-edged sword; policies that help the middle class might harm the working class, those that advantage men might disadvantage women, systems that benefit mainly white people might discriminate against black people, and so on. As a result, one of the fundamental dilemmas faced by the discipline of Social Policy has been how it handles this double-edged character. In response we have seen the emergence of many critical, ideological and philosophical, traditions within the discipline, most notably Marxism, feminism, anti-racism and, more recently, the green movement. But welfare has not been dragged down under the weight of its own contradictions, it still denotes a generally 'good thing', and the discipline of Social Policy also appears to have survived, if not completely unscathed, at least intact in its broadest essentials. How are we to account for this strange ability to survive? Part of the answer has to do with what we might call its unique 'ideological tunnel vision', which has kept it on course and striving doggedly towards the light. But this vision was precisely the cause of Titmuss's scepticism in 1964.

> There is an assumption that the establishment of social welfare necessarily and inevitably contributes to the spread of humanism and the resolution of social injustice. The reverse can be true. Welfare can serve different masters. A multitude of sins may be committed in its appealing name. Welfare can be used as an instrument of economic growth which, by benefitting a minority, indirectly promotes greater inequality. Welfare may be used to serve military and racial ends – as in Hitler's Germany. . . . Welfare may be used to narrow allegiances and not to diffuse them – as in employers' fringe benefit systems. . . . What matters then, what indeed is fundamental to the health of welfare, is the objective to which its face is set: to universalize humanistic ethics and the social rights of citizenship or to divide, discriminate and compete.
>
> (Titmuss, 1964)

So in studying Social Policy we necessarily begin with a problem. It is this problem, concerning the 'ends' of social policy, that the present book seeks to address.

I have suggested that whilst it is possible to criticise the 'anti-social' character of the policies of the Thatcher governments, this is not my primary objective. I also suggested that the government and its sup-porters might well claim that rolling back the state, increasing inequality, advancing private ownership and reasserting family values are fundamentally *'social'* policies embracing *social* priorities. In fact, this is precisely what they do claim. 'Free markets and limited govern-ment', it is suggested, will maximise a range of essentially 'social' priorities, 'better than any known alternative' (Barry, 1987, p. 26). The claim is that markets create choice and freedom, that inequality is the spur to initiative and that, together, privatisation and domestication enhance personal responsibility and family values. 'Not only mere eco-nomic realism, but also a more deep-seated moral regeneration,' as Green puts it (Green, 1987, p. 218, but see also Friedman, 1980; Thatcher in Ungerson, 1985; Minford, 1987).

But this is hardly satisfactory. Neo-liberal social theory, with its emphasis on individualism, freedom and choice, runs into difficulties with 'the social'. Hirsch has criticised the modern neo-liberals' tendency to assert the 'law of the market' and the pure doctrine of self-interest without any accompanying 'social' considerations – indeed, his analysis of the 'crisis' of liberal capitalism rests upon his argument that liberal capitalism progressively erodes its own 'social' and moral foundations. He writes 'the principle of self-interest is incomplete as a social organis-ing device. It operates effectively only in tandem with some supporting social principle. This fundamental characteristic of economic liberalism . . . has been lost sight of by its modern protagonists' (Hirsch, 1977, p. 12; see also Taylor-Gooby, 1983). And as Barry has acknowledged, 'liberals have recognised that there is some truth in the frequent accusation of "economism", i.e. that they have no *social* theory apart from the application of economic principles to all social phenomena', and he goes on to add, 'almost all liberals would now concede that economics alone is not a sufficient base to found a social theory' (Barry, 1987a, p. 25, emphasis added). Yet the many 'silences' in liberalism cannot simply be filled with a 'social' content, precisely because liberalism has long seen its central task as denying the authenticity of 'socially inspired' forms of order.

Above all, however, it is in Hayek's work, especially *The Mirage of Social Justice* (Hayek, 1976) that one of the most insistent rejections of 'the social' can be found. For Hayek 'the social' is a very specific concept, once it is extended beyond its literal connotations, 'pertaining to, or characteristic of the structure and operations of a society', then for him it ceased to be meaningful. His objection to its more general use was that it seemed to hold 'society as a whole' responsible for the welfare and material condition of each subject and suggested that society 'should be deliberately directed to particular results', that is to say, planned (Hayek, 1976, pp. 78–9). The very idea was anathema to Hayek's brand of individualism. On this reading then, liberal philosophy cannot construct for itself an adequate theory of 'society' or of 'social' order, capable of supplementing economics simply by drawing on concepts and principles taken from a 'social' discourse. For, by claiming that values, ethical principles and a social morality underpin our ideas of social order, a social discourse presumes that conceptions of society rest upon firmer foundations than the instrumental individualism posited by modern neo-liberalism. As we have seen in Hayek, 'the social' is merely, 'something which has developed as a practice of individual action in the course of social evolution' (p. 78).

Thus, the claim that the neo-liberals are promoting a new, specifically 'social', order, or the suggestion that 'society' features at all in their legislative programme, is at best disingenuous. After all, as Barry himself has remarked, 'there is no collective organic entity called "society" or the "public" which is not reducible to individual experiences' (Barry, 1983). Likewise, it was none other than Margaret Thatcher who, in 1988, solemnly declared that there was 'no such thing as society' (*Sunday Times*, 9 November 1988). The same year, during her controversial speech to the Assembly of the Church of Scotland, Mrs Thatcher went on to claim that it was, above all, within the family that the 'nursery of civic virtue' lay, and consequently upon the family that governments ought to build their policies for 'welfare, education and care' (Thatcher, in Raban, 1989). So if Thatcherism considers society a fiction and if New-Right governments have directed policies, not towards society itself but, rather towards some of its smaller 'platoons' – the family and the neighbourhood, (Hurd, 1988) – then this must represent the very essence of an 'anti-social' policy.

From this perspective, it might seem that 'anti-social' policies are neither specifically harsh, sectarian nor vindictive. They are simply policies ignorant of 'society' or, to go further, they are policies designed to dissipate the spurious or allegedly harmful collectivities of a bygone age and replace them with new realms of choice and freedom. Of course, for the Prime Minister and her colleagues 'the social' and socialism have always been synonymous and they have often declared themselves determined to eliminate socialism (see Tebbit, 1988).

'Anti-social' policy, in this sense, becomes simply the collective name given to policies guided by another political rationality – a rationality derived from liberalism and classical political economy and oriented to the needs and demands of the individual, his [*sic*] family, his property and his immediate community. In this use of the concept, 'anti-social' need not spell something unpleasant. Nor, unlike the terms 'anti-racist' or 'anti-communist', need it indicate a complete opposition, in this case an opposition to the idea of society. Put simply, the anti-social refers to a kind of absolute individualism; to individual freedom, individual choice and the ability to enhance one's welfare. Somewhat paradoxically, however, these represent some of the highest ideals of 'the social' itself. For liberalism, therefore, perhaps the irony of 'the social' is that its highest attainment is its dissolution, just as for liberals the true object of the Welfare State, 'is to teach people how to do without it' (Peacock, 1961).

This is all very fine, but of course a political community without some foundations of collective welfare and a range of democratic rights could turn out to be very unpleasant indeed – 'solitary, poor, nasty, brutish and short', to borrow Hobbes's famous phrase. The niceties of neo-liberal philosophy notwithstanding, 'anti-social' policy has another, much simpler, meaning: namely, policies to create avarice and discontent, institutions to foster inequality and discrimination, structures to centralise power and cultivate authoritarianism and, perhaps above all, welfare that ignores need and responds only to consumer demand backed by hard cash. This 'anti-social' legacy of the New Right is undoubtedly much more real and immediate. Yet it would be a mistake to overlook the more specifically historical, discursive and ideological transformations undergone by society and 'the social', if only because it is from these that many of the underlying principles for the development of welfare are derived. For, as Titmuss has already assured us, what *really* matters in the study of social policy, is the objective towards which the face of welfare is set.

Restructuring 'the social'

This is not all there is to it, however. Liberals, in government and out, are seeking far more than the dissolution of a political philosophy. They have their sights set upon a political movement, upon the social structures, institutions and discourses of collectivism. 'The social' is being actively reconstituted and reconstructed, and with it, society also.

But if society is restructured and 'the social' as a distinctive discourse dispersed or transformed, the reference points of social policy will have disappeared. Entering these difficult times, social policy's moral vision will become simply kaleidoscopic. Its reassuring tunnel vision will no longer dictate a course and the light at the end of the tunnel will have gone out. A relatively coherent discourse of 'the social' is crucial to the survival of the discipline of Social Policy but, at the beginning of the 1990s, its future is uncertain. In the chapter which follows, some of the levels and dimensions of 'the social', suggesting a number of its political and ideological roots, are considered. The chapter concludes with a brief sketch of the problems faced.

As was suggested earlier, I am acknowledging and using the adjective 'social' as a particular kind of constructed concept. Using the concept this way, I have in mind 'the social' as an arena – society, or 'social' space, the 'social' terrain. Just as society itself is a fabricated entity (rather like our concepts of the nation, or the national interest, considered earlier), 'the social' is similarly formed. Perhaps we can say that wars and legal systems typically form nation-states whereas ethnic identities, cultural traditions and social policies form societies. The discipline of social administration has had no difficulty with this formulation, 'the social' is a field of work or an area of activity. Just as the term 'business administration' spells administration in the field of business, 'social' policy and administration refers to policy and administration in the 'social sphere' – that is to say, society, or some component part of it (See Slack, 1966, p. 17). A similar point has been made by Parker, who argues that Social Policy is a 'field of study' (Parker, 1974). This is fairly straightforward; all that is suggested here is the additional idea that 'the social' is itself a field, a 'zone of intervention' or a 'political terrain'. It forms the battlesite for a range of competing political programmes, it is the space for which they compete. And as victories are secured or defeats registered, or simply as the balance of power shifts in the conflicts running throughout 'the social', its meaning and significance is inflected in different directions.

So 'the social' is constituted by power relations, formed by the ebb and flow of political forces. Like any other domain, if it is to serve, it must remain in subjection. This is one meaning, one level of significance, of the constructed idea of 'the social'. A second meaning involves understanding 'the social' not only as a terrain but also as a form of rationality, as a discourse or political language. This discourse takes the form of a loose affiliation of normative values, principles and objectives. We can say, therefore, that we have a 'social' discourse, that is, a normative political language to describe the appropriate structure and organisation of society. The discourse draws upon the disciplines of sociology, politics, economics, psychology, philosophy (more recently, Marxism, feminism and ecology) and has, we might claim, the discipline of Social Policy as its most practical embodiment.

To invoke the language of 'the social' has always been to speak for 'the people', to speak for their collective needs and aspirations, their institutions and values, their collective well-being. Or has it? Is this not precisely the enduring myth of 'the social', the very object of Titmuss's scepticism in 1964? Yet, notwithstanding Titmuss, in the above sense, 'the social' has typically featured as the limit to a practical debate about the common good. It effectively 'policed' what it was possible to say. Arguments which did not address themselves directly to the normative principles and objectives provided by 'the social' might not seem relevant, worse still, they might prove positively harmful, being preoccupied with 'philosophy', or 'Marxism' or, indeed, 'economics'. The discourses barely connected – as C. S. Loch, President of the Charity Organisation Society, recognised in 1910. 'Economic science does not supply the key to the social problem, it has been preoccupied with things rather than with men' (Loch, 1910).

Yet all this might change. 'The social' may have emerged in a burst of radical energy as 'civil society' declared itself 'a very Eden of the innate rights of man', the exclusive realm of freedom and equality (Marx, 1976, p. 280), but in the era of late capitalism and the extended state, the 'free spirits' of 'the social' have become colonised and contaminated. Capitalist relations of production, economic inequalities, state patriarchy, bureaucratic regulation and political intervention have usurped the supposed radicalism of 'the social'. Instead it has become a cultivated terrain and a sanitised discourse. Above all, it has been disciplined.

'The social' has always been a specifically fabricated ideal, never a blank space. It does not emerge uncontaminated from the mists of history. Like any society, 'the social' is constructed by particular forces at particular times and, like any society, is saturated with political intrigues, conflicts, alliances and memories. 'The social' comes to us loaded with meaning and significance. Here lies a clue to the normative and benevolent idealism historically associated with 'the social', for it spoke in the name of rationality, security, civilisation and freedom against the confining order of feudalism and the violent uncertainty of the 'state of nature' (see Frisby and Sayer, 1986). As we shall see, part of the problem of getting to grips with 'the social' lies in discovering its hidden meanings and understanding their significance. Yet, just as society itself is constructed on the basis of a series of relations, only some of which predominate, so the ideals and principles of the 'social sphere' are unequally weighted. The forms of power, the political relations, the ideologies, discourses and practices comprising 'the social', are not all of equal significance. To employ Gramsci's concept, a 'war of position' is taking place throughout 'the social'; hegemony (ideological and political domination) is being gained and lost, 'the social' is constantly in flux, although certain meanings appear to endure more readily than others. Understandably, the social and political forces which have the largest hand in the shaping and reshaping of societies are also the most effective manipulators of 'the social'.

Here, of course, lies the dilemma of 'the social', for the very forces which gave birth to this constellation of principles, practices and ideals may now be transforming it in fundamental and irretrievable ways. In the course of this book I attempt to interpret this evolution of 'the social' by tracing the development of an 'anti-social' policy – not, it must be said, an 'anti-social' policy taken to mean simply the dark side of the Welfare State, the flip side of the welfare ethic or even some teleological journey inexorably retracing T. H. Marshall's steps from citizenship and social equality to feudalism and servility. Rather, this pursuit of an 'anti-social' policy proceeds by way of an analysis of the punitive and coercive elements of state intervention, by way of the penal and deterrent features of social administration – in short, by way of an analysis of the inherently disciplinary relations of policy. I am by no means suggesting that these disciplinary features necessarily represent the whole of the policies in question, nor even that they always invalidate such benefits as are delivered or distributed, but they are seldom insignificant. As I suggested earlier, whilst this book takes questions of social policy and welfare as its substantive concerns I am, strictly, less directly concerned with issues of need or with rights than with the roles they are made to play and ultimately, less preoccupied with poverty and inequality than with the ways in which they become sites for political intervention, how they become incorporated into social and political discourses and transformed into a power relationship. This is the real meaning behind Titmuss's cautionary tale of welfare. What counts is what is done with it.

As I shall be showing, in different periods and contexts the disciplinary characteristics of welfare may ebb or flow. On occasion, the 'severities' of policy may appear quite contrary to a principle of welfare and it is then that we gain a glimpse of the 'anti-social'.

In a sense, this returns us to where we started, to the New Right and its political project. Thatcherism and its 'anti-social' policies can be taken as a sign that certain transformations at the heart of 'the social' are taking effect. 'The social' has not been banished (nor socialism extinguished, for that matter) but different discourses inhabiting its space and mobilising alternative norms, values, practices and objectives have begun to acquire its legitimacy. Poverty and inequality, authoritarianism and greed, racism, sexism and capitalism, hitherto thought quite incompatible with the spirit of 'the social', now seek justification in its name. The 'anti-social' has come of age.

But perhaps all is not lost. The reference to *different* discourses, or *alternative* norms, does suggest some remaining potential to the social. After surveying the evolution and development of the disciplinary 'welfare state' and the emergence of an 'anti-social' policy, we turn finally to consider just what this submerged potential might be.

2

The difficulty with 'the social'

The greatest semantic difficulty arises, inevitably, with the word 'social'. Nor is it made any easier today by the fact that so many disciplines, professions and groups claim it as a Christian name and, indeed, flourish it about as something distinctly different.

(Titmuss, 1974, p. 24)

This chapter is concerned with the emergence of what we might call 'the social' both as an *arena for* and as a *mode of* political intervention. This issue is fundamental in any attempt to delineate, theoretically and politically, the appropriate terrain and purposes of social policy. The adjective 'social' is frequently attached to all manner of regulative interventions into societies and populations. Yet seldom is the nature (or logic) of these 'social' practices made particularly explicit. This might strike us as surprising in the applied social sciences, a series of disciplines which claim to base their very *raison d'être* upon the integrity of this sphere of political, economic and moral rationality.

So what does this concept 'social' mean? What does it refer to? Within the field of social policy and administration, indeed throughout the entirety of the social sciences, we are accustomed to frequent references being made to the adjective 'social'. It has, seemingly, acquired a somewhat taken-for-granted status within the disciplines constituting the social and human sciences. As Donzelot remarks, 'we only have to open any newspaper to realise that the concept of the social covers such a range of meanings that it can easily be taken for a catch-all term' (Donzelot, 1979, p. 80). We accept, frequently and without much dispute, that the concept refers to, or pertains to, humans

11

as social beings or to 'society'. This latter term we claim to know well, it refers to something tangible, something concrete; the body of the population; the community of persons or subjects.

However, in different respects, 'the social' is both more and less than this. It is more in so far as 'the social', clearly a constructed arena, reflects its own quite particular processes of development, and any reference to 'the social', therefore, brings into play many important relations of power, knowledge and discipline. We are, in short, talking about much more than 'society in general'. Yet, at the same time, 'the social' refers to something rather less than society in general. It is not, to adopt Minson's phrase, entirely 'coterminous with the field of social relations', rather, it carries a more restricted meaning (Minson, 1985, p. 9). Yet the very polyvalence of 'the social' is indicative of a range of relations and connections requiring exploration to see if there is not 'a coherence and an effective articulation [to] its diverse senses' (Donzelot, 1979).

As will become clear, 'the social' emerged as a virtual ideological by-product of certain political interventions into the ordering of the population. As such it performed a role of naturalising and legitimating those interventions by reference to its own normative rationality. Today in the related disciplines of Social Policy and Social Administration and in the practice of Social Work it continues to play much the same role.

But these are not the only 'interventions' to which 'the social' is subject. Indeed, part of our difficulty today (and it is a particularly acute problem for applied social studies and the policy sciences) concerns precisely how and why 'the social' is changing now. It is clear that in recent decades, 'the social' has for the first time featured as an object of knowledge. The proliferation of forms of mass communication, the burgeoning information technologies and the related success of the social sciences in opening out 'the social' as an object of political and economic calculation mean that there are no longer so many dark recesses within the social sphere. The whole is emerging into the light; intelligible and calculable. We need to ask important questions about how strategies of domination and the power relationships they mobilise are able to traverse 'the social' and about the changes they are able to effect.

I shall demonstrate that the central issue that any analysis of contemporary 'social politics' must deal with involves the intensification of disciplinary relationships across 'the social'; the ever-tightening grip exerted upon 'the social' by forms of power and, finally, the expulsion from 'the social' of any autonomy or spontaneity that would allow us to see in it anything other than the effects of a successful domination. That these are vital issues for the field of social policy is without doubt.

We desperately need to break open 'the social' in order to comprehend what holds it together and how power relationships are insinuated within it and mobilised through it. We especially need to know how political, economic or 'personalist' rationalities (the discourses of the state, the market and the individual, respectively – perhaps the most powerful discourses at play within 'the social') gain ascendancy over one another through 'the social' and how, in doing so, they are able to transform it, reconstitute it or align it with new ideas and processes. In different periods, these hegemonic contests have taken different forms. The conflict between a traditionalist moral economy and the utilitarian political economy during the early nineteenth century were instrumental in the constitution of a political discourse on the 'Social Question' itself. Subsequently, liberalism and collectivism, have found 'the social' to be their major battleground. In the course of their skirmishing, it has been further developed and modernised (Yeo, 1979). And of course, in a period when the apparent contest between the discourses of the market and competitive individualism and those of state collectivism (conducted within, throughout and by constant reference to 'the social') is having so significant an impact upon social and political relations and social policy development, we are quite entitled to ask some rather searching questions of 'the social'.

Confronting civil society

In the late eighteenth and early nineteenth centuries, political economists and philosophers frequently referred to 'civil society', hoping to counterpose it (the domain of the 'free' individual) to the state. Civil society was considered as an almost naturalist arena, the sphere of private interests, desires and aspirations. In some respects, conceptions of 'civil society' might be seen to represent an important precursor to our more modern notions of 'the social'. Conversely, the state – the site of politics – was seen as an essentially separate institution, above and beyond the mass of personal and localised disputes of a population. In fact, as Marxists, feminists and pluralists alike have shown, this 'liberal' picture of the autonomy of the state, though fundamental to the Western political tradition, is profoundly misleading. But in their concern to dispute the impartiality of the state, critics often failed to pay sufficient attention to the model of civil society which was installed. We need to devote some attention to this side of the 'classical' equation. For to assume that the actual body of persons (to which the concept 'civil society' referred) possessed the same purposes, communal integrity and value frameworks as those attributed to them by philosophers intent on founding a basis for the particular political authority of the state, is to invite a profoundly idealist and tautological reading of history. Of course, such privileging of the political philosophers' visions of political authority is far from uncommon in the social and political sciences, but a highly unsatisfactory way of comprehending the development of a social order.

The effect of such idealist readings of social history is to attribute purposes or intentions to social institutions and latent meaning to contingent historical processes. In fact, as we shall see, 'the social' has evolved gradually and contingently – as a *space* – a surface upon which political forces have sought to inscribe certain meanings. Where they have been successful then 'the social' has acquired new significance. Beyond this strictly contingent development, its evolution has embodied neither a central theoretical principle nor an overarching philosophical ideal. Minson has underlined the point, 'social and political arrangements are not exemplifications of a general figure, society, with some overall character most fully expressed in the modern age; they are just – arrangements' (Minson, 1985, p. 82). Even so, one image of 'the social' has been effectively sustained and, paradoxically, all the more so to the extent that the state has expanded and developed its forms of intervention, and the market economy has tightened its grip over the means of subsistence. This is the image of 'the social' as separate or autonomous; the sphere of the personal and of human relations. It is, of course, the most enduring myth of 'the social'. Somehow, the very quantity and diversity of social relations seem to defy the existence of any unifying or originating principle or ideal.

Just as the development of the human sciences was occasioned by a series of significant developments within Western culture (Foucault, 1970), so we need to examine the construction of 'the social' as a central category in contemporary thought. Neither the human sciences nor the social discourses inherited a blank space constituted in advance, they did not pursue a trajectory previously established. Rather, their development reflected processes of conflict and correspondence as they came to define themselves in relation to the field of available human knowledge, in relation to each other and in relation to their objects. They represent a contested terrain constantly undergoing change and development. Likewise, for Donzelot, 'the social' needs to be *situated* in terms of its own particular conditions of emergence and *understood* in relation to its subsequent expansion and development.

'The social' is not society understood as the material and moral conditions that characterise a form of consolidation. It would appear to be rather the set of means which allow social life to escape material pressures and politico-moral uncertainties; the entire range of methods which make the members of a society relatively safe from the effects of economic fluctuations by providing a certain security – which give their existence possibilities of relations that are flexible enough, and internal stakes that are convincing enough, to avert the dislocation that divergences of interests and beliefs would entail.

(Donzelot, 1980, p. xxvi)

'The "social" is a distinct domain,' affirms Hirst, it does not refer to the whole of society (Hirst, 1981, p. 68). 'The social' can be seen to emerge within an historically specific conjuncture, in relation to the several attempts to resolve the 'social question'. This is to say, the problematic question of population management and political order which the late nineteenth century defined in 'social' terms. Donzelot's point is that,

The 'social' is the product . . . of a series of innovative interventions directed towards particular social evils. The social realm is an *artefact*, conditional on the appearance of certain forms of social organisation and certain objectives: mass education, the supervision of 'private' conducts in childrearing and health, public health measures, and attempts to eliminate pauperism.

(Hirst, *ibid.*)

This series of measures (amongst others) can be said to constitute 'the social' at its point of origin. Subsequently, the significance of social discourse has grown considerably. The coherence and integral nature of 'the social' rested not upon any particular political ideology or governmental programme, nor did it have any 'unity of design or single locus of direction.' (Hirst, 1981). Rather, and this is the crucial point, the coherence of 'the social' lay in the considerations of political order and integration, wealth and authority that it inspired in an age when they seemed to be under some considerable threat. From this limited point of origin, the most astonishing thing, for Donzelot, about 'the social' is 'the status that [it] has won in our heads, as something we take for granted' (Donzelot, 1980).

From these quite specific beginnings, 'the social' has truly blossomed to incorporate virtually all aspects of modern life – our loyalties, aspirations and well-being. The chatter of social discourses now completely surrounds us; at home, at work, in the media and the supermarket. Within these social discourses we find the values that make our culture whole. Always a contradictory ensemble, they provide the yardstick by which the programmes of competing political groupings are judged. Simultaneously, they supply the basic vocabulary out of which the languages of politics and morality are constructed. The myth of their longevity and ubiquity endorses our sense of common humanity, their continued presence as ideals is held up as testimony to our presumed progress. Yet we are rightly sceptical of these social discourses and the values they have come to embody – the more so to the extent that they appear to celebrate certain ideologically charged, and frequently profoundly 'anti-social', ideals.

We know very well that 'society' is no spontaneous or natural construction. Its emergence and its contemporary existence are clearly the result of certain military, economic, political, ideological and legal developments. And if our concept 'social' is in any way to reflect these developments, then it too must encompass the military, economic, political and ideological dimensions of social order. If the concept 'social' has any meaning then it must embrace those relations of power and authority by which societies are formed, transformed and sustained. Just as we are unable to freeze our concept of society in a single moment, neither can we embrace this or that aspect of 'the social'. It comes to us as a whole. It also comes to us from the past, any concept of 'society' will represent, often in a highly selective and prioritising way, certain aspects (values, relationships, institutions, etc.) of the collectivity to the relative exclusion of others.

Yet the problems with this notion of 'the social' are more complex. As we shall see later, ideals of welfare frequently reflect more than just beneficence, welfare must not be invested with a 'halo of altruism' and it is not indivisible. Furthermore, 'what is "welfare" for some groups may be "illfare" for others' (Titmuss, 1974). Similar problems relate to 'the social'. We cannot detach from the adjective 'social' all those negative, uncomfortable, punitive and coercive references with which it is associated.

Taken as a whole, these remarks on the concept of 'the social' force us to recognise in it both a complex series of references and a particular kind of constructed historical pedigree. This is to say, despite the normative framework of a great deal of work within the social and human sciences, the 'social' is not an unambiguous concept. There are many dimensions to it; the following discussions form part of an attempt to elaborate some of these.

Dimensions of 'the social'

'The social' and society

The first dimension of 'the social' relates to the idea of society itself. For Hayek, this was the only meaningful interpretation of 'social'

(Hayek, 1976), but for our purposes it is important to examine how a category established politically – the population – is reconstructed as a moral entity through the discourse of 'the social'. The population category is numerical and political, defined both by reference to ideas of territory and notions of political authority. According to Kay and Mott, the population category represents, 'the first and most fundamental category of modern political thought . . . the first category of political order' (Kay and Mott, 1982, pp. 85–6). Yet the population category is typically presented as a natural and near spontaneous emergence, a simple mass of persons or bodies. The science of demography, by its treatment of the population as a simple 'aggregation of human beings' (*ibid.*), has facilitated and reinforced the naturalistic representation of the idea of population thereby obliterating both its military/territorial aspect and also its political and disciplinary character.

For Kay and Mott, the failure to recognise political authority and the failure to recognise disciplinary order in the formation of populations are fundamental errors. Overlooking the latter (discipline and order) implied a failure to see something that was plain even to Malthus in 1798, whereas failing to acknowledge the former (political authority) implied accepting the inversion of political authority upon which modern liberalism is based. For, despite liberalism and social contract theory, the state should not be seen as the legitimate crystallisation of the political authority of a population; rather, the population typically forms the *object* of a prior political authority.

These remarks lead us to consider the coherence and integrity of our concept of 'society' itself. Whilst the category 'population' implies the existence of a prior sovereign authority and the ideals of 'nation' and 'race' a sense of biological and territorial identity and purpose, the concept 'society' presumes to represent a relatively integrated *moral* community. This presumption requires some further consideration for accepting this ideal of 'society' as a relatively harmonious community of interests overlooks the critical significance of important social divisions, primarily of class, gender, race and, increasingly, age.

Whilst differing perspectives within sociology have detailed the transition from gemeinschaft to gesellschaft conceptions of 'community' or, alternatively, from mechanical to organic foundations of social order, at an ideological level, it is the integrated moral community to which 'the social' aspires. This much is evident in work which endeavours to outline a normative philosophy of 'welfare' within the applied social sciences (Marshall, 1963; Robson, 1976; Weale, 1983). It is not difficult to identify similar aspirations in much of the initial advocacy of 'community care' (Plant, 1974; Scull, 1977). Yet, notwithstanding the precise 'social' guarantees institutionalised by reference to a 'social commitment to welfare', it is none the less true that commentators adhere firmly to a normative framework (social democracy) within which conflicts of interest and other divisions can be accommodated or resolved (Robson, 1976; Room, 1979). This is not the place to develop in any depth the critique of the normative frameworks of social democracy and welfarism. All that needs to be achieved here is to signal certain problems associated with the adoption of an integrated and harmonious conception of 'society' as the objective and *raison d'être* of welfare discourses.

As I pointed out earlier, society (and the social sphere which pertains to it) is a constructed entity. It is founded upon political, economic and, frequently, military relations. Historically, an economic conception of the objectives of territory and population became fully articulated at the same time that the modern social order became firmly established. Economic processes, imperialist traditions, conflict and conquest play a major part in laying the foundations of societies (Mann, 1987). Similarly, the social structure and internal composition of society are determined by relations of class, gender, race and, as is now increasingly being recognised, age. Our *collective* designation of these relations – as 'social relations' – is fairly meaningless. In this sense 'the social' simply throws a veil over a series of discrete processes. We may well wish to use the term 'social relations' as an umbrella term for a whole series of processes that we do not fully understand, but otherwise the analytical utility of the term is strictly limited. It obscures rather more than it reveals.

In many respects this is the key to the basic weakness of 'the social'; the veil of ignorance it draws over specific social processes – power relations, conflicts, hierarchies, structures of patriarchy or institutional racism – obscures the very relations that should be examined. A politically paralysing blindness, which inclines us to take an idea of *society as a whole* as the basis of analysis, is induced. This blindness makes us neglect the differing perceptions and experiences of different groups, constituencies and communities and leads us towards an essentially pluralist assumption about the equivalence of all sets of social relationships. The effect of this, of course, is to obliterate fundamental inequalities, and overlook political and ideological relations. Racism and sexism are ignored and the significance of central political and economic disciplines is underplayed within the social disciplines. We hardly need catalogue the attempts by Marxists, feminists and anti-racists to demonstrate the conflict and coercion integral to so much that goes by the name of social policy.

Clearly, the point of all this is not that we should simply try to reconstruct some new and suitably 'sensitised' ideological discourse with which to replace 'the social', but rather that the specific processes (conflicts, hierarchies, ideologies) that have hitherto been blanketed by our comforting discourse of 'the social' should be more fully spelled out. We should more readily acknowledge the tendency of Social Policy to sustain prevailing ideologies, hierarchies and inequalities through its failure adequately to appreciate their origins and significance. Such analyses should help to show that society's social relationships are frequently determined by racist, ageist or other discriminatory beliefs and practices, that its forms of cohesion are typically unfair, unequal and hierarchical and that its apparently benign primary ideological discourse – 'the social' – is at best ambiguous and misleading and at worst disciplinary and coercive.

In short, therefore, images of 'society' and 'the social' are appearing which contrast fundamentally with the benign, harmonious and 'liberal-progressive' representations of the social order with which we are familiar. As we shall see, these coercive aspects of the 'liberal-democratic' regime bear more heavily upon certain members of the population than others. Precisely where its integrative moral order is least secure, the liberal – democratic regime becomes all the more punitive and disciplinary. Hence, around society's key social divisions – the 'fault lines of the social' – a whole array of mechanisms and procedures (disciplinary, ideological and administrative) are deployed – with profound consequences for some sections of the population.

It follows, then, that if we can meaningfully speak of an 'integrated moral community' – society – or even of a normative moral framework which underpins the contemporary Welfare State, this is something which certainly does not derive from the political or economic foundations of the social order. Or rather, if it can plausibly be claimed that a normative *social* order stressing liberal–democratic values does exist, then we must assert that it has evolved, on the whole, *despite* the political and economic foundations of society.

The integrated moral community of the Welfare State appears ever more elusive when we examine the political and economic relations at play within society. Not only is 'the social' thoroughly suffused with economic and political rationalities, but the political and economic institutions of society are themselves part of a dense web of economic and political relations, whose influence might extend to all levels of the social formation (nations, regions, corporations, firms, communities, families and individuals). Obviously, the ramification of these relations has a direct bearing upon people's lives, their aspirations and standards of living and, ultimately, upon their welfare. One could almost say that these political and economic relations, and the conflicts and struggles around them, constitute the entire field of social relations. There may be no necessary centre to these conflicts and struggles, no single 'eye' to the 'storm' produced by conflicts over and resistances to forms of discipline, but it is possible to locate certain focal points of power and authority (the state, the market, social class and the family) and certain key dynamics (capitalist relations of exploitation, imperialism, patriarchy and racism).

It is difficult to understand how these political and economic relations, the forms of discipline mobilised, and the conflicts which clearly surround them, can be seen as entirely consistent with a normative and integrative conception of 'the social'. The division of society by a series of differentiated political and economic interests situates major sources of antagonism within the social order, and the idea of contradictory class interests seems quite subversive of an integrated and coherent conception of 'the social'. Furthermore, what is true of the antagonisms generated at the specifically economic level of society is equally true of those social divisions which, although frequently structured throughout by social and economic inequality, are further overlaid and compounded with a racial, sexual or generational dynamic.

The reason for developing these points is not to suggest that certain forms of social division are in any way politically or analytically prior to the others, rather that each (as well as other divisions occurring along certain 'fault lines of the social', be they socio-economic or occupational, generational, consumption-oriented, regional, ethnic, religious or sexual) constitutes a potential source of instability within 'the social'. Moreover, as social divisions giving rise to ideological disaffection, oppositional consciousness and/or outright resistance amongst sections of a given population, their very existence is indicative of a profound failure at the level of the society's mechanisms of integration and its normative commitments to democratic citizenship.

As Therborn has made clear, the attainment of full *social* democracy is intimately linked to a certain 'broadening of the nation' which is achieved by the political incorporation of previously unrepresented elements, by material incentives and by sponsorship of hitherto disaffected interests. Nevertheless, it is clearly significant that the most enduring criteria for political exclusion, namely class, race, and sex, remain, even within the social democratic polity, the most potent sources of social division (Therborn, 1977). Continuing evidence of such persistent, fundamental and dynamic forms of inequality undermines the 'social' claims implicit in both the 'welfarist discourse' of Social Policy and the politically integrative frameworks of social democracy.

In effect, faced with a political culture (social democracy) with such highly conditional integrative mechanisms, and forms of 'welfare' which ignore the most vital and dynamic inequalities, one is inclined to suspect that social democracy and welfare capitalism are little more than the mechanisms by which political order is imposed, hierarchies legitimated and social discipline circulated. (I shall be developing these issues in later chapters.)

The social and the national

The above points lead to our second area of concern regarding the constructed pedigree of 'the social' for, as well as involving 'racial' and crudely territorial considerations, ideas about nationality also embody rather more sophisticated ideas of political authority and political allegiance.

'Nation', like 'community' or 'society', embodies an idea of unity, of a whole significantly greater than the sum of its parts, perhaps even 'indivisible before God' – an idea, interestingly, rejected by both Benthamism and Thatcherism. But to entertain such notions requires us to suspend critical disbelief and embrace wholeheartedly liberalism's idealist fallacy that a nation might spontaneously constitute itself by some collective act of will, or perhaps even by some form of 'social contract'. (I shall be returning to this question.)

As we are well aware, however, no such events actually occurred. 'Nationhood' and citizenship can only be fully understood in the context of a legacy of acts of power, violence and coercion – that is to say, war (Mann, 1987). It should come as no surprise that Westminster's principal justifications of the Falklands/Malvinas Conflict took the form of a defence of the 'rights' of the 'islanders' (see Barnett, 1982). Likewise, the South African government's policy of apartheid is evidence enough of the coercive and/or restrictive implications of certain conceptions of nationality and citizenship. Furthermore, wars and international crises have often proved to be the catalyst for a good many of the celebrated welfare institutions of the British state (Titmuss, 1955; Myrdal, 1960). The equation, of course, is not all one-way, important social policy initiatives have been defeated or delayed by such conflicts and crises (Thane, 1982). Nevertheless, the general point holds true; much of the content and character of British social institutions and domestic social welfare ideologies derives from the country's particular legacy of imperialism and war (CCCS, 1982; Williams, 1987).

Yet these examples are important not simply for the ways in which they demonstrate the coercive and frequently racist aspects of apparently benign notions like 'citizenship' and 'nationhood' (every inclusion is an exclusion; all boundaries have two sides), but especially for the way in which they raise important problems for our idea of 'the social'. Nationality and citizenship seem to provide the biological and geographical, but especially political and economic, boundaries to 'the social' itself. Bearing in mind the observations made previously, this would seem to imply a fairly violent gestation for 'the social' and also that its boundaries, once formed, must be scrupulously policed. This obviously helps ensure the exclusion of 'aliens' but also provides the context within which the duties and responsibilities of citizens might be defined.

This is, in fact, what we find. The much heralded 'birth' of the postwar Welfare State provided the occasion for a significant and notably more restrictive redefinition of British citizenship. The 1948 British Nationality Act concluded reciprocal agreements with former colonies regarding rights of entry and abode and, in creating a new legal status – Citizen of the United Kingdom and Colonies – removed wholesale the rights of those who were previously known as 'coloured' Commonwealth citizens – the inhabitants of the former colonies. Such measures indicated the willingness of Britain to renege on its Commonwealth commitments when convenient, but they did not yet show just how far it would be willing to go (Sivanandan, 1976).

The 1948 Act must be seen as an important corollary to the enhancement of citizenship status for UK citizens; it underlines the important nationalist dimension in conceptions of 'the social'. In historical terms, however, the 1948 Act was by no means the first step. In 1905, following considerable anti-Jewish agitation involving large sections of the Labour movement and the TUC supported by influential Fabian intellectuals, the Conservative government had passed an Aliens Act. The Act did not specifically identify Jews as 'aliens' but sought to exclude those deemed 'undesirable immigrants': those without the means of supporting themselves and their dependants, or those likely to become a charge on the rates or otherwise a 'detriment to the public'. As Cohen concludes:

> English welfare was to be denied to the foreign sick and the foreign poor. This was a direct forerunner to the present Immigration Rules which prevent the entry of anyone who may have 'recourse to public funds' or may in any other way become a 'burden to the state'.
>
> (Cohen, 1985)

Although the Liberals had opposed the Act whilst in opposition, they enforced it the following year when in office. Hence, to the already exclusive character of the 'Liberal Welfare Reforms' was added, 'a principled belief in entitlement to welfare benefits by nationality'. In turn, 'nationality' became a crucial qualifying condition for the cele-brated benefits of the reforming Liberal government (Williams, 1987; Cohen, 1985). Clearly the 'presence test' initially proposed by the Conservative government in its 1985 *Reform of Social Security* Green Paper has a long and ignominious history (HMSO, 1985b, para. 2.87).

The development of law and practice in immigration policy has con-tinued in the increasingly exclusive direction outlined. This policy and practice were continued after 1948, initially with more and more restric-tive quotas, later with explicitly racist checks and controls. Since the late 1950s and early 1960s these latter measures have been very much fostered and fuelled by the emergence of markedly racist ideologies and the activities of strongly nationalist political groupings. In the mid–1960s, Enoch Powell had become the centre of gravity for much of the political agitation arising from questions of race and nationalism. Significantly, his 1968 'rivers of blood' speech led to one of the more innovative social policy initiatives of the incumbent Labour government (Bridges, 1975; Loney, 1983). Although again, this only goes to illus-trate the strong connection between 'the social' and conceptions of nation and citizenship.

Yet is is not simply a question of particular racist stereotypes or assumptions, rather the *whole* political discourse of immigration has been overtly and covertly racist (Reeves, 1983; Miles, 1987). The most obvious instance of this is the common claim that some limitation of the numbers of coloured immigrants is necessary in order to preserve good race relations 'at home' – in other words, an immigration colour bar. The argument surfaced prominently in debates surrounding the 1968 Commonwealth Immigration Act, which extended restrictions to people with British passports but without 'substantial connections' with Britain, and the 1971 Immigration Act, which 'extended and formalised the racial basis of immigration legislation' by removing rights of access and settlement from all Commonwealth citizens bar those with parents and grandparents born in Britain. It was clear that limiting coloured immigration was the legislation's objective (Moore and Wallace, 1975).

The argument favouring an immigration 'colour bar' in order to preserve 'social order' has resurfaced periodically, particularly in the run-up to the 1979 general election and during the debates which pre-ceded the 1981 Nationality Act. The argument allows an important shift to take place within racist discourses, as Barker and Reeves, in their different ways, demonstrate. Specific racial stereotypes, aspects of superiority/inferiority or race hatred, need not be invoked. The discourse simply identifies difference, in Thatcher's terms 'alien cul-tures', as the problem. The focus of concern, unashamedly, is with the distinctiveness of the British race and nation, our institutions, character and culture (Barker, 1981; Reeves, 1983). As Miles has put it:

> Within the formal political arena there have been few references to inherent biological inferiority to legitimate the demand for exclusion. Rather, the migrants have been simultaneously racialized and signified as the cause of economic and social problems for 'our people'.
>
> (Miles, 1987)

In a very important way, this blend of 'new racism' ties conceptions of 'the social' to ideas about British character and culture and notions of race and nation. Others are defined outside this, different and incompatible.

Throughout the 1960s and 1970s (and 1980s), therefore, these racist and nationalist discursive formulations of the politics of immigration and race relations were making the key ideological running. Furthermore, the particular direction of immigration policy itself was largely dictated by political agitation seeking restrictions, controls and limits upon coloured immigration. Finally, as Miles argues, the 1981 British Nationality Act 'brought nationality law into line with the racist categories constructed in earlier immigration law and immigration rules' (Miles, 1987).

This brief legislative history and the accumulating evidence of racist and discriminatory social practices and beliefs strongly support the view that markedly nationalist sentiments underly a great deal of contemporary social discourse. Making the theoretical point, Giddens (1982) has remarked that, 'Struggles to achieve citizenship rights have almost wholly been carried on within the bounds of Nation-states. And the very notion of citizenship has come to be defined in nationalist terms.' The capacity of these explicitly 'social', implicitly nationalist discourses to pass themselves off as non-ideological, or 'natural' and even positive, manifestations of political solidarity is worthy of more extensive examination, (see F. Williams, 1987), but I have only sufficient space here to consider the significance of this interweaving of 'social' and 'national' discourses.

As Myrdal recognised in 1960, the welfare state is clearly nationalistic:

> The democratic welfare state in the rich countries of the world is protectionist and nationalistic. The peoples in those countries have achieved economic welfare at home – economic progress and a substantial increase in liberty and equality of opportunity for all within their boundaries – at the expense of indulging in nationalistic economic policies.
>
> (Myrdal, 1960)

The passage of time might have made us rather more sceptical with regard to the 'democratic' pretensions of the Welfare State, and from the perspective of the late 1980s it is clear that the increasing liberty and opportunity have been rather less equally distributed than might have been hoped. Nevertheless, in pointing out the legacy of imperialism and exploitation upon which the developed nations have depended – and still do – Myrdal drew attention to an important feature of the Welfare State which, despite his efforts, continues to be largely neglected by analysts of social policy. Likewise, what Mishra calls the 'ethnocentrism' of British social administration (Mishra, 1982) has, suggests Williams, blinded it to 'the international context of its welfare state and the racism of the welfare state's policies' (F. Williams, 1987).

Indeed, Social Policy has tended to convert social welfare's ethnocentric and nationalistic orientation into an ideology all of its own. This ideology commonly goes under the title of the consensus model of welfare. Beyond recalling a supposed golden age of political agreement, the consensus model is frequently said to represent a time when progressive and realistic welfare objectives were achievable. In this way, the consensus model attaches to itself the unquestioned virtues of a sensible pragmatism. In Reeves's terms this consensus ideology would undoubtedly represent an instance of 'deracialised political discourse' in that the nationalist – and especially racist – impact and significance remains implicit. Of course, this is not always the case and there are notable, quite explicit, exceptions. As the Beveridge Report is often pointed to as a crucial foundation document upon which the post-war Welfare State is based (again very much a product of wartime experiences) it would seem a good place to start.

Pinker sought to give Beveridge the benefit of the doubt, arguing that Beveridge was 'appealing to sentiments of communal and patriotic loyalty which were inclusive rather than exclusive, reaching out to an ideal of international welfare' (Pinker, 1979, p. 24). This may well be so, but the dream of 'international welfare' seems to have fallen a good way short in practice. The Welfare State seemed insular and ill-prepared for the role it was expected to play. As Jones (1977, p. 155) has observed, 'The Welfare State was somehow insufficient or inappropriate to cope . . . with the consequences of New Commonwealth immigration. [It] was not, after all, the comprehensive, open-ended, recipe for social reconstruction that its champions had originally forecast.'

We do not have to look too far for an explanation for this particular inadequacy on the part of the Welfare State, the ideals embedded within it were drawn from solidly British stock – an imperialist tradition impervious to the specific needs and priorities of black immigrants. As Beveridge, in a far from infrequent expression of nationalist sentiment, put it:

In seeking security not merely against physical want, but against all these evils (Want, Squalor, Ignorance, Disease and Idleness) and in showing that security can be combined with freedom and enterprise and responsibility of the individual for his own life, the British community and those who in other lands have inherited the British tradition have a vital service to render to human progress.

(Beveridge Report, 1942, p. 170)

Beveridge's remarks were no isolated example. Elsewhere, 'ensuring the continuance of the British Race and of British ideals in the world', was Beveridge's description of the vital, though unpaid, work allotted to housewives and mothers (Beveridge Report, 1942, p. 52). On the same theme, it is clear that considerations of 'national interest' weighed heavily upon Beveridge's support for family allowances and maternity benefits, so it is very difficult to disassociate the British ideology of social welfare from strongly nationalist concerns. Indeed, as Williams has argued, nationalism and racism 'were intrinsic to the welfare state', and to the ideal of social welfare itself (F. Williams, 1987).

Where Pinker, in seeking to defend the Beveridge Report's social welfare ideals, suggests that Beveridge saw the creation of the Welfare State in Britain as, 'a partial fulfilment of the wider aims of the Atlantic Charter', he merely unveils an even greater problem. The 'common cause' to which Beveridge referred becomes rather more Anglo-American – or perhaps simply welfare-capitalist – than internationalist. The European Recovery Programme (the 'Marshall Plan') provided the vital economic platform for Britain's post-war recovery. Hence the presumed relation between social welfare ideals and international politics might require some reconsideration. It was not that the (allegedly) British ideals of social welfare provided the ideological foundation for an international political settlement, as both Beveridge and Pinker seemed to imply, but rather the Marshall Plan which provided the general ideological and political framework within which particular national policies and provisions found their place. As Mann has suggested, 'sociologists are prone to forget that "evolution" is usually geo-politically assisted' (Mann, 1987, p. 351). Perhaps we can say the same thing for ideologies of 'the social' and conceptions of welfare. The two main planks of the post-war Welfare State, the National Insurance Scheme and the National Health Service, embody this notion of *national* welfare quite admirably. They provide ample evidence of the relationship between social discipline, full employment, and a particularly British ideology of social welfare.

As we have seen, two decades of relative economic well-being rather endorsed this framework of social welfare and the ideology of national, as opposed to international, collectivism it embodied. Continued, although relatively low, rates of economic growth, the expanded public sector, full employment, rising real incomes and rising standards of living appeared to obviate the need for further structural reform of the British economy. Amongst sections of the Left, a certain complacency became evident, Crosland arguing that Britain was no longer a capitalist society; that the Welfare State had solved the major social problems of poverty and social deprivation and that further redistribution from rich to poor would serve no useful purpose (Crosland, 1964, pp. 29, 123). Continued, planned, economic growth, it was assumed, would provide the answer to all remaining social problems.

On the Right, however, these decades of so-called 'consensus politics' witnessed the crystallisation of a profoundly nationalist welfare ideology. Under the guise of an ostensibly non-ideological, even non-sectional, approach to policy questions, the framework of consensus politics appeared to vindicate the sensible pragmatism of the Welfare State. In turn, this sensible pragmatism was effectively exploited by the Conservatives' political advocacy of 'one nation'. This brand of Toryism, planted firmly upon the promise of continued economic growth and an attainable cycle of rising expectations, sought to depoliticise social and economic policy-making, or rather – which amounted to the same thing – to submerge it within a traditionalist conception of the national interest. The popular, and quite misleading, expression of this involved the idea that 'we' were all becoming middle class. In this way, a firmly British and manifestly individualised and consumerist conception of social welfare came to be installed at the core of welfare ideology articulating British ideals and cultural values.

This advocacy of 'one nation' was only sustainable with the assumption of economic growth. In this context, Barker's analysis has sought to show how the latent nationalism of British political ideology provided a seedbed for what he has called the 'new racism' manifesting itself more and more virulently throughout the 1970s and 80s (M. Barker, 1981). This potent blend of racism and nationalism became increasingly strident in the early 1980s at the time the British Nationality Bill was going through parliament and during and after the Falklands/Malvinas Conflict.

Yet perhaps the signs were all there. The important relationship between citizenship and inclusive conceptions of welfare has already been noted. Yet, even in the very heart of 'one nation' Toryism in the late 1950s and early 60s, the writing was on the wall. According to Hall *et al.*, 'the two topics most calculated to catch the imagination of grassroots Tories at the Party Conference were crime and immigration.' Racism itself was, of course, neglected, being part of what actually defined the nation, 'but the existence of Blacks as a problem was tacitly acknowledged' (Hall *et al.*, 1978, p. 234).

Subsequently, of course, this Conservative nationalism and the latent racism of British social and political culture, firmly established through three decades of a post-war settlement that effectively insulated the majority of the British population from external 'competition', was hijacked from within. A more potent blend of nationalism and racism surfaced, fuelled by perceptions of economic recession, social disorder and imperial decline. The tendencies identified by Myrdal in 1960 appeared to be coming to fruition. The citizens of the affluent countries, he argued, had expanded their economic fortunes but concurrently narrowed their social vision, they found it much easier to blame 'foreigners' for the difficulties they faced (Myrdal, 1960, p. 115).

As Miles has shown, debates surrounding the Nationality Bill and the Falklands/Malvinas Conflict provided the critical opportunity for these ideological discourses to pour forth. Defending her decision to despatch the Falklands' task force, Mrs Thatcher told the House of Commons, 'the people of the Falkland Islands, like the people of the United Kingdom are an island race. Their way of life is British, their allegiance is to the Crown' (Barnett, 1982). In a sense, this told us who 'we' were; the objective of the British Nationality Act had been to tell us who was not 'one of us'. While the Falklands debates gave full reign and expression to the racist and nationalist categories so central to British experience and culture, the 1981 British Nationality Bill imposed its own more restrictive definition of who really 'belonged' to the British Nation (Gordon and Klug, 1986).

Commenting on this Act which, by bringing nationality law itself into line with prevailing racist and nationalist ideological discourses, appeared to validate and endorse the peculiarly exclusive conception of 'the social' operating within British culture, Dixon has remarked:

> The crucial irony of the 1981 Act is that it is designed to define a sense of belonging and nationhood which is itself a manifestation of the sense of racial superiority created along with the Empire, while simultaneously it cuts the ties of citizenship established in the same historical process. The ideology of Empire is reconstructed: while Thatcherism rejects the essential expansionism of Empire in favour of 'isolationism', its supremacism, chauvinism and racism are preserved.
>
> (Dixon, 1983)

In these ways, ideologies of 'the social' came to take on a markedly more racist and nationalist character in the 1970s and 80s. It was not that Thatcherism itself had wholly redefined the political and ideological terrain, rather that right-wing politicians and commentators had been able to take advantage of crucial social and political tensions within British political culture, tensions exacerbated by the international economic recession and its domestic repercussions. In the process, the latent racism and nationalism endemic in British culture – attitudes and ideologies that social policy and the 'welfare state' had, at best, only compounded and, at worst, intensified, as the contest for 'our' scarce resources became more acute – had been exploited in an attempt to re-establish allegedly more traditional values and a more authoritarian social order. That these tendencies were always within the scope of 'the social' is without question, that they have come so prominently to the fore in recent years underlines quite emphatically enough the limitations of the rather more benign conceptions of 'the social' with which social policy has typically sought to associate itself.

The social and the state

The political discourse of liberalism fails, on the whole, to acknowledge the state's foundation of the space of civil society (and implicitly of 'the social') itself. Earlier, we saw how philosophers and classical political economists employed the idea of civil society so as to differentiate it from the domain of the state. In this conception, civil society ('the social') is seen as the repository of freedom, private interests and passions. The two essential pillars supporting this vision of 'the social' are the family and the economy. The role of the state, although practically and theoretically vital, is both overlooked and misunderstood in liberal discourse.

At the outset, it is clear that our conception of 'the social', incorporating both household and economy, dramatically cross-cuts modern liberal conceptions of the public and the private. Contemporary political philosophers, alert to feminism's critique of the patriarchal formation of 'society' (and therefore of 'the social'), recognise in the 'public/private' division a more fundamental challenge to the coherence of 'the social'. To adapt Deleuze's remark, the social is indeed a 'hybrid domain' (Deleuze, 1980, p. x). These themes will be returned to later; for the moment it is enough to outline briefly the manner of the state's establishment of 'the social'.

In attempting to chart a field of 'social' politics it is not difficult to detect the more significant ideological themes, sites and institutions. Yet of all the key sites upon which social practices have been played out, the family appears as one of the more prominent. We should not be concerned with this or that specific family form, but rather, with the family as a site of social practices and the centre of a political discourse

(Donzelot, 1980). The historical centrality of the family – as a transmitter of cultural values and a major influence in the formation of traditional notions of 'community', as a site for the transfer of property and as a focus for authority and 'political' loyalties – is quite clear (Laslett, 1974; Shorter, 1981; Donzelot, 1980; Gillis, 1981). 'Centuries of complaint' about the dislocation of family ties is indicative not only of the political significance of the family and its proximity to ideas of social solidarity but also of certain longstanding vulnerabilities at the very heart of 'the social' (Pearson, 1983).

Undoubtedly a great deal of the concern regarding this perceived social malaise can be attributed to a fear of the newly emerging proletariat, the dangerous classes of the new urban centres and the demoralised poor who, in Britain at least, so preoccupied the Poor Law Commissioners. Yet, whilst strategies of social reform affected families of differing social classes in quite different ways, it is true that the family (as the site of a certain pathology and an instrument of remedial intervention) became, as never before, an object of concern.

Yet what presented itself as the 'crisis' of a certain family form and a fundamental rupture in the mechanisms of social cohesion was in fact no more than the emergent symptoms of a certain political and economic *decentring* of the family. This decentring reflected the emergence of new forms of political authority consequent upon the rise of the modern state and a changing mode of production. In the process, the family ceased to conform to a general 'model' of government (sacrosanct, autonomous, a domain unto itself), in which the 'head of state' was deemed to resemble the paternal head of a family. Even the working-class family was affected by these changes although, in its case, its relative privacy derived from its poverty and its insignificance. Henceforth, the family became an *instrument* of government: 'the privileged instrument for the government of the population and not the chimerical model of good government'. Foucault proceeds to demonstrate the ways in which the family thus became the appropriate site for the location of interventions within the body of the population, citing the emergence, during the late eighteenth and early nineteenth centuries, of concerns regarding mortality, marriage and vaccination (Foucault, 1979, p. 17). Later in the nineteenth century, and reflecting the ascendancy of liberal individualism, statutory authority began to transcend further the unique authority of heads of households by amending the law in the fields of divorce and inheritance and by establishing the property rights of married women. Some of these themes, clearly, have been more thoroughly and specifically developed by Donzelot (See Donzelot, 1980, p. 48 *passim*).

The economic decentring of the family can be seen as a reflection of changing modes and relations of production: specifically, the gradual replacement of the domestic basis of production (Smelser, 1968; Medick, 1976; Anderson, 1976), the associated growth of a specifically sexual division of labour (Burman, 1978) and also the growing commercialism of markets. The transformation of the family's direct links with production relations signalled other important changes which, in turn, provided the basis for the further development of industrial capitalism. As Creighton has suggested:

> It is not enough to argue that the crucial stage in the transformation of family relations came with the removal of work from the home to the factory. This criticism is incomplete for the real significance of factory employment was that it represented the final stage of the longer process which divorced the workforce from the means of production and so was the decisive step in the transformation of labour as a commodity. It was these changes which finally brought an end to the collective interest of the family in private property and to the role of inheritance in reproducing certain social relations of reproduction and a certain type of family structure.
>
> (Creighton, 1980, p. 132)

The decentring of the family led to a steep rise in the number of labourers who were increasingly detached from their 'pre-economic' loyalties; this, in turn, facilitated the transformation of labour power into a simple commodity. This 'commodification of labour' is central to the political economy of capitalism. However, commodification established a principle of formal *equivalence* between workers which became incorporated into conceptions of 'the social'. This remained a tense and contradictory equivalence, for it was cross-cut by patriarchal ideals regarding gender roles and complex conceptions of status and 'respectability' deriving from a developing division of labour.

We find a complementary conception of the equivalence of political subjects within the social contract tradition. This tradition of political philosophy advances a model of political order and authority which establishes a degree of formal equivalence between persons in a given population. The equivalence was formal, however, in so far as it reflected classical liberal conceptions of the rational individual, the possessor of capacities, rights and responsibilities. The significance of contract theory lies in the way it has served to legitimate existing forms of authority and also formally establish a single focus of authority – the state – to which disparate persons could henceforth relate as individuals.

A particular construction of 'the social' connects the market with the frameworks of economic individualism. 'The social' operates to obscure the tense and conflictual character of market relations; to infuse these same relations with a logic of social necessity (the 'need' for incentives and for punishments, especially those of profit and poverty, and for the penalties of indolence and inefficiency; the 'need' for hierarchy and the relatively sacrosanct nature of existing statuses – employer and employee). The ideological effect of 'the social' in relation to the market might simply be to 'socialise' it, to incorporate the tense, competitive and individualist character of market relations within the diversity of 'human nature'. As Marx argued in *Capital* vol I: 'The advance of capitalist production develops a working class which by education, tradition and habit looks upon the requirements of that mode of production as self-evident natural laws' (Marx, 1976, p. 899). To a degree, expressions of 'the social market' begin to attain this naturalisation of market relations.

Marx, of course, had no illusions about the real character of this domain. The 'social sphere', ('The sphere of circulation or commodity exchange') is seen as 'a very Eden of the innate rights of man.'

> When we leave this sphere . . . a certain change takes place, or so it appears, in the physiognomy of our *dramatis personae*. He who was previously the money owner, now strides out as a capitalist; the possessor of labour-power follows as his worker. The one smirks self-importantly and is intent on business; the other is timid and holds back, like someone who has brought his own hide to market and has nothing to expect but – a tanning.'
>
> (Marx, 1976, p. 280).

It is at this point, that the fundamental inconsistency at the heart of contractarian social theory lies. The inaugural social contract, from which the sovereign state was said to derive its authority, presumed, for its legitimacy, the existence of precisely that rational, capable and right-bearing individual that the contract was supposed to create. Despite this weakness, however, the contractual model of society firmly endorsed the principle of the formal equivalence of citizens. In this, a key element of the foundations of the contemporary liberal-democratic Welfare State was laid in place. The expansion of a conception of citizenship and its incorporation, during the twentieth century, of a series of new 'social rights', (Marshall, 1963), testifies to the strength and persuasiveness of this liberal conception of the individual.

In contrast, the Marxist conception of equivalence encapsulated both the reduction of the labourer to a quantifiable unit of labour-power and the collective experience of social class that the new relations of production imposed. Yet in both cases, the state performed a fundamental role, on the one hand, underwriting the forms of legal equivalence upon which contractual relations within the market rested and, on the other hand, representing a unique source of authority which could, if necessary, forcefully confront the radicalised elements of the new proletariat.

Through its maintenance of these principles of political and economic order the modern (constitutional) state obtained a powerful rationale for expansion. Subsequently, when the state began to embark upon direct interventions into the immediate circumstances of the population, by reference to established principles of political and economic order, the discourse of social welfare can clearly be seen as a convenient vehicle for the maintenance of economic relations and the consolidation of political power. It seems plain that the state remains absolutely central to any meaningful conception of 'the social'. We have found this to be true in terms of the two conventional pillars of 'the social' – the family, and the market economy.

As we have seen, the authority and integrity of the modern family is thoroughly underwritten by statutory powers and interventions. The significance attached by feminism to the family as the principal site of women's oppression can be understood in this light. The patriarchy of the private family, through which social order was maintained and government conducted, has been transformed into a state patriarchy (Donzelot, 1980; Borchorst and Siim, 1987). State activities and laws fundamentally reinforce prevailing (and patriarchal) conceptions of gender. The policing of the family, therefore, turns upon a particular disciplining of gender. Furthermore, this disciplining of gender is clearly a feature of both state social policy and labour market relations – from child care policies and the structure of social security to the social and economic implications of the division of labour in a 'gendered' labour market. It hardly needs emphasising that sexism and discrimination are inherent in both areas of life, the private (family and economy) and the public (the political). It is undoubtedly necessary to develop a specifically patriarchal dimension of 'the social' at greater length but, as the preceding discussion suggests, patriarchal relations are sustained by and through the family and the labour market both of which derive their essential authority, order and significance from the state.

Finally, but closely related, the state also represents the formal source of authority from which, in liberalism's terms, the rights and capacities of citizens are derived or, in Marxism's terms, 'the commodification of labour-power for the market' is assured. It is, for these reasons, impossible to ignore the state in any treatment of 'the social'. 'The social' does not emerge as a free series of ideas, an autonomous perspective from which 'state intervention' might be judged, it does not 'speak for itself' in this way, but rather comes to us already constituted in terms of the state, a feature that recent social policy commentators have readily endorsed (Taylor-Gooby, 1981).

The social and socialism

A fourth area that merits some consideration here is the apparent relationship between socialism and 'the social'. It is important to clarify these relationships because it is often presumed that the rise of the 'social state' and the development of a specific discourse and politics of social welfare can be explained by reference to the growth and development of socialist parties and socialist movements. However, Balfour's oft-quoted remark that 'social legislation . . . is not merely to be distinguished from socialist legislation but is its most direct opposite and effective antidote.' (Balfour, quoted in D. Fraser, 1973), suggests that there is rather more to it than this.

Discourses of social welfare are closely tied to the fortunes of a social-democratic political culture and to a range of values centring upon individual rights and freedoms, equality of opportunity and distributional justice. Socialist political movements and organisations are not irrelevant to the development of such principles and such a culture, but the two are premised upon quite different theoretical and political analyses, different conceptions of the place and significance of moral and philosophical values and differing conceptions of political practice.

It is difficult to do justice to distinctions between socialism and social democracy, or 'revolutionary' struggle and social reform in just a few pages. Socialists and Marxists have seldom had much time for the 'philosophical idealism' of their contemporaries (Marx and Engels, 1967). It was not that Marxists harboured a disdain for philosophy, simply that philosophy and the political and ideological values to which it gave rise had to be grounded upon the political consciousness, experience and conditions of life of the working class. For, just 'as philosophy finds its material weapons in the proletariat, so the proletariat finds its intellectual weapons in philosophy' (Marx, quoted in McLellan, 1975, p. 98).

Central to Marxism's rejection of 'critical or utopian socialism' lies the latter's alleged abandonment of a politics centred upon class analysis and the real historical bases of social order. Instead, as Meiksins-Wood argues, those who Marx and Engels ironically referred to as the 'True Socialists', 'take on trust the illusion . . . that it is a question of the "most reasonable" social order and not the needs of a particular class and a particular time' (cited in Meiksins-Wood, 1986).

Whilst concepts of human welfare and emancipation certainly featured as part of the heritage of values Marxism shared with other varieties of socialism during the nineteenth century, the ideal of the 'most reasonable' social order was not one of them, not least because it implied that the question of social transformation was a quantitative rather than qualitative affair. As I shall show, however, the presumption of gradual or incremental change was often central to the 'revisionist' or social democratic political philosophy.

There is, as I suggested earlier, a relationship between these traditions, but this is only part of the story. In fact, analyses and political tracts attributing a specifically 'social' interest to the working class certainly predated the development of a 'scientific' socialism. Fourier and the Saint-Simonians in France and the Owenites in Britain were articulating an idealist and utopian socialism premised, not upon the development of a political struggle through which emancipation might be achieved but, rather, upon a synthesis of class interests that anchored a harmonious social order around the core liberal values of justice, freedom and equality. Likewise, Bauman's analysis of the 'economisation' of labour disputes in the early nineteenth century demonstrates quite clearly how questions of political conflict were effectively ruled out and replaced by calculations of the 'fair' price (Bauman, 1982, pp. 107–9).

An essentially similar point was made by Marx in his own critique of the 'Programme of the German Workers' Party' (or 'Gotha Programme'). In the 'Gotha Programme' Lassalle had developed a simplistic analysis of capitalist production, claiming, ultimately, that labour (the working class) was the source of all wealth. He went on to develop what was, to Marx, a crude and class-essentialist model of politics and social transformation, arguing that capitalism would be overcome by the workers obtaining the full value of their labour and attaining the liberal democratic freedoms enjoyed by the bourgeoisie. The suggestion that quantitative additions to the well-being of the working class and that a commonality of political interests constituted on the basis of bourgeois freedoms, were any substitute for genuine socialist struggle and revolution was anathema to Marx. It was precisely this 'commonality of interests', that went by the name of 'the people' in Kautsky's 1891 'Erfurt Programme', that Engels objected to: 'The people in general', he queried, 'who is that?' (Przeworski, 1985).

The preceding discussions should be enough to indicate that the political and ideological traditions of socialism and social democracy, whilst deriving from a similar conceptual heritage, and overlapping in certain important ways in certain contexts, do, in fact, represent significantly different traditions. These distinctions become clearer when we turn to consider the analyses of Bernstein, whose name has in many respects become synonymous with 'revisionism', and of the Fabians. Bernstein's revisionism and Fabian planning were based upon an explicitly 'social politics' and a socialisation of capital. According to Kolakowski, Bernstein 'attempted to combine socialism with liberalism and looked to social legislation as a means of reform' (Kolakowski, 1978 vol. II, p. 101).

Like the celebrated founders of Fabianism, the Webbs, Bernstein centred his political theory upon a conception of 'the social' – a sphere of ideal or universal political interests detached from the interests of any particular class. And his economic theory – like that of the Fabians – differed significantly from the economic theory of Marxism. He simply quantified the concept of 'surplus value' – clearly central to Marxism's analysis of exploitation – to give the impression that it represented no more than 'an index of social injustice' in which the working class were the most revolutionary because they were the most suffering. Fabian economic theory, such as it was, likewise digressed from Marxist political economy by its conception of surplus value, which was understood as if it were a kind of 'rent' accruing to capitalists through their ownership of assets productively employed within the market place (Durbin, 1985). This particular interpretation of Fabian economic theory explains, up to a point, their emphasis upon nationalisation (or socialisation) of capital assets as a way of securing for society as a whole the profits of industry. Furthermore, implicit in this Fabian conception of nationalisation there lie two clear ideological assumptions; the first about the 'common interests' of society as a whole and the second about the neutrality of the state.

For Bernstein, socialisation replaced socialism as a central political goal and his case for social legislation centred upon moral and ethical commitment rather than the political interests of the working class, thereby establishing an independent or 'voluntarist' social politics. Similarly, Fabian conceptions of the common interests of society and the neutrality of the state were combined with an historical analysis which transformed the materialist conception of history by allowing human actors, especially educated and socially aware ones, greater scope to effect social change. And, as Lee and Raban remark, this is very clearly an important element of the legacy bequeathed by Fabianism to post-war social policy and administration (Lee and Raban, 1988, p. 25).

The alleged 'voluntarism', 'revisionism' and 'moralism' of social-democratic politics drew a range of criticisms from Marxists. Lenin, in particular, resented the revisionists' emphasis upon political alliances with the reformist bourgeoisie (Lenin, 1968). But it was the revisionist parties' pursuit of a politics of compromise that neglected the specific interests of the proletariat in favour of appeals to the 'people as a whole' that distinguished them radically from their Marxist contemporaries. However, as Przeworski acknowledges, the revisionists were caught in a rather acute electoral dilemma; their political appeal addressed itself to 'the masses', 'the people', 'consumers', 'taxpayers' or, simply, 'citizens', rather than to the working class as a specific political force.

> By broadening their appeal to the 'masses,' social democrats weaken the general salience of class as a determinant of political behaviour. . . . To be effective in elections they have to seek allies who would join workers under the socialist banner, yet at the same time they erode exactly that ideology which is the source of their strength among workers.
>
> (Przeworski, 1985, p. 29)

Despite attacks from the left of the political spectrum, social democratic discourses and political strategies evidently flourished in a number of countries. In Britain, for instance, the Fabian tradition emerged fairly strongly, supported by the experience of the liberal welfare reforms of 1906–14 which promised 'a more peaceful route to a rather different kind of socialism, the socialism of active and responsible government' (Lee and Raban, 1988, p. 35). By 1918, the Fabian imprint upon the Labour Party's policy-making was abundantly clear. The 1918 manifesto, *Labour and the New Social Order*, located a social politics squarely at the heart of British socialism. Subsequently, Keynesian economics, which emerged in the later 1920s and 30s, provided social politics with an economic discourse through which it could be expressed and within which its socio-political strategy could be situated. Keynesian economics seemed to validate the social-democratic approach to government and its assumption of the basic neutrality of the state.

> From the passive victim of trade cycles, the state became transformed almost overnight into an institution by which society could regulate crises. . . . Society is [no longer] helpless against the whims of the capitalist market, the economy can be controlled, and the welfare of citizens can be continually enhanced by the active role of the state: this was the new discovery of the social democrats.
>
> (Przeworski, 1985, p. 36)

With their adoption of Keynesian techniques of economic management and a reformist social politics aimed at the 'general welfare', the social-democratic parties had all but realised the strategy that had earned the contempt of Marx and Engels many years before. They had trimmed their ideology, dusted off their 'social' figurehead, broadened their appeal and set a course for the 'most reasonable' social order. Stephen Yeo has provided an interesting summary of developments during these years, drawing particular attention to the transition from a 'socialist' to a 'social' politics that was taking place.

> What was going on . . . during the late nineteenth and early twentieth centuries was a scramble for socialism – as imperialist as the contemporary scramble for Africa. An attempt was being made to take its germs away

from working-class hosts and to vaccinate the body politic with them in harmless, even health-giving forms. There was an attempt, partly successful, to de-class the idea of socialism, or to nationalise it; to suggest loudly and clearly that it was a 'good thing' as an idea, even a necessary idea, but not attached to working-class interests or associations.

(Yeo, 1979, p. 67)

From this point, the political discourse of social democracy adheres more directly to party political fortunes. Yet, as an analysis of 'social democracy' or 'welfare capitalism' would show, the significant developments within the field of social democratic politics need not be seen exclusively in these terms. In particular, one is apt to lose sight of a discourse of 'the social' and a specifically social politics if a too pragmatic party political focus is adopted. Despite a common ancestry and an early process of evolution that initially tied socialism and 'the social' together, it is clear that they have now gone their separate ways and that 'the social' has developed a pedigree, a history and a potential of its own.

The social and welfare

I have examined four dimensions of 'the social', but there remains one important aspect to be considered. This concerns the ideological concept 'welfare', probably the most important dimension of 'the social'. The idea of welfare is closely linked to the ideal of the 'good society' (a principal object of philosophical endeavour). As I have pointed out, 'the social' represents a domain of activity (the social realm), the forms of activity (social work, social intervention) as well as a rationale for these activities. 'The social', is clearly a fabricated entity, it forms part of a broader discourse on the maintenance of order in society. The idea of welfare (as practice or ideal) is often assumed to have some especially significant contribution to make to 'the social'; it specifically addresses itself to a principle of collective well-being (Thoenes, 1966; Pinker, 1979). But this is not the whole of the story. Amongst other things it is at least clear that welfare is not one-sided and indivisible. For, as I mentioned above, (see Titmuss 1955; 1964; 1974) on occasion, it has taken some particularly punitive and coercive forms.

Nineteenth-century references to 'the social' were essentially references to a problem – often expressed as the 'social question'. The 'social question' reflected a series of inter-related problems centred upon poverty and the challenges that poverty was thought to pose for the security of property, moral and political order and society. Yet if 'the social' once referred to the specific question of poverty and associated problems of political order, we need to know how and why it has come to assume its more contemporary definition embracing issues of 'general solidarity and the production of a lifestyle'. That is to say, questions of welfare (Donzelot, 1980).

In a sense, tracing the metamorphosis of 'the social' involves us in examining the development of different general strategies of government (see Garland, 1985). Formerly, these strategies can be said to have consisted in exploiting poverty, instituting mechanisms of social and political marginalisation and meting out punishment; later collective mechanisms of welfare were applied, and, more recently, the strategy has been to foster rather more individualist images of well-being. With each strategy, the significance and implications of 'the social' have shifted markedly, ideals of welfare altering accordingly. The important point, however, is that we have inherited a concept with which we associate our ideals of well-being and of the 'good society' and whose expression we take to imply notions of altruistic benevolence and progress whereas, in fact, its origins lie in forms of discipline and coercion.

Since the late 1960s, social policy analyses have increasingly acknowledged the growing importance of ideological conflict in policy formation. Undoubtedly, such work reflects the rising ideological tension manifesting itself in British politics specifically regarding the role of the state, the balance between public and private sectors and the role and responsibility of the individual in the production, delivery and consumption of welfare (George and Wilding, 1976; Watson, 1980). Yet it is possible to go too far. While it is clear that new social policy initiatives can be said to reflect new ideas about welfare, and that all manner of ideological demands are placed upon the state on grounds of 'welfare', to what extent are these exclusively, or even primarily, responsible for the new and emergent patterns of social organisation?

Although it is quite inadequate to attribute all social change to the force of moral and ideological argument, it is not uncommon to encounter demands around questions of 'welfare' elaborated upon the basis of some alleged characteristic of individual or collective human existence – that is to say, characteristics of 'the social' (for instance, need, justice or freedom).

Attributes of 'the social' are often taken as given, the role of social policies being to assist in the realisation of these states or conditions. Yet there are important logical and political problems with this approach to policy making. Very conservative forms of thinking are encouraged – welfare ideals are often based upon traditional or existing ideas about society and social structure. In 1931, in the course of an analysis of what he referred to as the 'religion of inequality', Tawney remarked that, 'to convert a phenomenon, however interesting, into a principle, however respectable, is an error of logic. It is the confusion of a judgement of fact with a judgement of value' (Tawney, 1938, p. 28). Although it has a wider general application, Tawney's point was specifically directed at those conservatives who believed that the simple existence of a given (unequal) distribution of income and wealth, largely understood as a 'natural' phenomenon – the result of fortune and/or differences in talents or aptitudes – legitimated the existence of inequality itself. By this means specific social arrangements might be naturalised and socialised; the simple fact of inequality could be crystallised into a principle fundamental to the social order itself.

In a similar manner, notions of welfare might be appropriated by the ideology of inequality and the idea of welfare henceforth understood solely as an element in a discourse organised around principles of hierarchy and social differentiation (the 'natural order', the necessary incentive of inequality) (see Von Leyden, 1976; Joseph and Sumption, 1979; P. Green, 1981). In fact, in welfare capitalist societies this is virtually what we find; welfare develops an almost schizophrenic duality. On the one hand it approximates to an idea of the 'general' welfare of society – usually subordinated to the particular interests, the wealth and well-being of the more affluent sections of society. On the other hand it comes to refer to the specific measures, institutions and policies designed to handle the casualties of this society. There are, therefore, two welfares, the one that stands as a symbol of the well-being of the wealthy, of social order and harmony, and the welfare of the poor which pursues these same goals by coercion when it fails to attain them by compliance.

Whilst these particular conceptions of 'welfare' correspond to a certain model of 'the social', they do so, as we have seen, only to the extent that they commit an essentially conservative error of logic. Unfortunately, however, critics have often been guilty of a rather similar error. Conservatives and traditionalists have often moved complacently from 'is' to 'ought', (from descriptive to normative statements) whereas critics and social reformers have often moved mistakenly in the opposite direction, assuming that what *ought to be* would become what *is* (or what will be). Despite Titmuss's warning about the importance of distinguishing between, 'philosophical tomorrows and the current truths of reality' (Titmuss, 1974, 1987b), it is hardly necessary to look very far for examples of this tendency in mainstream social policy (cf. Marshall, 1963, 1972; Robson, 1976; Pinker, 1979; Jordan, 1987). Within the Social Administration tradition, the marked emphasis placed upon values and normative philosophies is indicative not only of a certain rigidity in received notions of welfare, but also of a somewhat inflated optimism regarding the power of benevolent idealism.

This assumption about moving from *ought* to *is* mobilises a particularly virulent form of idealism involving the establishment of fixed and preconceived notions of 'the social' towards which welfare policies and institutions are said to gravitate. While ostensibly forward-looking, this model of idealist reform is equally conservative in so far as it envisages progress in social reform to be the result of moral forces working throughout history. Today's welfare policies are always the result of yesterday's ideological, moral and political frameworks. In a very real sense, the tradition is always addressing yesterday's social concerns.

The conservative and teleological weaknesses of such approaches to the development of welfare are evident enough and need not be developed here. For our part, we are especially concerned with the bond established between 'the social' and conceptions of welfare. Ideals of societal welfare are themselves integral to 'the social', and particular welfare programmes or policies derive their legitimacy from 'the social'. Furthermore, their compatibility with aspects of 'the social' is often the source of their political appeal. 'The social' provides both a yardstick and also a testing site for competing welfare strategies. Yet it cannot be seen as a static entity, it evolves so as to reflect dominant welfare ideologies. 'The social' itself is neither a programme nor a policy, but the terrain *on* which they compete and *for* which they contest. It is always the result of previous successful dominations.

Ideologies of welfare and the policies and programmes to which they give rise endeavour to construct alternative models of 'the social'. These alternative models, frameworks for the organisation of social relations, may be general or quite specific. They carry, explicitly or implicitly, favoured models for the future governance of human conduct. In this sense they have to be seen as utopian, driven by idealist principles, in the same manner that Bentham's model prison, the panopticon, Robert Owen's 'new community' or Marx's 'communist society' were utopian (Morris and Patton, 1979; Minson, 1985).

In addressing the organisation of social relations, ideologies of welfare deploy normative principles which serve as the basis of social policies and by which attitudes, behaviour and activities might be judged. In turn, these judgements, the prologue to forms of control, mobilise strategies of normalisation comprising both sanctions and incentives. In effect, philosophies of the 'good society' promoting happiness, harmony and order and embodying normative principles of welfare, operate as implicit police principles which entail a certain degree of regimentation or normalisation. Techniques of normalisation operate by specifying norms and setting up techniques, 'for distinguishing and correcting individuals deviating from these norms' (see Donzelot, 1980; Minson, 1985).

However, in a curious fashion, an analysis of strategies of normalis-ation returns us directly to the 'is/ought' question. Normative principles of welfare establish a foundation, reinforced by a range of incentives and sanctions, upon which a host of social relationships and aspirations may be based. With such institutional and discursive supports, 'ought' might well come to resemble 'is'. For instance, the supposed 'failings' of the poor might become the basis for more and more intrusive regimes of control, in the course of which further 'failure', more intensive stigma and an entrenched sense of powerlessness come to compound an original problem of poverty. The teleology is completed when powerful vested interests insist that this state of affairs is somehow natural or inevitable. Such an arbitrary means of determining the principles of social order and the ideals of welfare was precisely Tawney's target in 1931. For our own purposes, the example simply demonstrates the close relation between ideologies of welfare and the broadly defined social field. Particular ideals of welfare (welfare as well-being – the good society) are inscribed upon 'the social' itself, in turn the institutions and mechanisms of welfare policy derive their legitimacy, objectives and support from prevailing conceptions of 'the social'.

Developments since the 1960s, however, have raised important ques-tions about the meaning and coherence of 'the social' and the underlying values and principles of welfare to which it is related. These develop-ments can be attributed to two connected processes. The first is the fragmentation of the welfare ideal, the second what we might call its secularisation.

The question of fragmentation has to do with the diversification of the actual objectives of welfare. The problem reflects Donzelot's concern, referred to earlier, regarding the shift from a politics of poverty to a politics of consumption and lifestyles (i.e. the politics of welfare). Although it would be quite wrong to infer, from Donzelot's remark, that former welfare strategies possessed any neat unity of purpose, problems of poverty no longer command the same significance and contemporary welfare strategies seldom achieve the same singular focus of concern. Growing individualism and a recognition of the potentially divisive character of welfare have undermined welfare's unity of pur-pose; in turn its political confidence has been shaken. All manner of (social) demands become pressed in the name of welfare. In a quantitat-ive fashion, this proliferation of welfare discourse undoubtedly broad-ens and enriches our conception of 'the social', but at the same time it rather robs welfarism of its historic sense of moral purpose (however misguided that may have been). This takes us to our second question, the secularisation of the welfare ideal.

The idea of the 'secularisation' of welfare is not intended to suggest that welfare formerly possessed a proud moral and philosophical heritage which has now slipped into a tortuous cycle of bureaucratic and self-interested decline, or that the history of welfare is not also one of discipline, coercion, exclusion and punitive control. Rather, the point is that whilst it was once possible to equate welfare with certain fundamental moral and philosophical precepts, even if at times somewhat punitive ones, it is no longer clear that this is the case. Even the Poor Law, for so long the harsh secret of social policy, formed part of a political project encompassing aspects of societal order and well-being. It was a mistaken and ideologically flawed utilitarianism, but none the less ambitious for that. It is questionable whether contemporary social policies embody such coherent moral and political purposes explicable in terms of 'welfare'. Indeed, today, it is arguable that the very idea of welfare has been all but dissipated. Residual elements may still be found, some sheltering amongst the rationalist and pragmatic activities of the modern state and others submerged beneath strategies of wealth accumulation in which welfare has come to mean little more than prosperity and personal well-being. Despite their manifest inadequacies and often heavy-handed coerciveness, modern philosophies of welfare have never previously been reducible to this.

It might be protested that contemporary forms of welfare become comprehensible through the perspective of individualism, albeit a rather inconsistent individualism, and perhaps there is some truth in this. But a sense of an intended, even planned, welfare outcome, even the starkest and most disciplinary form of welfare, seems lacking. Welfare as such, appears more and more the incidental by-product of politics and economics; it commands neither the attention nor the esteem credited to former welfare programmes. In a veritable sea of moral demands, welfare has no particular claim to authority, no particular sense of direction. If individualism is the key to the social and political developments of the late twentieth century, then welfare has truly been decentred; it has lost its legitimacy, or perhaps it is just a subsidiary project for the management of discontents. These developments have profound consequences for the relations between welfare and 'the social', for we are witnessing the decentring, even the expulsion, of traditional conceptions of welfare from 'the social'. This is an issue I shall pursue later.

We are left with a predominantly statist tradition of social welfare policy, practice and analysis that has come to bear precious little resemblance to its manifest ideals. It can no longer claim to preside over an integral ideal of 'welfare' at all. Indeed, 'the social', to adopt Marshall's phrase, 'is no longer a bearer of the welfare message' (Marshall, 1981). Only in this light does the extent of the marked transformation we are witnessing, become apparent. Formerly, this 'welfare message' represented a large part of 'the social' – it was undoubtedly also harsh, disciplinary and frequently punitive, but a welfare message none the less. The two aspects were indispensable features of the same project. Liberal historians, keen to emphasise the power of a benevolent idealism, have undoubtedly overestimated the significance of these elements of welfare and understated their more coercive features. But as Stedman Jones has shown, discipline and welfare were but part and parcel of the same *social* development.

> Looking forward to the creation of the Welfare State [historians] have concentrated upon proposals for old age pensions, free education, free school meals, subsidised housing and national insurance. They have virtually ignored parallel proposals to segregate the casual poor, to establish detention centres for 'loafers', to separate pauper children from 'degenerate' parents or to ship the 'residuum' overseas. Yet, for contemporaries, both sorts of proposals composed parts of a single debate.
>
> (Stedman Jones, 1971)

Nowadays, the debate is not one in which welfare plays any significant part. In what Titmuss referred to as the 'public burden model of welfare' (Titmuss, 1967), conservatives and neo-liberals discovered a lever with which to prise welfare away from the 'national interest', away from ideals of national well-being and, ultimately, away from 'the social'. The ascendancy of economic individualism and consumerism has led not merely to a redefinition of the ideal of collective welfare, the central premise of the welfare state, rather it has all but killed it off. Welfare no longer entails the principle of an adequate standard of living, or condition of existence, in which all are able (or expected) to share, it has instead become the exclusive privilege of a mass of isolated and competitive individuals. In short, welfare no longer speaks for the collective satisfaction of common needs, but for the maintenance of private differentials, the attainment of secular privileges and personal desires, and above all, for the individual's freedom to consume. Having developed together, almost hand in hand, welfare and 'the social' have largely parted company within the ascendant politics of social policy. Only the ideological symbols remain; *social* security, *national* health, *comprehensive* education – echoes from a time when 'social' meant more than the aggregation of individuality.

Of course, these processes pose major tensions for 'the social'. In later chapters I shall endeavour to develop them further by reference to changes in contemporary social policy, but now I must assess what this rather long examination of the dimensions of 'the social', has shown and draw this chapter to a conclusion.

Conclusion

I have now considered five major dimensions of 'the social'; that is, five important ways in which a discourse of 'the social' is constructed. These different dimensions need not be entirely consonant with one another, nor do they exhaust the possibilities of 'the social'. The often implicit naturalism of 'the social' and its incorporation of many informal even 'familial' characteristics conducive to an ideal of welfare (Jordan, 1987), frequently militate against an awareness of the constitutive role played within it by both the state and the market. Conversely, an appeal to 'social' justice frequently serves as the basis for resistance to the incursions of the state or the market. Furthermore, whilst the pluralist categories of the prevailing political culture, with its consensual strategies on conflict resolution and formally egalitarian conceptions of citizenship, underline a rather benign attitude towards the social order, this can only be experienced as profoundly alienating by those who do not (or cannot) share these perspectives. Yet, it is still within a discourse of 'the social' that answers are commonly sought. Paradoxically, 'the social' seems both cause and solution to political problems of this order. This perception is reinforced by cultural assumptions and forms of expression that imply a common experience of social existence, alongside ideologically charged notions of 'everyday life', 'reasonable' expectations of rewards and 'acceptable' standards of living. In Gramsci's terms, these common cultural assumptions and forms of expression, as well as the political and economic mechanisms by which they are daily verified, constitute a prime foundation for that 'chain of ideas' or 'spontaneous consent' through which effective hegemony is established (Gramsci, 1971; Hall *et al.*, 1978). In the process the 'fault lines' of 'the social' are smoothed over, and challenging images or critiques become submerged. Hence, 'the social', both as a terrain of struggle and an object of struggle, plays an important role in deflecting and reconstituting political objectives, ideologies and ideals.

Despite a certain superficial familiarity, therefore, the enigmatic character of 'the social' has had a major influence upon contemporary political philosophy, culture and strategies. An important effect of this is, as I have shown, the naturalisation of relations of competition and inequality, and the legitimation of mechanisms of discipline and forms of authority.

In their various ways, both political philosophers and social theorists, have endeavoured to account for the nature of political and economic relations in democratic capitalist states, but it is apparent that without an adequate contextual analysis of 'the social', as both a zone of intervention and a form of political rationality in itself, these accounts will be rather limited. And, as we have seen, the discourse of the social sphere engineers a remarkable conciliation between the critical demands and aspirations emanating from tensions within society, and certain received normative principles of social justice, economic rationality and political order. That this 'conciliation of interests' taking place within and throughout 'the social' not only avoids significantly challenging the existing structures of state and society but in many respects actually strengthens both is a profound testimony to its political utility. Its strength, the rationalities it embodies and the practices it deploys, derives from the persuasive ideals and objectives which have long constituted the Western tradition of political philosophy. However, like a cuckoo secretly maturing in the nest of another bird, 'the social' has, for some time, been ejecting rival discourses whilst consuming all that had hitherto sustained them.

This is important; it had previously been assumed that the political stability experienced by the developed capitalist nations in the late twentieth century could be attributed to economic growth and the political structures of liberal democracy. However, it now becomes clear that this political order has less to do with democracy than with 'the social'. And, as developments in contemporary western nations currently suggest, it is 'the social' as opposed to democracy which is proving indispensable. In later chapters, I shall endeavour to develop these issues.

3
The emergence of a disciplinary social policy

So far I have considered several different dimensions of the contemporary 'social sphere' and in the process outlined some new configurations of disciplinary power peculiar to the liberal-democratic Welfare State. These forms of power appear to supply their own justifications; they are, at one and the same time, components of an ideology and yet intensely practical measures. My objective in this and following chapters is to chart the growing prominence and increasing sophistication assumed by disciplinary techniques within a burgeoning social politics during the nineteenth and early twentieth centuries. Yet, when we examine this 'intensification' of disciplinary controls during a period which saw rapid development in the fields of commerce and industry and a significant expansion of state activity, a deeper and more fundamental project emerges. In short, we need to understand the development of the 'social sphere' as a disciplinary event in its own right. In constructing an account of origins of 'the social', we shall see both processes of class formation and the complementary mechanisms and techniques of individualisation developing and interacting.

As both an ideology and a form of power, 'the social', has been found to rest upon essentially disciplinary techniques and forms of intervention. We now need to consider how these mechanisms of surveillance, normalisation and judgement evolved in the context of nineteenth-century Britain. How, indeed, their development represents nothing less than the achievement of a practical ideal of social order and the forms of practice, knowledge and administration needed to sustain it. We are, in effect, examining the ways in which a generalised terrain of social problems ('the social question') came to be the accepted target of a regime of state interventions. Put another way, we might say we are describing the rise of the 'social state'. A form of state in which government activity is centred upon a series of *socially constructed and defined* objectives, pursued through the techniques of *social administration*.

The political and economic context for this rising preoccupation with ostensibly 'social questions' is provided by the emergence of a capitalist mode of production and its attendant class structure in Britain. The inherently disciplinary character of 'the social' undoubtedly derives from the complex societal transformations that were occurring and creating the kind of political and economic order within which capitalist relations of production, reproduction and exchange might thrive. The related emergence of discrete sciences – political economy for the government of wealth, demography and statistics for the government of population – testifies to the close connections between the development of capitalism and the emergence of a uniquely 'social' form of discipline. The subsequent preoccupations of social reformers – health, morality, idleness, problems of social class – in general, problems that cohered under the rubric of 'the social question' and which Foucault has referred to as 'bio-political' interventions, might all be related to this more fundamental capitalist transformation of social order (Foucault, 1980).

The first 'interventions' of what we can properly call the rising 'social state', therefore, have to do with the enhancement of forms of discipline attendant upon the development of capitalism and, in particular, the facilitation of conditions for the exploitation of labour. Ultimately, as Garland has argued, the crucial feature of this new terrain of social policy lay in, 'the establishment of mechanisms of security and integration, which could overlay and reorganise the effects of the labour market while maintaining its basic capitalistic terms' (Garland, 1985, p. 231).

A supply of labour did not simply exist, untapped, ready and willing to offer itself up for exploitation at the moment that the productive forces demanded it. Rather, this supply of labour power had to be created. The working class, figuratively speaking, had to be pushed into the factory; and, where 'factories' still exist, it still does. To achieve this political orchestration of economic pressure, all social relations within the emerging industrial society had to be brought within the disciplinary relations of capitalist political economy. Social relationships had to be infused with a new form of power, a form of coercion – frequently subtle, occasionally brutal, but usually effective – complementary to the exploitative conditions of the labour market. In this way, the state, in the first primitive forms of social policy became directly involved in the conditions under which labour power was produced (see Kay and Mott, 1982; Novak, 1988). It became involved in dictating the terms of subsistence – the conditions of material existence and necessity – for a whole class. The significance of the reform of the Poor Laws in 1834 lies here. As E. P. Thompson has remarked, the Poor Law Amendment Act was 'the most sustained attempt to impose an ideological dogma, in defiance of the evidence of human need, in English history' (Thompson, 1963, p. 276).

Ideological dogma it certainly was but, more to the point, it was also the core to a uniquely disciplinary political project. The exponents of capitalist political economy, the rising class of neo-liberal intellectuals, demanded a system of social policy which would complement the labour market. A system which, by imposing throughout society as a whole the disciplinary relationships of the factory and workshop, applied sanctions against those resisting this economic pressure and, therefore, helped assure the acquiesence of the working class as a whole. The Old Poor Law, with its traditional and customary practices, its regional variations and its arbitrary and undiscriminating distributions had to go. Its place taken by a more cohesive and calculated system of social policy which would combine the poverty and subsistence of the working class with the discipline of the capitalist economy, and in so doing, force the working class to give freely of their only possession, their labour. All restraints upon the 'free play' of economic forces were to be removed by the creation of what Bentham saw as a 'disciplinary continuum' which stretched from the workhouse and the prison to the 'freedom' of the market place (Bahmeuller, 1981; Melossi, 1979; Evans, 1982).

It is this 'disciplinary continuum', the first manifestation of a specifically 'social' policy, with which I am concerned. Not with its ideal form as dreamt up by Bentham but with its actual existence as it evolved, from philanthropic and early social scientific attempts to grapple with the related problems of pauperism, criminality, vice and immorality in the early nineteenth century, into a cohesive and nationwide system of social discipline. So enormous a political project – the social and political accommodation of labour to capital – could not realistically be achieved through a simple politics of repression and exclusion, yet neither could it be achieved solely through the individualised work of private and philanthropic associations.

It follows, therefore, that three important shifts lie at the heart of the social and political transformations we are addressing. First, a shift from strategies of exclusion and repression to policies of regeneration, inclusion and rehabilitation. Second, a shift from individualist techniques of control rooted in classical liberal jurisprudence and emphasising the absolutist fictions of 'rational economic man', moral choice, individual responsibility and consequential notions of guilt and desert, to essentially collectivist forms of social intervention focusing more directly upon the normative and behavioural characteristics of given populations. And, third, a shift from typically private, philanthropic and evangelical avenues of contact, coupled with juridical modes of access, to essentially statist, administrative and bureaucratic forms of 'social' intervention.

The discourses of poverty and criminality are uniquely suited to the elaboration of these transformations. For, aside from the fact that the respective discourses are often so closely associated that they are commonly taken to be referring to the same set of phenomena, whilst the discourse on poverty can be said to define a material and economic boundary to social order, the discourse on crime defines a moral and ideological one. Taken together they form perhaps the two most crucial dimensions of social order in which qualitative shifts in social discipline and changing practices of social intervention might be most readily discerned (see Jones and Williamson, 1979, page 69).

Different authors, located in differing political or theoretical traditions, have expressed the combined effect of these several transformations in terms of the progressive enhancement of the frontiers of democratic citizenship (Marshall, 1963), the 'incorporation' of the working class (Hearn, 1978) or the 'legalisation' of the working class (Edelman, 1980). I, on the other hand, intend to view these several changes in terms of an intensification of disciplinary mechanisms across society, transformations collectively comprehensible in terms of the rise of a new form of *social* state and new strategies and logics of *social* control.

A shift from strategies of repression to strategies of incorporation, involving selective promises of conditional well-being, best describes the transformations occurring. But it is important to emphasise the disciplinary character of these new arrangements. If we go to the trouble of pinpointing the 'essence' of modern conceptions of 'the social', we should be aware of the fact that few look upon these developments in anything other than a thoroughly positive light, and my objective here is to reveal its disciplinary – in other words its 'anti-social' – nature. And this is precisely the task I now turn to.

Class and classification

Commentaries upon 'the condition of the poor' and the 'state of public morality' as evidenced by growing rates of criminality jostle with one another for prominence amongst the political discourses of early nineteenth-century Britain. Consequently, it is not difficult to detect the repressive features of early nineteenth-century interventions into questions of poverty and criminality. On the one side, the Poor Law Amendment Act of 1834 might be thought to stand in a league of its own although, undoubtedly, the harsh principles of the statute were tempered by the vagaries of its actual implementation (Brundage, 1978; Digby, 1978). A similar situation prevails with respect to the Criminal Law. The severity of the law and the large number of capital offences were offset by the oft-remarked reluctance of juries to convict or judges to confirm sentence in cases where statute allowed for the imposition of the severest penalties (see Hay, 1975; Thompson, 1975; Weisser, 1979). Furthermore, the Criminal Law was a blunt instrument, lacking an insight into – or even a means to investigate – individual character. Consequently, geared primarily to retributivism, it had no means other than simple deterrence, with which to effect reform. Yet in the absence of effective policing or anything that might reasonably be termed a 'strategy' of punishment or prevention, even deterrence was not very effective. It was this gross inefficiency in the use of force which prompted Beccaria, and later Bentham, to propose a more rational system of penality.

However, if the Criminal Law was blunt, the Poor Law itself was a rather unsophisticated instrument, relying as it did upon a wholly negative application of force against the mind of the pauper. In effect, both systems of law lacked mechanisms that would make their administration anything but negative and repressive. Yet, even when they began to acquire reformist characteristics, these seldom tempered the harsh and repressive features of the twin systems of law. On the contrary, their major significance was in rendering 'social' coercion all the more *effective*.

At the heart of the new methods of social discipline being developed for the containment of the problems of pauperism and criminality, lay principles of classification. It was classification in the penal system which gradually enabled the authorities to separate the 'vicious and degraded' from the 'reclaimable', and classification which, within the Poor Law, might help distinguish the 'feckless and idle' or the fraudulent 'clever pauper' from the 'genuinely needy'.

Throughout the first half of the nineteenth century efforts were made, first by philanthropic societies and only later by the state, to undertake the complex task of classifying the impoverished working class. The whole endeavour of these philanthropic reformers has been described as an immense exercise in 'social scientific imperialism' (D. Fraser, 1973), whilst their political ambitions were made quite plain in 1833 as the Annual Report of the Statistical Society of London remarked, 'the science of statistics differs from political economy . . . although it has the same end in view' (Statistical Society of London, *Annual Report* 1833). As Foucault has observed, in this early phase in the development of capitalism, the accumulation of capital and the amassing of populations (as labour supply) were but two sides of an equivalent process. The examination of the 'conditions' of populations was expressly (and often it was very explicit) an examination of their quality and productive capacities. Moral prerogatives slipped easily into economic ones. 'The new science was to have demography at its core . . . and its end was the production of what was later to be called *useful* knowledge' (Cullen, 1975). For whom such knowledge was actually destined to be useful was presumed to be so self-evident as not to require elaboration.

The forms of classification attempted emerged primarily from the interaction of two opposing discourses of class: the first an essentially pre-sociological series of ranks, classes and grades, and the second a counterpart of the emerging self-consciousness of the modern proletariat, the state's political discourse on the (potentially) 'dangerous' working class (Bauman, 1983). The interaction of these two discursive themes may well have produced their most precise results within the walls of the nineteenth-century prison but, under the auspices of a nascent science of demography, the immense labour of charting the 'darkened terrain' of the working classes, as the prelude to the application of a Benthamite science of morals and legislation, was just beginning.

The most usual subject of this early statistical endeavour was the working-class community, its gradations of vice and virtue. In conjunction with the work of the social investigators, the machinery of the Poor Law and police fabricated a wholly new and synthetic discourse of class focusing upon the working classes primarily as a social and political threat whilst retaining a uniquely 'sociological' preoccupation with what contemporaries referred to as the preservation of 'peace and plenty' (Cullen, 1975). It is in this light that one can better understand the introduction of the first Official Census in 1801. For, whilst the important work of Malthus, *An Essay on the Principle of Population*, 1798, (Malthus, 1970) was no doubt influential, Cullen has argued that the writings and arguments of John Rickman, 'rooted in the confused and dangerous external and internal political situation of the mid 1790s', were probably more significant.

These insights into the links between the statistical and 'reform' movements are confirmed by the working-class subject matter selected by the social investigators and philanthropists, and also by reference to the predominant fears and concerns shared by the 'respectable' and 'propertied' who saw the 'dangerous and criminal classes' as the fundamental threat to their perception of English social order and peace.

In the London and Paris of the late 18th and early 19th centuries, people often saw themselves as threatened by agglomerations of the criminal, vicious and violent . . . it was much more than a question of annoyance, indignation or personal insecurity; the social order itself was threatened by an entity whose characteristic name reflects the fears of the time – the dangerous classes . . . even where the term is not explicitly invoked, the image persists of an unmanageable, volatile and convulsively criminal class at the base of society.

(Silver, 1970)

Yet it was not only in respect of crime and criminality that social investigation flourished, for a common set of social attitudes with regard to social problems was shared by the reforming bourgeoisie, state servant or philanthropist (Ritt, 1959). Statistics of criminality and pauperism were approached essentially as *class* phenomena, couched in terms of strong moral abhorrence and coupled with the need for discipline, instruction and reform. Marx's dictum (from *The Civil Wars in France*) that 'every social form of property has morals of its own', is borne out in the reports and statistical compilations of the early investigators, which gave social reformer and philanthropist alike broad licence to intervene. On the basis of such research and intervention, the foundations of an entire state sociology of social classes were laid.

Class, no doubt, features only as a fictional collectivity within an ideological representation of the social order, yet it became a reality, more to the point a problem, through the labour of enquiry and intervention invested by philanthropists and reformers. This is the point, the modes of intervention (investigation, treatment, reform, control) constitute precisely the objects of their own concern. And for the early nineteenth century, the objects of concern were classes: the 'pauper class', the 'dangerous and criminal classes'. This was so even though the acts, states and transgressions – crime, vice and poverty – which provided the organising principles for these classes were themselves understood individually, on the basis of profoundly moral aetiologies.

From a brief review of the activities of these early reformers it becomes clear that the constituted image of the problem social *class* as an object of investigation and manipulation occurred prior to the emergence of the problem individual. Only later did the detailed exposure and attempted reformation of these classes help found the individual as a valid object of enquiry and treatment. This is no more than we should expect for, as was suggested at the beginning of this chapter, in many important ways, the processes of class construction and the techniques of individualisation developed closely together. So when Foucault refers, in *Discipline and Punish*, to the individual as, 'the fictitious atom of an ideological representation of society', yet also a reality, 'fabricated by a specific technology of power . . . called discipline', (Foucault, 1977, p. 194), he is no doubt correct but he is talking of a later development in the history and refinement of 'the social'. Nevertheless, his remarks on the fabrication of subjectivity are no less true of classes, the agglomerates from which the details of infamous individuality were drawn.

The pioneering work in charting the character and extent of the 'criminal classes' seems to have fallen to the early nineteenth-century statistical societies. Whilst principles of classification found increasing application in the management of prisons and, later, of workhouses, the statistical societies concerned themselves with the 'criminal classes' as groups of the population at large and with the districts in which they lived. Theirs was a sociology of class that also served as a rudimentary criminology.

Close relationships developed between social reformers in and out of government service, as Cullen has argued, 'the same men tended to recur in all those avenues leading to the generation of social statistics' (Cullen, 1975, p. 27; Corrigan, 1975). Similarly, chief constables, prison governors and chaplains, and officers of the Poor-Law unions were prominent amongst those presenting papers to the meetings of the provincial statistical societies. Yet the limitations of existing criminal statistics were frequently alluded to and, in view of the purposes that reformers had in mind, the existing material on the 'criminal classes' was far from adequate. Philanthropists and social reformers alike demanded greater insight into the lives and conditions of the poorest classes, the better to pursue their strategies of classification and reform. In outline at least, therefore, an entire science of pauperism and criminality was embarked upon. In 1839 Rawson, the secretary of the Royal Statistical Society, remarked, in the Society's annual journal, that whilst the few details available in the Home Office criminal tables afforded material for a number of important analyses, it was, at the same time, 'important to bear in mind those boundless influences of residence, occupation, association, domestic habits and social position of which it is almost impossible to give any statistical representation' (*JRSS*, vol. 2, 1839, p. 319). Detailed study of every facet of the lives of the poor would, it was presumed, bring forth a solution to those social evils and moral vices so frequently attendant upon poverty. Investigators of the poor were themselves to reach a similar conclusion.

The state's own discourse upon the 'dangerous and criminal classes' lacked the depth and familiarity of that produced by the statistical societies. By the 1840s, these societies were already gathering material upon what they saw as the moral depravity of the lower classes – a condition of which pauperism, illiteracy, crime, vice, idleness and, in later years, 'socialism' were but the outward signs. A vast machinery of disciplinary social intervention for the reformation of character, the organisation of moral instruction, popular education and literacy, the regeneration of religious enthusiasm, policing and sanitation and the reconstruction of established notions of hierarchy and political order was being set in motion (Graff, 1977; Donzelot, 1980).

Like the philanthropists whose work they paralleled, the early social investigators assumed the confidence of an authority derived from their social position and sense of mission. This enabled them to overcome the opposition of those households they visited. Investigators reported that, 'much suspicion and reluctance were first encountered', and, despite vows to objectivity, were moved to anger and contempt on discovering 'untidy dwellings', 'wasteful expenditure', 'evidence of drink' or children 'improperly schooled'. Enquiring as to the habits of the parents or the religious instruction of children, their knowledge of the Ten Commandments or their ability to answer simple questions of religious doctrine, 'our agent was universally regarded as interfering with what they thought he had no concern and they gave answers which he knew in a great majority of cases to be false' (*JRSS*, vol. 1, 1839, p. 357). In tones of satisfaction, however, the investigators reported on 'males who had a trade' or 'females who could sew or knit', on membership of savings banks or friendly societies and upon satisfactory levels of literacy. In many respects the information collated by the statistical societies reveals the same ambiguous preoccupation with factors of *class* and *character* that come to play such an important part in poor relief discourse in the second half of the nineteenth century. In turn, these concerns with morality and character helped pave the way for that transition from a perception of criminality and poverty as class phenomena to a new view of them as located firmly within the individual.

Significant steps forward in regard to the state's own production of statistics occurred in 1857, the year following the passage of the County and Borough Police Act, which established police forces in all counties and boroughs of England and Wales. After 1856 an 'Introductory Report', highlighting the more significant trends and developments, was added to the Home Office Criminal Returns, thereby supporting Burton and Carlen's claim that:

the main function of the [Reports] . . . was to provide and publicly propagate knowledge of social conditions that would shape the technology of social engineering. Their contents became the discursive armory of the political scene. As such the enquiries had a clearly dual function of not only creating information but also manipulating its official reception.

(Burton and Carlen, 1979)

The year 1856 also saw the first entry of the 'criminal classes' into the statistical discourse of the state, whilst in 1857, the 'Census of the Criminal Classes' began. The 'criminal classes' had only a temporary residence in this official criminological discourse, however, for within the methods being developed for their analysis and treatment were also accumulating the ideological forces for their diffusion. The 'Census of the Criminal Classes' finally disappeared during the 1890s, later Victorian society being more preoccupied with supposedly 'dangerous' individuals, the 'hardened' or 'professional' criminals. Criminality, once looked upon as an almost natural state of the poor, gradually came to be seen as a condition presumed to be affecting only a small but desperate sub-class at the base of society (Gatrell and Hadden, 1972; Ignatieff, 1978; J. Davis, 1980; Gatrell *et al.*, 1980).

The disappearance of the 'criminal classes' from the criminological discourse of the state and the emergence of the individual offender announced the victory of a certain strategy of social reform focusing upon classification and social division. 'Character' and morality became the keys to effective social discipline, the objective being to isolate and control the hard-core criminal, the deviant poor and the 'undeserving' in order to concentrate a strategy of rehabilitation upon those remaining. Such systems of classification and partition were undoubtedly fairly arbitrary, the more so to the extent that the supposed hardcore of criminals and paupers were themselves, as we have seen, somewhat fabricated entities. Despite this arbitrariness, however, classification and social division served as vital pre-conditions for the success of the strategy of social reform and the resolution of the 'social question'. Similarly, while the discipline achieved through the respective systems of police and Poor Law was often crude, it was none the less an indispensable foundation for the organisation of all social policy.

The political economy of the Gospel

Eventually, the production of more thorough taxonomies of paupers and criminals – of the working class – and more elaborate systems of classification led to a more rigorous investigation of their differences, these investigations giving rise to the formation of a knowledge of individual characteristics and circumstances. Through such advances in social scientific taxonomy and the emergence of more specific versions of the theory of social causation, the class-centred interventions of the early nineteenth century gave way to a more relational practice of intervention which came to form the basis of the 'case-centred' approach of the Charity Organisation Society. However, this gradual shift from class to character, from repression to casework, from pauperism to pathology, in sum, the move from a view of pauperism as the result of a single general cause to the idea that its roots lay at the midst of a complex interaction of social, individual and environmental factors and 'categories of need', represents only one of the routes by which a disciplinary social administration came to rest, eventually, upon a detailed process of investigation and interrogation – the study of character and casework.

It might be objected that this interrogation of individual character had always featured as an important component of alms giving and charitable relief. Lis and Soly, discussing the 'social contract' between rich and poor during the Middle Ages, indicate that the 'political economy of the Gospel' (Symons, 1849) revealed a certain reciprocity between the rich and poor. Within this relationship, the poor were certainly the 'passive agents of spiritual action', but, 'the alms they received brought spiritual value to their donors'. Rich and poor appeared to need one another, 'spiritual and material poverty were complementary. And after all, alms assured . . . the maintenance of social equilibrium' (Lis and Soly, 1979, pp. 22–3).

However, the poor were only assisted on displaying appropriate habits and customs and on condition that they submitted themselves to the superintendence of the church authorities. Of course, some means of ascertaining the character of these applicants had to be found (Salter, 1926; Lis and Soly, 1979). Yet whilst such examinations certainly drew attention to the authorities' reluctance to distribute relief entirely indiscriminately or without some, albeit token, recognition of moral or religious authority, they appear trivial when compared with the pauper 'tests' developed later in the nineteenth century. Furthermore, moral investigation within early charitable endeavour served more as a confirmation of circumstances than as the prelude to positive assistance. Nineteenth-century philanthropists began to develop their rigorous examinations with a view to distinguishing those upon whom their time would be wasted from those whose character and efforts rendered them worthy of a little investment.

Nevertheless, it is beyond the scope of this account to develop in any further detail an analysis of the historical pedigree of philanthropic endeavour. Rather, my objectives here are to examine this legacy of charitable practices at the point at which they combined most fully and coherently with an individualising moral 'science' of social classification and casework which, developing throughout the nineteenth century, formed the basis of a disciplinary social administration.

Believing he was witnessing the passing of an important epoch in European government – the epoch of the patriarchal system of government described by James Mill – J. C. Symons pointed to what he believed to be a vital gap in the state's array of measures for the combating of pauperism, crime, indigence and disorder. Symons did not share Mill's faith in the principles and practices of political economy *alone* as a means by which the evils emanating from the opposition of rich and poor, might be tempered. He felt, above all, that a union of interests could be most effectively secured through the development of a range of juridico-moral techniques of identification and classification combined with active social interventions. In articulating the age-old problem of political order and social security through the problem of pauperism in this way, Symons stood at the very intersection of two historically significant relief practices. The older religious discourse of worldly poverty and piety opposed to a heavenly salvation endorsed, in very practical and immediate terms, the respective statuses of rich and poor. The newer discourse reflected in political economy and echoed throughout 'scientific philanthropy' favoured a more mortal conception of rehabilitation in the here and now. The establishment of a variety of 'reformatory institutions' throughout the country, encouraging attitudes of self-help and respectability, for instance Bentham's 'disciplinary continuum', would seem to represent the most complete realisation of this strand of relief practice.

Symons argued that, 'the power of the higher orders will mainly consist in chastening and Christianising that of the lower', yet along with like-minded contemporaries he rejected all universal panaceas – such as those advocated by the new generation of political economists – as solutions to the evils of pauperism. In a similar vein, the Reverend J. Tuckerman argued, 'panaceas are the bane of most reformers. . . . The evils under which we suffer are manifold, and manifold must be the remedies. No one, two, or three reforms . . . will suffice for the purpose; the evil must be met by a combination of appliances' (Tuckerman, 1833). The 'social question' was reconstructed and was no longer to be understood as a single great tension at the very heart of civil society but rather as a complex of factors which, collectively, resulted in pauperism. The aetiology was often crude, and moral and religious factors frequently weighed heavily upon the reformer's understanding, but nevertheless a new preoccupation can be seen to appear in relief work. The eighteenth century's discovery of the 'vices' – the pathological components of the new modern individual – and the nineteenth century's discovery of the dangers of 'class', paved the way for a new secular preoccupation with reform and rehabilitation – 'cure'.

A text which appeared in England in 1833, during the deliberations of the Commission on the Poor Laws and one year before the passage of the Poor Law Amendment Act, demonstrates very effectively the new preoccupations of philanthropy and, above all, the new discourse on 'cure'.

> Are the evils of poverty dependent, in part, on the moral condition of the poor? And who can doubt this, that knows aught of the state in which many of them are; who knows how ignorance has brought among them vice and idleness, in some cases an utter prostration of character; a recklessness, a moral death, an extinction almost of natural feeling. . . . How is this to be cured?
>
> (Tuckerman, 1833)

The new discourse of 'cure' – 'cure' as the strategic objective of moral policing and social intervention – was the element that tied together the two historical strands of relief practice. Although the emergence of a preoccupation with 'cure' marked a shift away from the rigidly ordered hierarchy entrenched within earlier patterns of relief giving, there are grounds for supposing that the new 'apparatuses of relief' may have been more effective in maintaining relations of hierarchy and the standards of respectability, morality and sobriety, so enthusiastically promulgated by philanthropists and bourgeois commentators, than were their forerunners (Gray, 1977). Yet 'cure' stood in a complex relation to the new disciplinary and classificatory system of scientific relief practice rooted in the principles of political economy and translated into policy through the Poor Law Amendment Act of 1834. 'Cure' implied a rather more interactive mechanism than the political economists envisaged. Bentham's proposals for a national organisation of poor relief supplemented by a regional matrix of panopticon workhouses in which a regime of machine-like discipline was to be sustained represented, perhaps, the most comprehensive application of the principles of the new political economy yet, even so, had little by way of 'cure' to offer.

Bentham hoped that his panopticon, whether as penitentiary or workhouse, would reform, certainly its 'moral architecture' was designed with this in mind. Yet despite its almost omnipotent surveillance, its insistence upon industry and regularity, there was little in it, save the certainty of further repression, to cultivate attitudes of 'voluntary' obedience amongst its inmates. Furthermore, as historians who have researched the development of the modern prison have indicated, even in their most ideal manifestations, such institutions failed lamentably to reform (Foucault, 1977; Ignatieff, 1978; O'Brien, 1982).

Despite the power relations, contrived through the model architecture advocated by Bentham and a whole new generation of civic architects, it seemed that the project of reform rested, as often as not, upon the moral and even spiritual relay afforded by the prison visitors and the chaplain. For Bentham, 'inspection' referred to a feature deriving from the careful design of institutions; for Chadwick and the Poor Law Commissioners, inspection and discipline were relationships made possible by the efficient administration of well-regulated workhouses, but for the more mainstream of English reformers, philanthropists and 'tories', inspection had traditionally implied a somewhat more human relationship and discipline referred ultimately to a discipline of the self (Crowther, 1981).

However, although the discourse of reform or 'cure' rested fairly uneasily with the full implications of the system of repressive deterrence derived from the new relations of political economy, a more fortuitous tactical alliance could be forged between the proponents of primitive forms of relief visiting or 'casework' and those early nineteenth-century social investigators whose disquiet about the moral condition of the poor has been well reported. Motivated as often by moral tragedies as by material deprivations, the social investigators are likely to have agreed with Symons's remark that, 'the exhibition of evils is of little use save it tends to remove them' (Symons, 1849, p. 9). Hence a combination of talents profitable to both philanthropist and statistician recommended itself. To the former this liaison offered methods, the confidence of scientific practice, the quantification of results as well as a certain authority deriving from the mastery of technique. To the latter it offered the opportunity provided by the great laboratory that was working-class life, a deeper understanding of the practicalities of reform and the opportunity to develop methods for the study of aetiology. In the cross-fertilisation of these two practices, it is fair to say that the modern discipline of relief management, a discipline that was to become social administration, was born.

Yet if this alliance of old and new strategies were thought to contain the seeds of a solution to the problem of pauperism, then it becomes necessary to examine just what proposals emerged for sealing the gap which had been identified in the state's defences against poverty and disorder. More than mere 'system' was seen as necessary to overcome moral decline and weakened social ties, but indiscriminate relief-giving was viewed as worse than useless. A more selective and discriminating practice, better suited to the regime of political economy and its competitive and promotional environment, was required. Repression and deterrence alone would not suffice, but should serve as the backdrop to attempts to develop new relations between rich and poor. In one of his more basic, yet nonetheless fundamental, 'Hints to Philanthropists', Davis had remarked:

> Though the fear of punishment may deter from atrocious and criminal
> actions . . . to produce in the labouring classes a superior line of conduct

and to fix in their minds and hearts good principles and virtuous habits,
we ought to have recourse to rewards. . . . Nothing will so forcefully excite
a spirit of virtuous emulation among the poor as the bestowing of certain
marks of distinction by the rich as well as their granting pecuniary rewards
to those who have best deserved them.

(W. Davis, 1821)

In this advocacy of classification, of social division and of the need
for systems of incentives, an entire philosophy of disciplinary social
administration was outlined. It was, however, manifestly clear to contemporary social economists that existing institutions were ill-equipped
for the task in question and fundamentally deficient in regenerating the
necessary community of interests. This was a judgement as critical of
past relief practices as it was of the New Poor Law with its singularly
hostile regime.

The regeneration of morals stood out above all as the primary task
of the reformer. The Poor Law offered one remedy in the form of the
crushing of pauperism and the building of the workhouse 'Bastilles'
(Digby, 1978) as the state's first line of defence against the pressure of
need, but a gentler, more effective, instrument of intervention which
would work more directly upon the morals of the poor and cure their
vices, seemed more appropriate. For, as Cormack has explained,
'pauperism was not merely poverty; it was moral degradation. And the
object of the reformer therefore was to rescue character – to regenerate'
(Cormack, 1945). Yet the Poor Law and philanthropy were not competing alternatives, as many contemporary philanthropists in their frequent
castigation of Poor-Law methods tended to imply. For whilst, in a very
immediate sense, the Poor Law was the basis for the ordering of class
relations in the nineteenth century it also served as the foundation from
which the more selective interventions of the philanthropists could
begin. The two methods of reform occupied a complementary relationship although few allowed that this admitted of any compromise in the
profoundly moral aetiology of poverty. According to Tuckerman in his
'Introduction' to *The Visitor of the Poor*, 'poverty and its attendant
evils spring rather from moral than physical causes, and by moral
appliances should their removal be sought.'

Investigating the poor

A solution had to be found. Contemporary social reformers were seeking to transform the character of relief strategy rather than its overall
social objective. Like the newer generation of penal reformers, the
social reformers were seeking to change the nature of the political

investment made by 'authority' in the social relations of class society by the specification of new forms of influence and new ideological objects to which it might usefully be applied. Despite their observation that idleness and immorality were evils 'not of the mind, but of the soul' (Gerando, p. 49), Tuckerman and his contemporaries cannot exactly be said to have 'rediscovered' the *soul* as the true object of reform (something not uncommonly attributed to penal reformers, see Foucault, 1977; Ignatieff, 1978), for, given their religious roots and overwhelmingly 'moral' preoccupations, they would always have seen the soul in close relation to the sins of the body. Rather, this generation of religious philanthropists were important for turning a long-standing religious association into a secular strategy of social reform. Henceforth, social reform would rest upon new moral sites of power. The social philanthropist hoped that, in future, the poor would no longer be merely confronted by the governing classes but would be drawn into an infinitely more productive and useful arrangement with them.

> The failure of the existing instrumentality bids us consider what new measures may be devised. Now what is this failure of? Coercion. Force. And the failure of coercion or force suggests the employment of the mild and caring agencies of benevolence; or if force be still in some degree necessary, let the force be so directed as to remove, not aggravate the evil. . . . For a remedial then, let a system of prevention be tried. Let the schoolmaster and the visitor of the poor take the place of the gaoler.
>
> (Tuckerman, 1833, pp. x-xi)

And with these words Tuckerman commended de Gerando's guide to the visitation of the poor to his contemporaries, pausing only to launch a discreet attack on those Benthamite reformers who sought to systematise poor relief yet who simultaneously paid little attention to their moral reform. The author of *The Visitor of the Poor*, on the other hand, 'really knew the poor . . . he was therefore qualified to write of them' (*ibid.*). To this end, the furtherance of a knowledge of the poor and the selection and promotion of those deemed sufficiently worthy, de Gerando's book was delivered to its readership in the manner of an early manual on the art and science of the visitation of the poor.

It is not the purpose of this analysis to investigate the explicit political differences and the conflicts between advocates of alternative methods of pauper management, in any event the lines of opposition are often far from clear. Rather, my objective is to examine the evolution of disciplinary techniques through ostensibly 'welfare' policies. The opposition between the Poor Law and philanthropy provides an opportunity to examine the emergence of a singular disciplinary strategy throughout the interaction of two supposedly alternative systems. Whilst Chadwick and the Poor Law Commissioners had sought to compel the cessation of charitable relief to the poor, preferring the unitary discipline of the 'workhouse test', the authors of the 1834 Act, 'allowed a place for charity over and above the minimum requirements of the law' (Young and Ashton, 1956, p. 50).

My concern then, is with the increasingly complementary relationship between two principal relief discourses. In terms of the refinement of disciplinary power within the systems of poor relief, this synthesis proved to be a very productive association. A deterrent relief system, reinforced by a system of individual supervisions, would yield a host of highly effective associations, techniques and sites for the application of social discipline. In the following few pages this general synthesis of procedures, or languages and, ultimately, of a knowledge of the poor will be examined through a brief analysis of the emerging science of pauper investigation, the 'science' that was to become the new discipline of social casework. Although a new knowledge of the poor was certainly in process of forming, as in the case of the 'criminal classes' discussed earlier, it seems clear that private associations, philanthropic and visiting societies were developing a far more systematic knowledge of the poor than the state and the Poor Law authorities. As Williams has confirmed, the Poor Law

> did not require the development of a knowledge about paupers. Such knowledge would require documentary support in the form of dossiers on paupers. But the general mixed workhouse only kept a stocktaking record of paupers in the form of an admission and discharge register. . . . The workhouse before 1870 was dedicated to a blind repressive discipline.
>
> (K. Williams, 1981, p. 118)

By contrast, the work of the philanthropic and pauper visitation societies was positively sophisticated with its endeavours to distinguish gradations of vice and virtue. Indeed, so extensive were the enquiries that the philanthropists were required to undertake prior to offering the poor any material assistance that it is surprising that any assistance was ever given. This being said, however, many of the considerations recommended to the nineteenth-century philanthropist bear an uncanny resemblance (in substance if not in precise form) to both the interrogation of status and intentions that precedes the demonstration of an entitlement to social security and to the enquiries that feature so prominently as aspects of social casework in the twentieth century.

Nineteenth-century philanthropists were warned of the dangers of 'indiscriminate alms giving', instead, they were told, 'Charity alone does good.' Charity considered all the facts and extended its purview to the future whereas alms giving catered only for the pressures of the present (Gerando, 1833, p. 38). Alms giving could no longer be left to the simple whim and fancy of the bourgeois classes, henceforth, charity would have to be precisely organised and administered. The harm done by the indiscriminate alms giver was said to be visible in the outward appearance of every demoralised pauper. The 'vain and meddlesome bounty' of the unenlightened bourgeois had seemingly done far more than just permit the failings of the poor to go unchecked; it had robbed them of their independence, of their will to labour. In short, nothing less than the very morals of the poor themselves were placed in jeopardy by indiscriminate alms giving (*ibid.* p. 42).

Philanthropists were carefully taught how to discriminate between genuine need and pretence; they were warned to be alert: 'importunity itself is sometimes a sign that should put you on your guard.' But, above all, they were encouraged not merely to wait for need to present itself; true philanthropists were expected to seek out the genuine poor for themselves. 'It is in their dwelling places that you must investigate which is the reality and which the phantom' (*ibid.*).

From this point the pauper investigation begins in earnest. Nothing is taken for granted. All the elements of domestic life – thrift, need, virtue and sobriety – must be examined for what they might reveal of the character or true circumstances of the members of the household. When questioning members of particular households, philanthropic investigators were encouraged to solicit precise information regarding the relationship of each to all the others in every supposed 'family' relationship. 'Beware', the investigators were warned, 'how you become an accomplice in a conspiracy against the most holy ties of nature' (*ibid.* p. 43). In dealing with the poor, therefore, nothing had to be taken at face value. Indeed, as if the investigators really needed to be told, de Gerando later added that, 'the poor will sometimes seek to deceive you' (*ibid.* p. 99).

In all cases, therefore, the philanthropist had to delve beneath the surface presentations and seek to appraise the true character of those whose claim to assistance was under consideration. The interrogation of 'character' held central place, for philanthropy admitted only a very limited form of 'real poverty'. Yet the general 'science' of relief administration that grew up in the effort to identify these 'real causes' was of fundamental importance in that it was intimately tied to the political and ideological objective of recasting the hierarchy of relations that prevailed between rich and poor. Thus, even accepting the substantial part of an eighteenth-century 'materialistic' understanding of poverty seemed not to preclude the foundation of a highly discriminatory relief administration. 'There are three causes of real indigence. Inability to labour, insufficient produce of labour and absolute want of employment' (*ibid.* p. 44). It followed, therefore, that all other poverty was no more than the failing of individual character or industry and required assistance that was more directly moral than material. However, even the supposedly legitimate forms of poverty had to remain suspect until fully proven – and proof itself was no simple matter. The general categories of legitimate poverty broke down into a number of more specific disadvantages and conditions, each of which was capable of a variety of interpretations. It is unrealistic to assume the absence of strikingly moral preoccupations within the character assessments of the investigators, particularly as their interventions were an express contribution to a moral discourse with a moral objective in view and all the doubtful idiosyncracies of a supposedly human 'nature' to be wary of.

The full character of these investigative techniques becomes apparent on examination of the schedule of enquiries proposed even for the case of 'real poverty'. To take the issue of 'poverty due to inability to labour', investigators were reminded that inability to labour might be either temporary or long-lasting, absolute or partial. The investigators had to judge for themselves, 'you must go to the bedside of the sufferers . . . on different days at different hours . . . you must question the neighbours, you must bring a physician' (*ibid.* p. 44). Yet the task is not complete simply upon making a correct diagnosis, for the objective is remoralisation and, having provided a potential remedy, the investigator must always oversee its application. To do this effectively philanthropists were reminded that everything possible had to be known about their charges: 'a thousand things . . . nearly their whole lives' (*ibid.* p. 45). Knowledge, then, became the key to philanthropy. Knowledge as power and the core of a crucial political relation. This was no mere knowledge for its own sake but, in a class-ridden society, the most basic of all knowledges. Ultimately, nothing less than a complete science of the poor was anticipated.

The parameters to this knowledge were clearly given by the laws of political economy and the canons of respectability and morality. The question of poverty was to be firmly situated within the relations of the labour market and the philanthropists were confidently assured that, 'the price of daily labour is *naturally* regulated by the sum necessary for the support of the generality, and it is found insufficient *only for cases of exception*' (emphasis added, *ibid.* p. 45). It followed, therefore, that genuine poverty could only be the result of improvidence in the rearing of children, irregular habits of employment or problems of aptitude or application. In accordance with the accepted canons of political economy it is not difficult to see how the principles of disciplinary supervision were to cajole and correct the recipients of charitable assistance into the habits and manners appropriate for members of their class. But above all, visitors of the poor were urged to pay especial attention to the women, 'on account of their sex'. An especially stringent supervision of mothers and wives was called for, because 'misery may lead a woman to a still greater misfortune than poverty. It may expose her to seduction' (*ibid.* p. 46). There seemed no task quite so important as the supervision of mothers and, through them, the family as a whole. Around the mother an entire family history – a moral history – was to be constructed.

> Learn how she has lived, in order to better ascertain how she lives now. . . . How do the husband and wife live together. . . . Study the internal habits of the family. . . . Be assured, nothing is so common as to exaggerate poverty.
>
> (*ibid.* pp. 47, 55)

In scrutinising each household, 'penetrating their internal history and studying their domestic relations', investigators were called upon to examine a myriad of tiny details of domestic life because 'improvidence has its peculiar signs' and the investigator had to become a veritable expert in the ways of the poor. 'You must examine the dwelling, see how the furniture is arranged, look at the linen, and, obtaining their confidence, learn how they combine their scanty means . . . find out if the rent is regularly paid, and if the family is peaceable and regular in its habits.' The poor, it is suggested, 'will tell you all their imprudences under the reviving hope of being assisted', and the opportunity to deliver a stern lesson in morals and economics was not to be squandered (*ibid.* pp. 48–9).

Behind this careful scrutiny of each and every applicant for assistance there lay one motive above all others, the discovery of vice. This task was rendered all the more difficult because

> Vice is almost always concealed. . . . We must observe carefully. . . . We must watch for those inadvertences which the most cunning cannot avoid. We must mark whether our sudden appearance to them seems to agitate them, and what impression our words make; we must surprise them in those actions which they thought would be concealed from us; we must find out their connections in life and the kind of characters they have most frequent intercourse with.
>
> (*ibid.* p. 50)

And in these ways the investigator was to scrutinise the poor so as to classify them most accurately, in order that they might be most effectively assisted. Matters of distress and human character being what they are, however, it is readily admitted that the understanding of the causes and effects of poverty and pauperism is by no means absolute. It was for these reasons, therefore, that the judgement and discretion of the individual philanthropist was so crucial. Despite the almost doctrinal clarity of the written discourse on the visitation of the poor, the multifarious conditions under which the latter lived implied that remedies were neither clear-cut nor easily found, strict rules of practice were displaced in pursuance of achievable objectives. But it was the visitor, first and foremost, who had the responsibility of making this apparatus of investigation and remoralisation work. Indeed, herein lies the very weakness of the entire strategy.

The labour of reform: the burden of philanthropy

Despite the claims of its many and varied proponents, the voluntary visiting agency could never effectively accomplish the nationalisation of relief practice upon which the new industrial order would come to depend. On the contrary, the visiting agencies were almost entirely local in their scope and aspirations. Furthermore, they demanded too much from even the most experienced philanthropists to provide a workable alternative to the Poor Law. The system of visiting and the personalised authority of the philanthropist working under a charitable scheme was far too idiosyncratic; it accommodated too readily to the specific circumstances and deficiencies of the poor themselves and required too great an investment on the part of the philanthropic agencies. The project of reform aspired to by the political economists, on the other hand, demanded that the poor themselves should make the greatest contribution to their own rehabilitation and that much less, politically or economically, should be required of the governing classes.

The lesson taught by philanthropy was that, above all, the poor themselves should be invigorated and encouraged to develop proper habits of industry. Yet if this were so, why did the greater part of the burden of relief work seem to fall upon the rich and propertied? A really effective system of discipline could not be set up by a corps of investigators: rather, the poor had to be set to work at their own remoralisation. The activity of home visiting could not be made the mechanism by which the relief apparatus was to work, in so many respects it was too inefficient; every characteristic had to be registered, every transaction closely supervised, every statement corroborated. More suitably, the burden of non-compliance had to be made to fall more directly upon the poor themselves. The problems inherent in the supervisory discipline of charitable relief could not be resolved within the framework of philanthropy.

The new generation of philanthropists had fashioned a huge charitable apparatus resting upon the accumulation of a vast quantity of detailed information that amounted to a virtual science of pauperism. In this sense, the work of the visitors of the poor complemented the work of those statisticians who had already begun to make a science of criminality. On the basis of this new realm of knowledge they hoped that the causes, effects and remedies of their respective problems could be suitably calibrated as a prelude to their elimination. However, as we have seen, the system of investigations each envisaged required too costly an intervention on the part of authority, and their patterns of supervision were far too cumbersome to imprint themselves firmly upon the social relations of the working classes and the poor.

Lessons from philanthropy

My remaining concern is to discover what might be learned from this highly interventionist precursor of a disciplinary social policy. Or, more specifically, whether in its detailed interrogations, supervisory procedures and strategic objectives can be identified the formulae of a more cohesive *modern* system of discipline.

I have already pointed out that the key to the assessment and classification of the poor rested upon an examination of moral character, whilst labour or, more precisely, the willingness to labour, served as the vehicle of rehabilitation. 'There is only one way of discerning the truth', noted de Gerando, 'see if the poor who are capable of labour, accepted it with pleasure and executed it with zeal when it is presented to them' (*ibid.* pp. 50–1). A familiar test indeed.

If we pursue the legacy of investigative philanthropy still further, we will not be surprised to encounter rather more examples of crucial judgements pertaining to the character and 'worth' of the poor being derived from conventional assumptions regarding hierarchy, inequality and the social order, bourgeois morality and, above all, the framework of political economy. The poor had to know their place and, philanthropists were assured, 'they will receive more advantage from us when recognising our superiority.' After all:

> The poor, on many accounts, are like children, they have want of foresight and are ignorant; they easily allow themselves to be carried away; they need to be supported, restrained, directed; they need more than a benefactor, they need an instructor.
>
> (*ibid.* pp. 107–8)

But knowing their place was never enough on its own, the poor had to *accept* this place willingly and, above all, *act* as if they knew it. From the philanthropist's point of view, these requirements and conditions, the constraints under which the poor were to exist, declared loudly and clearly the overriding purposes of 'true charity'. For the essence of 'true charity' is best represented in the form of a disciplinary schooling of the working classes by the governing classes, in the basic elements of political economy and morality. Something approaching complete control of the poor was aspired to. Thus, 'if we can only obtain the direction of the affairs of a poor family we should, in the first place, endeavour to teach them the science of economy. The least attention to it makes a wonderful difference in their affairs' (*ibid.* p. 153).

Such remarks, together with constant reminders to be wary of 'easy kindness', help us redefine the philanthropic task. Its central objective appears to have been one of reconciling the poor to the privations of their lives and to unending labour. Rehabilitation and 'true charity' sought to convince the working classes that none of the benefits of life – for them at least – came without effort. 'True charity', therefore, merged imperceptibly with Smiles's doctrines of self-help and worked upon the minds, aspirations and future possibilities of the poor rather than upon their more immediate physical and bodily wants. This disci-plinary application of the principles of political economy is suggested in the philanthropists' attempts to construct budgetary tables for the poor. These tables were designed to encourage foresight and self-restraint in the expenditure of poor families. In practice, however, they frequently revealed a far greater preoccupation with the outgoings than with the income of the poor.

Abstinence, method and the (permanent) deferment of indulgence became the basic elements of a project that sought to make a science of thrift. In the past, relief had placed its emphasis upon the sustenance of the body; 'true charity', on the other hand, was to focus upon the mind as its frame of reference. This shift in the practice of charity away from emphasis on physical sensations and the body to emphasis on the mind coincided with a series of similar shifts occurring within a number of nineteenth-century institutions concerned with the problems of social order and population management, foremost amongst which were the prison, the workhouse and the school.

Visitors of the poor were instructed to unmask contrivance and false-hood in pauperism and in applications for relief whenever they encount-ered it. This was not only because such applications were considered fraudulent but, more seriously, because they were seen as a form of self-deception, a denial of realities – moral standards and the principles of sound political economy – that were self-evident to the non-depraved sections of the population. On the one hand, pauperism was decried as an abuse *to* the poor, on the other hand, the language of vice, responsibility and moral failure asserted the culpability *of* the poor. Pauperism emerged as none other than the worst form of *self-abuse*. Through the discriminating and disciplinary exercises of philanthropy, the poor were to be returned to society, reconciled to its beliefs and divisions and rendered content with their lot. This 'rehabilitation' was not to be secured by ideological conditioning but by the more direct method of confining the poor to their allotted place within an industrial society. This place, the poor were assured, was predetermined and unalterable. To fail to accept it was to exclude oneself from the means of subsistence, to suffer voluntarily and unnecessarily. In any event, the spectre of the workhouse helped remind the pauperised, and beyond them the entire working class, of their 'proper place' within the social system.

As I have said, the new philanthropy could no longer be realistically considered as a thorough-going alternative to the Poor Law, but neither were the 'visitors' and 'social investigators' merely supplementary. Rather, philanthropy and the Poor Law were complementary, their respective disciplinary strategies becoming more and more interdependent. Together, the Poor Law and philanthropy pursued the socio-economic 'rehabilitation' of large sections of the pauperised working class, bringing about, in effect, their transition from a dangerous, criminal class to the modern industrial working class, a class whose accommodation to industrial capitalism was gradually being secured and who looked increasingly to the existing social structure for the realisation of virtually all their major aspirations.

Throughout the whole of this accommodation, or modernisation, of the nineteenth-century working class, the role of the visitor of the poor continued to assume a quite central significance.

> After the visitor has studied the situation of the poor and found out their wants, he must endeavour to discover the most economical means of assisting them. He must teach them economy, the spirit of order and foresight and how to preserve their self-respect and dignity . . .
> extraordinary results are not necessary . . . it is sufficient that each member of the family fulfils well in the very humble sphere which is assigned to him, the post to which providence calls him, and comports himself as an honest and useful man. *This is what the true interest of the family and the general order of society demands.*
>
> (*ibid.* pp. 150–1, emphasis added)

4

Discipline and division in the nineteenth-century Poor Law

The feature that many contemporaries claimed was lacking within the Poor Law, formed the very heart of the philanthropic strategy for dealing with pauperism. While the Poor Law sought, essentially, to confine the problem of pauperism within the repressive environment of the workhouse, philanthropy sought to 'humanise' – or perhaps we should say 'socialise' – the discipline of industrial society through the improvement of morals, the enhancement of the capacities of the working class and the dissemination of knowledge.

Knowledge of the poor was a vital component of philanthropy for it helped refine the classificatory principles which dictated the pattern of relief administration. As has been suggested, this was always a particularly pragmatic knowledge, closely tied to the administrative process, seldom questioning its categories and perpetually reinforcing the original moral divisions upon which its system of classification was based. Knowledge and education were deemed important in two further senses in addition to the way in which they registered the progress of the 'science' of philanthropy. In the first place, as I have said, knowledge and education were crucial to the task of reforming and remoralising the poor. 'Helpable' cases were to be schooled in the basic elements of economy, instructed in budgetary method, advised about and assisted in the pursuit of new trades and taught the principles of christian morality. In the second place, knowledge and education were of central importance in the recruitment and training of philanthropists, the foundation of a body of theory and a range of techniques for intervening in the lives of the poor. Knowledge, in this sense, was the core of the developing discipline of philanthropy and the earliest form taken by social work as a professional practice.

There exist several authoritative accounts of the origins and development of social work in the nineteenth century, the rise of the Charity Organisation Society (COS) and the refinement of techniques of casework (Cormack 1945; Young and Ashton, 1956; Harris, 1972; Fido, 1977; Parry and Parry, 1979; Jones, 1983). My objective here is not to attempt to rewrite this history but, rather to concentrate upon the refinement of disciplinary techniques for visiting and investigating the poor and upon the new disciplinary science of social administration – a true 'anti-social policy' – which emerged as a result of the cross-fertilisation of the methods and tactics of pauper remoralisation and control used by the Poor Law administrators and the philanthropists.

Why does this amount to an 'anti-social policy'? In short, because it represents an explicit attempt to refashion 'the social', to turn it to another purpose. In constructing a primitive 'social' policy, reformers were reconstituting the very language and *raison d'être* of political order, purposes and meaning. Similarly, they were subjecting society itself to alien forms of authority and radically new political and economic forces. None of this is to suggest that 'the social' ever existed as an historically pure entity untainted by power, corruption and greed, rather, as we have seen, 'the social' is always the result of earlier successful dominations. But if 'the social' is never pure, how can we arbitrarily describe one historical form, rather than another, as 'anti-social'?

The answer to this question has to do with the emergence of new forms and relations of power. The transformations I have been examining bear witness to an intensification of disciplinary relations across society – relations which entrap and belittle human agents and which, as Foucault has remarked, sustain themselves by their own mechanism (Foucault, 1977, p. 177). Previously, when power had been visibly and ceremoniously held, it had always been possible to envisage its transformation; Marx and Engels' attempts in the *Communist Manifesto* to rouse the working class against the bourgeoisie typify this formulation of a pedagogy of the oppressed. But when power is neither localised nor the possession of any single agent, simple injunctions to rebellion or resistance lack clarity of purpose or direction.

In the new situation, the 'social interventionist' phase, discipline insinuates itself into the entirety of social relations, people become the bearers of their own discipline, increasingly forms of self-discipline become encouraged. Resistance or servitude both reinforce the patterns of subordination; the distinctions between oppressor and oppressed seem less clear cut, less tangible and are, therefore, less easily resisted. For all this, maybe they are even less offensive. The new discipline is more 'complete' but – and this is the key – it is also qualitatively different, for the individual becomes part of the arrangement of discipline. It is certainly no less effective – in fact, it is probably more so, for the transformations we are considering differ in that a new mode of domination, new techniques and interventions, are justified *in the name of 'the social' itself.* Thus, the new modes of domination and the developing techniques of disciplinary control have become vitally necessary, they are the essential frameworks of orderly coexistence, in effect, the *sine qua non* of society and 'social' life itself. In such a context, resistance becomes either pointless (a challenge to an entire social order), or impossible to conceive of (lacking a foundation independent of either 'society' or the disciplined individual). And it is in this fundamental closure of alternatives, this authoritarian and anti-democratic elimination of choice and freedom that the 'anti-social' of the new political relations lies. It also goes some way to explaining the difficulties facing a radical politics in modern society, but this is a theme I return to in the final chapter.

In charting the development of the leading edges of this new disciplinary power, one of the first tasks is to observe how the new ground rules of social order become established within a new politico-economic rationality. The ideological onslaught had already begun before 1832, but the Royal Commission on the Poor Laws provided a very suitable focus for the popular refashioning of ideas about poverty. In a manner not unfamiliar to us today, the poor were told that the state did not owe them a living. According to Berg, 'the working classes were to be informed of their true place in society: "it is high time to disabuse them of the disastrous fallacy involved in the word *Poor*," wrote one witness to the Poor Law Commission in 1833. The working class "were to be reminded that the poor man is not a pauper".' (Berg, 1980, p. 304).

Several preoccupations revealed themselves within the complicated investigatory and classificatory relief practices adopted by nineteenth-century relief agencies. These related to the visible adherence of the poor to standards of morality and respectability, to their soundness of character and, above all, to their willingness to work. These features of relief organisation are well known, because they are often reiterated, but another feature, perhaps the major concern of the relief administrator, consisted in the prevention, detection, control and repression of all forms of 'fraud', 'imposture' and 'abuse' of relief funds. Indeed, the wide definition given to the notion of 'abuse of public funds' is indicative of the fact that the conditions of subsistence and means of life itself for the working poor were being redefined. As the Poor-Law commissioners were to write in their final *Report* in 1834, 'it has never been deemed expedient that the provision should extend to the relief of poverty; that is, the state of one who, in order to obtain a mere subsistence, is forced to have a recourse to labour' (Checkland and Checkland, 1974, p. 334).

In order to understand this concern with poverty, pauperism and the alleged 'abuses' of the Poor Laws, we must situate this discussion within the context of the new industrial capitalist methods of production which engendered new forms of class relations and necessitated a new form of state. The new modes of production demanded an abundant supply of labour – acquiescent, mobile, yet collectivised. The labour force had to be accommodated to the new conditions of exploitation. The state was exhorted to assist in reformulating what Kay and Mott have termed the 'wider law of labour' – the broad political and economic context within which the labouring classes lived and worked; within which they were left free to satisfy their subsistence needs only through employment (Kay and Mott, 1982). The state was able to contribute to the process of transformation by reconstituting the formalised conditions under which the labourer was required to work. It could achieve this generalised orchestration of political and economic pressure by effectively tightening up on the conditions under which poor relief would be made available. Writing in 1849, J. C. Symons was adamant that the construction of this 'wider law of labour' was, above all, a task for the state, and that only in this way could a coherent, consistent and wholly legitimate influence be brought to bear – in the name of all and in the interest of all. 'We must have a central power as the *primum mobile* of all such policies . . . there must likewise be a central fund. Hence the necessity of a national rate. . . . The state alone, can, may and ought to do it' (Symons, 1849, p. 191).

Symons was acknowledging what Chadwick, Senior and the other Poor-Law commissioners had argued for most strongly in their Report. With the state directly involved in dictating the terms of poor relief on a national scale, it was, at one and the same time, underwriting the political economy of capitalist enterprise and redefining something that had hitherto hardly qualified as an 'abuse' at all as a threat to economic profitability and an affront to the state. The alleged 'abuse' of outdoor relief, which was thought to be widespread throughout the whole of the unreformed Poor Law, was a major loophole in the political and economic order of nineteenth-century Britain. Economic viability and political authority were both at stake in its proposed eradication. This, then, is the first level of significance of the question of 'abuse'.

The second level of significance for the question of 'abuse' of public funds relates to the attempted 'nationalisation' of relief practice after 1834. The political and economic transformations of the seventeenth and eighteenth centuries – the enclosure movement, urbanisation, industrialisation – had tended to sweep away the traditional common-law 'rights' of the peasant upon the land and the pragmatic reciprocity of the landlord-tenant or employer-employee relationship (Thompson, 1963, 1975; P. Hollis, 1973). In this context, the reform of the Poor Laws did endeavour to turn a highly variegated, essentially local and discretionary series of practices into a system that was, at least formally, national.

The Act of 1834 formally introduced a right to relief within a workhouse. Yet the severe discipline of the workhouse regime – the severity was intended to give effect to the principle of less-eligibility, the discipline to instil habits of industry – and the preoccupation with 'abuse' served as the means by which the formal right was for all practical purposes compromised and contradicted. As we shall see, the delivery of welfare through such essentially truncated rights has become something of a feature of the liberal capitalist state and it is in this context that the discourse on 'abuse' of public funds has played an important historical role. The discipline and severity of the workhouse regime – the essence, as Crowther has suggested, of the reformed Poor Law (Crowther, 1981) – were united in pursuit of a single series of effects. The workhouse sought to bring the disciplinary relations of the labour market into the field of subsistence relief and, to this end, relief was granted in an oppressive and disciplinary manner. The objective of guarding against forms of 'abuse' justified such excessive policy measures, which, in effect, nullified the formal right encapsulated in the Poor Law. This is the second level of significance of the discourse on abuse.

The third level of significance is closely related to the other two. It helps us to understand how a concern with the 'abuses' of the laws served as grounds upon which the petty, regulative and disciplinary workhouse regime could be justified. Developing an administrative system designed to cope with the most troublesome pauper, like always legislating for the worst possible case, suggests an approach to policy making in which order, security and, above all, discipline routinely prevail over welfare. As Crowther noted,

> The [Poor Law] Commissioners devised elaborate rules for the punishment of paupers who committed workhouse offences, including being noisy or dirty, refusing to work, swearing, malingering, attempting to enter the quarters of another class of pauper, and disobedience. Punishments ranged from making the pauper wear special clothes to reducing his diet for 48 hours, but serious offenders had to be sent before a Justice of the Peace. . . . Other petty regulations resembled the prison system: silent mealtimes, and control over the visitors and mail.
>
> (Crowther, 1981, p. 44)

As abuse had been successfully portrayed as endemic within the Old

Poor Law, and as the pauper had been characterised as a thoroughly disreputable, even criminal or dangerous type, so punitive measures had to be equally prolific. A certain self-fulfilling prophecy came to pass; the more vociferously the authorities condemned 'abuses', the more active they became in pursuing them and, not surprisingly, the more 'undeserving cases' they unearthed. Ultimately, the emphasis upon 'abuses' and the supposed moral dangers resulting from relieving the poor without requiring their industry legitimated the whole host of disciplinary policy measures which have become familiar components of the state's management of poverty. This, of course is the third level of significance of the question of 'abuses' within Poor Law discourse.

Eventually, pauperism and poverty as objects of a discourse, vital elements in a series of ideological preoccupations, became squeezed on two sides. On the one side they were bordered by a system of generalised repression and disciplinary control by which it was hoped to deter. On the other side they were caught up in and defined by a promotional and ostensibly preventive series of relations wherein the limited but 'respectable' aspirations of the working class were cultivated. These two complementary activities were to be secured through disciplinary systems of relief administration which, above all, were most scrupulous in policing the social, moral and political boundaries between the two social groups. On the one side, those considered 'merely poor' and, on the other, the 'pauperised'.

As one examines the various utterances made by contemporaries upon this question, it becomes clear how vital the line being drawn really was. In contrast to the strictly regulated entitlements of the reformed Poor Law, the old Poor Law and the vague sentiments which underpinned it came to appear as the real abuse. With its lack of systematic discipline or selection it failed to confront pauperism with sufficient rigour. As Chadwick and the Poor Law commissioners knew well, society as a whole was compromised because the administration of relief funds was not tight enough: 'the pauper must accept assistance on the terms, whatever they may be, which the common welfare requires. . . . Every exception, every violation of the general rule lets in a whole class of fraudulent cases by which that rule must in time be destroyed' (Checkland and Checkland, 1974, pp. 376–7). And if the same be said of society, every deviation from strict administration might well undermine the foundations of social order – 'abuses defended under the mask of benevolence' endanger the common welfare (*ibid.* p. 395) And in this enunciation of the link between strict administration and the common good, might be detected an early articulation of 'the social'. Henceforth, it would be possible to defend severity in the name of 'the social' itself, not so much because the poor themselves were deemed to need the discipline (although this was certainly so), but because society and the relations of order and power upon which it depended, were presumed to require the careful management of the poor.

It was in the Poor Law Report itself that this case for the management of the poor was most consistently and emphatically put. Following a chapter which outlined the historical development of the Poor Laws, Chapter 2 of the Report reaffirmed the sense of social danger consequent upon a lax administration of the Laws. 'The fund . . . is applied to purposes opposed to the letter and still more to the spirit of that law, and destructive to the morals of that most numerous class, and to the welfare of all' (*ibid.* p. 62). Such remarks were substantiated in the Report by observations from the reports and submissions of assistant commissioners who conducted the Poor Law Commission's survey and from 'evidence' from overseers and district relieving officers. The commissioners were somewhat selective in their use of evidence. 'There can be no doubt', the Checklands remark, 'that the Commissioners in their fact gathering were looking for bad practice rather than good' (*ibid.* p. 40). Whilst Blaug has added, 'the Poor Law Commission of 1834 . . . deliberately selected the facts so as to impeach the existing administration on predetermined lines' (Blaug, 1963, p. 177).

The 'abuses' that were found to exist under the Old Poor Law seemed to demonstrate the impossibility of administering a system of outdoor relief. Punctuated only occasionally by references to sound practices where strict principles were adhered to, the catalogue of 'abuses' continued. The submission of a particular assistant commissioner was cited in order to demonstrate the disciplinary failings of the old system. 'One man to every twenty would be required to watch the paupers living out of the parish, and one man to every hundred living in the parish; which is an expense of inspection which could not be borne. . . . Unless you have a considerable number of men to watch every pauper, you are sure to be cheated' (Checkland and Checkland, 1974, pp. 116–17). Yet these ratios of investigators to paupers sound positively ideal compared with Chadwick's own evidence.

> The outdoor relief in the City of London would require almost one man to look after every half-dozen able-bodied men, and then he would only succeed imperfectly in preventing fraud. They cheat us on all sides . . . with respect to the outdoor relief, there must, from the very nature of it, be an immense amount of fraud. There is no industry, no inspection, no human skill which will prevent gross imposition belonging to this mode of relief.
>
> (*ibid.* pp. 118–19)

The Poor Law commissioners were coming to the same kinds of conclusions as those being reached in the related field of investigative philanthropy. The task of disciplining the poor had to be reorganised into a task for the poor themselves. The immanent corruptability of the working classes seemed to render supervision almost superfluous to the disciplinary task, 'the permanent officers frankly acknowledge, that it is beyond the powers of any individuals to prevent an immense amount of fraud' (*ibid.* p. 118). For the commissioners, the conclusion was inescapable, whilst philanthropy had sought to combine 'assistance' with 'remoralisation' to the extent that the two processes became indistinguishable, so, for the effective operation of the Poor Law, relief had to become indistinguishable from discipline.

It was not simply that the older practices of poor relief were considered highly susceptible to 'abuse', but that the poor, in finding it so easy to 'abuse' the system, would come to rely upon it, would lose the virtuous habits of industry and thrift and would find their moral fibre rapidly weakening. Hence, in the reports of the regional assistant commissioners were to be found numerous testimonies of employers who seemed to be lamenting the passing of an age in which employees were reliable, deferential and hard-working, and the coming of a time when labourers were 'much degenerated . . . generally disaffected to their employers . . . working unwillingly or wastefully'. Still more 'evidence' indicated an even deeper malaise, not just an accumulation of individual acts of fraudulent abuse, but a structural and systemic pressure towards abusive expansion within the system as a whole.

> Relying on parish relief, [labourers] are indifferent whether they oblige or disobey their masters . . . until the system of allowances is abandoned the spirit of industry can never be revived. Allowance men will not work. It makes them idle, lazy, fraudulent and worthless, and depresses the wages of free labour. (*ibid.* p. 146)

Moreover, it was noted that parish settlement, and therefore entitlement to relief, could be obtained through marriage – 'another fertile source of fraud' – and this was alleged to produce temporary and unstable marriages of convenience which ended up depositing more and more persons upon the relief rolls. The process of moral corruption was believed to set in when the poor, having accepted the ill-conceived bounty of outdoor relief, became accomplices to their own decline. The relief applicant grew 'callous to his own degradation' and was henceforth unable to stop himself sliding into pauperism. As Chadwick himself remarked, 'the change that is made in the character and habits of the poor by once receiving parochial relief is quite remarkable, they are demoralised ever afterwards' (*ibid.* p. 174).

A change in the system of poor relief would, it was believed, remove the principal cause of moral decline by forcing each individual to rely upon his own efforts. It was abundantly clear that moral exhortation was hardly adequate to the task; the poor had to be actively engaged in the process of their own remoralisation; the poor certainly had to value freedom and independence, but they had to be encouraged and, if necessary, forced to be free and independent. Ultimately, the poor were to be ensnared in the task of their own disciplinary rehabilitation.

In criticising the Old Poor Law, the commissioners were aware that without system – strict adherence to regulations and an exhaustive, costly apparatus of investigation – it would be almost impossible to devise fair and rational means of distinguishing 'deserving' (or 'helpable') cases from 'undeserving' ones. However, with a system of relief that the commissioners intended to administer almost exclusively within a workhouse, such a strict regime of investigation, surveillance or inspection was less necessary. Under the reformed Poor Law, the commissioners intended to allow little by way of relief to be offered outside the confines of the workhouse, thereby obviating the need for such detailed scrutiny of the moral character of relief applicants. Only the informed personal calculation by the pauper himself could determine his entry into the workhouse. This insight, of course, supplied an essential principle for the operation of the workhouse system: less-eligibility. 'However diligent an overseer, or an officer for inquiry may be, there are numerous cases which will baffle his utmost diligence and sagacity: the only test of those cases is making their condition more severe than that of the lowest class of labourers who obtain their livelihood by honest industry' (*ibid.* p. 119; see also De Schweinitz, 1943, p. 121).

In outlining this principle, the commissioners were not acting without precedent. They drew upon the experiences of a relief scheme employed in Nottinghamshire and attributed to Sir George Nicholls. 'Knowing that it was impossible to refuse relief according to the custom and practice of the county', a means was devised whereby relief itself would be rendered 'so irksome and disagreeable that none would consent to receive it who could possibly do without it' (De Schweinitz, 1943, pp. 121–2). It was not surprising, therefore, that many Poor Law Unions adopted similar policies to discourage relief applications, although by no means a majority actually went to the trouble of building a workhouse (until or, in some cases, long after they were statutorily required to do so). Nevertheless, the commissioners made some use of this system of reducing relief applications, controlling 'abuses' and motivating the poor to action on their own behalf.

It is the study of bad paupers to deceive you all they can, and as they study more their own cases than any inquirer can study the whole mass of different cases which he has to inquire into, they are sure to be successful in a great many instances. The only protection for the parish is to make the parish the hardest taskmaster and the worst paymaster that can be applied to.

(Checkland and Checkland, 1974, p. 119)

Subsequently, when the commissioners moved on to elaborate the principles upon which their alternative scheme of relief might be based, they had it firmly in mind that the system must be construed so as to eliminate any uncertainty or localised discretion. Human judgements (save those of the paupers themselves) and personal discretion were to be completely eliminated and to this end a clear and rigidly simple conclusion suggested itself.

We see no remedy . . . except the general application of the principle of relief which has been so extensively tried and found so efficient in the dispauperised parishes . . . the able-bodied claimant should be entitled to immediate relief on the terms prescribed, whatever he may happen to be; and he should be received without objection or inquiry, the fact of his compliance with the prescribed discipline constituting his title to a sufficient though simple diet. (*ibid*. pp. 387–8)

As De Schweinitz has remarked, in more emphatic fashion, 'having revealed the weaknesses of the existing system and having expressed doubt about any remedy through the use of an administrative personnel, the Report described the operation in certain parishes of a device that seemed to provide a solution to the problem. This device was the workhouse' (De Schweinitz, 1943, p. 121; see also Bahmueller, 1981; and Evans, 1982, on the generality of functions ascribed to the new workhouse/institutional system of control).

Yet the workhouse itself offered little by way of incentives. In return for a pauper's acceptance of its harsh regime it provided a sparse form of subsistence. The relative pains and pleasures of the workhouse were left to the judgement of the pauper. This free, rational, calculating (Benthamite) individual was to weigh up the respective pleasures, pains, satisfactions and privations of the workhouse and come to his or her own 'informed' decision. This, or course, necessitated a certain degree of public awareness regarding the nature of the new institutions so as to facilitate the 'rational decision-making' of the poor. As Digby points out, however, a growing awareness of the conditions within East Anglian workhouses certainly enabled the poor to reach their decisions – decisions that would hardly have found favour with the commissioners. Several workhouses were attacked and burnt down (Digby, 1981).

Nevertheless, as regards scrutiny of relief applications under the new regime, all surveillance, investigation and inspection was to be concentrated within the one act of reflection by the pauper himself. All detection of weak applications, searching out of motives or the discovery and pursuit of alternative sources of income or relief became the pauper's own burden. Just as philanthropic relief administrators had discovered that moral character was the key to remoralisation and rehabilitation, so character, the pauper's supposed assessment of his own character, was the crucial factor concealed within the operation of the workhouse test and the pauper's decision to enter the workhouse.

Thus, whilst both philanthropy and the Poor Law seemed to have character assessment at the heart of their respective strategies, each used it in a different way. For philanthropy character was pliable, capable of re-education, the object upon which the relief administrator worked. Under the Poor-Law assessment of character, a poor labourer was either deemed capable of achieving sound industrious habits and of earning an income *and was, therefore, not a pauper at all*, or he was without such virtues, and of a character so irredeemable that he could knowingly surrender himself to the final degradation of the workhouse with its discipline, petty regulations and austere conditions. In short, for philanthropy, character was the object of remoralisation, for the Poor Law, it served more as the confirmation of vice (see McCord, 1976).

Although put to different uses, this common focus upon 'character' was to prove significant in the later decades of the nineteenth century. Despite the fact that during the second half of the century, the relief strategies of the Poor Law and philanthropy were in contest, because both organisations attached such importance to conceptions of 'character', considerable cross-fertilisation of principles, methods and practices took place. In the analysis of this productive cross-fertilisation of relief practices, I shall now turn to the later development of the Poor Law and philanthropy in order to consider the precise ways and means by which pauperism became thoroughly transformed. Gradually, pauperism would cease to be the attribute of an entire social class as philanthropists and reformers came increasingly to direct their attentions to the condition of the depraved and pathological individual.

It should be remembered that broad social, political and economic developments during the nineteenth century form the context within which these transformations occurred. But they are not the whole story. We must also have regard to the detailed, specific and inherently disciplinary interventions embarked upon by political authorities to contain and control an emerging field of 'social' problems as they manifested themselves in the conditions of life of the poorest classes in society. Organised, frequently, under the rubric of 'welfare', these interventions, as I argued earlier (see Chapter 3), have a great deal to do with the emergence of conceptions of the modern 'social' individual and, especially, with his or her supposedly 'deviant' counterparts. With these considerations in mind, I shall now consider these developing disciplinary discourses as they engaged with the difficulties confronting alternative relief strategies after 1834.

Poor Law strategy: success or failure

Despite the advocacy of the Poor Law commissioners, the 1834 Act did not sweep away outdoor relief. The Act's purposes were compromised in both principle and practice. There can, according to Williams, 'be no dispute that the formal power of the central authority was effectively restricted' (K. Williams, 1981, p. 68). But Williams takes issue with a number of authors (D. Fraser, 1976; Ashforth, 1976; Digby, 1978; Rose, 1976), all representatives of mainstream English historiography who, he believes, have tended to misconstrue the relief strategy pursued by the Poor Law authorities after 1834. For my own purposes, the significance of this debate lies in what it tells us about differing disciplinary strategies operationalised within the Poor Law and the lines of potential alliance that were opened up between the Poor Law and philanthropy.

Williams claims that the history of the New Poor Law cannot be read as a history of failure. Central to this claim is the status and significance of outdoor relief after 1834. Although, he suggests, 'many historians claim or assume that the recommendations of the 1834 Report included the abolition of outdoor relief . . . this assumption is untrue because the strategy of 1834 was preoccupied with *able-bodied males*' (K. Williams, 1981, p. 61, emphasis added). Williams's critique is centrally concerned with the development of disciplinary strategies within the reformed system. As I have said, the central objectives of the Poor Law commissioners were to affect the conditions of subsistence of the working class in such a way as to hasten their acceptance of disciplined factory work within a capitalist political economy. Such an objective required not the total cessation of all outdoor relief to able-bodied men but, rather, only its substantial restriction as a standard and accepted component in labourers' incomes. In this sense the restrictions imposed by the 1834 Act and subsequent regulations can be seen to have been broadly successful alongside changing patterns of economic activity and employment in the country at large (Berg, 1980).

Whilst it is certainly true that there existed substantial variation in the application of Poor Law principles and that the practices of local boards of guardians could vary enormously from area to area and from time to time, it is still possible, nevertheless, to form conclusions about effective strategy within the Poor Law. The workhouse was successful in helping ensure the subjugation of the male able-bodied unemployed and, by extension, the entire working class, to a regime of unremitting discipline whether in the labour market or outside it. Thus, the workhouse had an effect which reverberated throughout the working class for several generations.

In some respects the division between indoor and outdoor relief could be said to correspond to the division – often thought to lie at the heart of nineteenth-century relief policy – between the 'deserving' and 'undeserving' poor. In fact, practice was never so straightforward. Outdoor relief was widespread, but the workhouse was attempting to straddle two fairly incompatible tasks. Both of these tasks derive from settled and familiar institutional practices established long before 1834. Practices which, in the clamour of historical debate on the detail of the Poor Law, tend to get forgotten. On the one hand, the workhouse was to discipline and control – even deter – the incorrigibles, rogues, vagrants and 'habitual idlers' (a role closely akin to that of the sixteenth- and seventeenth-century institutions for the suppression of beggary, see Sellin, 1949). On the other hand, the workhouse operated as an institution for the sick and disabled, and a refuge for the incompetent (at which point it continues that tradition of institutions including almshouses, asylums, houses of industry and correction and charitable hospitals which comprise a large part of what Foucault has referred to as the 'Great Confinement', see Foucault, 1967). Indeed as Crowther has shown, the workhouses, like other institutions, often

> degenerated into mere receptacles: they housed, but made little effort to treat or cure the socially deviant or helpless. Incurable chronic cases filled the asylums; violent or habitual criminals the prisons. The poorhouses, as in Britain, housed mainly the long-term helpless paupers. Even the most elaborate systems of discipline had little effect on this type of inmate.
>
> (Crowther, 1981, pp. 65–6)

Yet, if the institutional tradition has changed so little despite the growing emphasis upon classification and the careful elaboration of disciplinary technique, and if the discipline of the workhouse was, as Williams has suggested, primarily blind and repressive, and, finally, if the major impact of the workhouse was to force the able-bodied male labourer to accept certain conditions of employment, then the limited direct experience of this group of persons of workhouse conditions would seem to suggest that one important function of the workhouse lay in its role as a potent physical symbol of deterrence. All this implies that the novelty and strategic significance of the post–1834 Poor Law lay, not in the development of disciplinary practices *within* the workhouses but in terms of the effects of a new system of discipline *outside* the workhouse, as reflected in the balance of power between employers and workers within the labour market and in the wider social relations of the labour market and between the social classes.

Too much consideration of the post–1834 Poor Law has focused exclusively upon the workhouse, yet the most vital effects of this instrument of discipline worked themselves out beyond its walls. My consideration of developing relief strategies and particularly the focus on the relief of able-bodied (i.e. unemployed) males, shows clearly that the significance of the Poor Law need not be read exclusively in terms of the single criterion of access to, or exclusion from, the workhouse and that wider social questions were involved. It is in this context that the question of outdoor relief – a disciplinary form of social intervention – becomes important. Outdoor relief was not important only because it was the main form of relief obtained by the majority of nineteenth-century paupers. Rather, the significance of the 1834 strategy lay in the framework it established for a nationalisation of relief practice to which an extensive series of disciplinary social interventions became attached.

Fixed upon a division of 'deserving' or 'undeserving' paupers, conventional Poor Law historiography has tended to emphasise the repression of the 'undeserving' – the idle, the vagrant, the vicious, the malingerer and the immoral – in short, the marginal groups or minorities, whilst remaining unconcerned with the effects of Poor Law discipline, generaliseable as a 'wider law of labour', across the field of class relationships and the social existence of the working classes as a whole (Novak, 1988). While it is never true to say that the refinement of disciplinary measures and their application to particular 'recalcitrant' categories of paupers is unimportant, the key question concerns the generalisation of these disciplinary techniques, their ramification throughout society and their multifarious applications in its future government. Through the strategy of 1834, therefore, a crucial aspect of the reorganisation of the conditions for the reproduction of collective labour power was secured.

Yet just as they had criticised the unreformed poor laws, contemporaries criticised the new system for lax administration, for being a burden upon the rates, for being a bounty upon idleness and for encouraging everything from fraud to crime and drunkenness. Such criticisms came from all sides, but especially from those who, for some considerable time, had advocated a more sophisticated relief strategy. Indeed the attacks of these 'scientific philanthropists', stressing the crudity of the Poor Law, its inadequate modes of investigation, unsystematic record keeping and the lack of training received by relieving officers, became rather more virulent as the century progressed (Mishra, 1969). Yet in the confrontation between these two discourses on relief, the system of administrative social discipline of the modern welfare state was formed – as Stedman Jones amongst others has observed (Stedman Jones, 1971, p. 257).

The 'rising tide' of pauperism and the 'crisis' of relief

The Poor Law continued to be attacked on both economic and humanistic grounds. Yet for my purposes the argument that the system continued to 'manufacture' rather than prevent or deter pauperism and that, in failing to reform the poor, it had seemed to have learned little from scientific philanthropy, is of prime importance (Fawcett, 1871; Strachey, 1907). For instance, the architects of the new Poor Law had been aware that a vigilant relieving officer was as important to the efficient running of the system of poor relief as a good governor was in a prison. In case some parishes or Poor Law unions had not appreciated the equation, the commissioners spelt it out for them: a good relieving officer could save the cost of his own employment and much more besides, by deterring frivolous or opportunist applications for relief. 'A considerable diminution would be effected in the rates, the really deserving poor would by this means have every proper attention paid to their claims and the dissolute and imposters would be detected' (Checkland and Checkland, 1974, Appendix A, p. 62).

The continuation of a vast margin of outdoor relief after 1834 might suggest that the exercise of the relieving officer's responsibilities failed to have quite the deterrent effect hoped for. If Williams's reinterpretation is introduced, however, then the substantial diminution in the amount of outdoor relief given to able-bodied adult males might point to an opposite conclusion. Nevertheless, given the ways in which the strategy of 1834 was applied, it became possible for philanthropists and reformers to argue that the Poor Law was both too strict and severe and, on the other hand, insufficiently rigorous, certain or effective. Many such criticisms tended to fall directly or indirectly upon the head of the relieving officer and, invariably, his ineffectual administration was held to be at the heart of the Poor Law's problems. While the new regulations of 1847 and 1852 went some way towards 'tightening up' Poor Law administration they did not go nearly far enough to satisfy a great deal of critical opinion. Mishra and others, for instance, have pointed to the prevalence of a belief that, by the 1860s, the Poor Law had already broken down, that the relieving officer's investigations were 'practically worthless in so far as the detection of fraud and imposture is concerned', and that this officer had become more of a welfare officer than a deterrent figure (Mishra, 1969, p. 93). Thus, from a number of quarters, a stricter administration was demanded. Boards of guardians were encouraged to appoint more relieving officers (on the understanding that they would be cost-effective) although, in practice, guardians were often very reluctant to act in a way that would make them so (Webb and Webb, 1929, pp. 145–57). The relieving officer was apparently failing to perform even the simplest supervisory functions over the operation of outdoor poor relief and the Poor Law authorities seemed little inclined to face these dilemmas.

Towards the latter part of the 1860s the 'crusade' against outdoor relief gathered momentum, partly in an attempt to further the disciplinary and institutional logic of the system and partly as a response to the stated deficiencies of the Poor Law Board's officials in differentiating between categories of applicant. In the first Annual Report of the Local Government Board, which assumed the functions of the Poor Law Board in 1870, this question was directly addressed. The evidence appeared incontrovertible, it was suggested that relief was granted, 'too readily and without sufficient inquiry . . . and [also given] in numerous instances in which it would be more judicious to apply the workhouse test' (*LGB First Annual Report*, 1871–2, p. 64). A circular issued on 2 December 1871 confirmed the new policy, insisting that 'measures should be taken not only to check any further increase but to diminish the present amount' (see De Schweinitz, 1943, p. 156). Finally, the rule was stated categorically in the Board's Third Annual Report. Henceforth, 'indoor relief shall be the rule and outdoor relief the exception' (*LGB Third Annual Report*, 1873–4, Appendix B, p. 142).

The situation which provoked this shift, or hardening, of Poor Law policy at the end of the 1860s – the decade that Rose claims witnessed 'the crisis of Poor Relief' (Rose, 1981) – assumed familiar proportions. All the dangerous and unpalatable signs of marginality, degeneration and vice were deployed once more as reformers sought for the words to describe adequately the grave social threat posed by this pauperised 'enemy within' (Keating, 1976; Procacci, 1978). Stedman Jones cites the words of Sir Charles Trevelyan, 'the doyen of relief experts', whose assessment of the situation, nothing if not extreme, is fairly characteristic:

> The rising tide of pauperism and crime threatens to overwhelm us . . . we shall surely be left behind in the race if we continue weighted with this

growing pauper semi-criminal class. . . . The pauper class of the
metropolis . . . are secured against starvation and need not even be
driven to the workhouse . . . the general result is a spreading decay of the
spirit of independence among our metropolitan poor, and a
demoralisation which threatens grave social consequences.

(Trevelyan, 1870, quoted in Stedman Jones, 1971, p. 244)

Both Poor Law and philanthropy were implicated in this crisis, however, and both were deemed culpable. The relieving officers may well
have been crude in their application of the regulations and somewhat
lax in their scrutiny of cases but many commentators favoured the
discipline of the Poor Law (with all its faults) in preference to a reliance
upon charity alone and the risky bounty of the 'indiscriminate alms
giver'.

The latter was a rather notorious folk-devil of the second half of the
nineteenth century. The character is never pinned down too precisely
but, as a persona, emerges from the host of factors typifying mid
nineteenth-century charity organisation. A combination of patchy,
often inadequate coverage, yet duplication and immense variation in
standards and procedures – especially in the urban areas – created a
situation in which, so it was alleged, the 'clever pauper' (another folk-
devil) could exploit all manner of relief agencies with impunity. Such
preoccupations, in a context of rapidly rising numbers of relief applications, spawned the publication of many books, tracts and articles
addressing the problem of pauperism and and consequent 'demoralisation' of the poor (Rose, 1979). Whether the accumulated proposals
improved upon those of de Gerando some forty years earlier is difficult
to ascertain. However, where the new texts did surpass de Gerando's
formulations was in their advocacy of a new relationship between the
promotional aspirations and practices of private philanthropy and the
more systematically punitive and disciplinary public relief agency – the
Poor Law.

In 1869, when public concern about demoralisation, pauperisation
and crime, about rising relief rolls and the need to systematise and
harmonise relief operations was mounting, new instructions came from
the president of the Poor Law Board regarding the appropriate relation
between the Poor Law and philanthropy (Chance, 1895). This intervention, the 'Goschen Minute' on 'Relief to the Poor in the Metropolis',
has attained a certain notoriety in the history of poor relief by virtue
of its attempt to delineate parallel spheres of responsibility between
the Poor Law and philanthropy. The 'Goschen Minute' formed a bridge
between two related discourses on poor relief allowing the cross-fertilisation of ideas and practices to develop between the two systems of
relief. Its significance in the formation of a peculiarly disciplinary and

divisive social administration in Britain derives from this. More ominously, the 1869 Minute helped create the conditions for the intensification of the crusade against outdoor relief. For, throughout the 1860s, the president of the Poor Law Board had sought to promote the recruitment of relieving officers and the enhancement of the investigative side of Poor Law administration. The reasons for both initiatives were often very explicit, the authorities were attempting to maximise the exercise of selective deterrence throughout the Poor Law system (Mishra, 1969, pp. 90–8; Webb and Webb, 1910, p. 103). The contents of the Goschen Minute were hardly new, but now they were given the sanction of official recognition.

However, the renewed deterrence of the Poor Law system made possible through the arrangements reached after 1870 with the charities, cannot simply be explained as an attempt to return to the 'principles of 1834'. On the contrary, rather more was at stake. The parallel operation of Poor Law and philanthropy made possible a new organisation of political and disciplinary effects throughout the Poor Law, a more deterrent public relief system could be developed based upon an 'extended and intensified workhouse test'. Henry Longley, a Poor Law inspector, neatly summarised the new relationship and its possibilities when he wrote:

> It is, in fact, the general existence of charity which strengthens the hands of the Poor Law administrator in adherence to rule . . . if the poor are given to understand that outdoor relief is to be granted only as an indulgence to deserving cases, it may be possible, in time, and when a more complete organisation of charity shall have been effected, to relegate such cases as those to the care of charitable agencies.
>
> (Longley, in *LGB Third Annual Report*, 1873–4)

While Goschen had envisaged the parallel operation of the two systems, Longley saw philanthropy as the rehabilitative supplement to a repressive and deterrent Poor Law. There was, admittedly, little new in Longley's desire to split the pauper class into the 'deserving' and 'undeserving' groups, but the ways in which these groups were subsequently treated within their respective avenues of relief reflected the establishment of a new connection between public and private morality in matters of relief practice and a reorganisation of the means by which sanctions, rewards and incentives were distributed amongst the working class. If the dichotomy of welfare and control, much beloved of twentieth-century social administration, has its roots anywhere, then surely they lie here in the complementary but separate formulation of a system of treatment and rehabilitation (philanthropy) and a system of discipline and punishment (the system of public relief, based upon the deterrent workhouse). Just as charity was to assist the operation of the Poor Law by removing from it the expense of a large number of 'curable' and 'deserving' cases, so the Poor Law was to provide the firm base for the successful application of charitable principles. The new parallel administrations helped to formalise, in ways that had not previously been possible, the regime of incentives and sanctions by which the disciplinary surveillance of the working class was effectively national- ised. A 'disciplinary continuum' was installed at the heart of the new social policy which sought to regulate the conditions of existence of the working class.

Central to the policy was the idea that the workhouse should feature prominently as the 'penalty for moral and economic failure' (Stedman Jones, 1971, p. 255), an arrangement which required that the symbolic power of the workhouse be revived. The poor were to be more effec- tively educated about political economy by being more sharply reminded about the workhouse. Such a plan necessitated the construc- tion of more workhouse accommodation and the maintenance therein of a sufficiently deterrent discipline, which, it was hoped, might force upon the pauper an appreciation of the desirability of relying upon his or her own resources (*LGB Third Annual Report*, 1873–4, p. 200). It was intended that these changes would remove the uncertainty from poor relief; the pauper was to be left in no doubt about what would follow an application for relief. To this end, it was suggested that a series of codes should be published in order to familiarise paupers with the rules of the system and, at the same time, that relieving officers should be issued with instructions encouraging them to increase the stigma of poor relief – not only as regards those within the workhouse, but *especially* regarding those in receipt of outdoor relief. The continu- ation of these concerns led the annual conference of Poor Law officers to propose, in 1878, the introduction of a 'pauper badge' for all recipi- ents of outdoor relief, whilst ten years later, the House of Lords Select Committee on Poor Relief favourably reported the attempts by metro- politan relieving officers to increase the stigma of outdoor relief (see Mishra, 1969, pp. 97–8).

The overall nature of the new relief strategy could be said to be 'educational', but a particular kind of 'education' was being orches- trated. Despite the concern with forms of 'knowledgeable discourse' regarding the poor, little real attention was devoted to what might be called the *causes* of pauperism. Of course, in one sense, these were held as largely self-evident (Stedman Jones, 1971, pp. 285–90). In another sense, given the authorities' fairly pragmatic interest in simple 'dispauperisation' or 'remoralisation', the causes of pauperism were implicitly posited in the discourses with which the authorities 'understood' their subject and evident in the practices they adopted to combat it, namely: too easy availability of relief and a deficiency of individual and collective moral virtue amongst the lower classes.

The body of philanthropic and quasi-social scientific knowledge of the poor was growing; at the same time the poor themselves were being made to acquire a different kind of knowledge – a knowledge of the stigma of poverty, of the stringent conditions of entitlement and of the punitive nature of the workhouse. This new knowledge was central to the operating principle of deterrence – indeed it is here that the significance of the proposed new Poor Law strategy lies. According to Williams, the new rules

> were so strict that very few working-class people would satisfy the specified conditions. . . . But the conditions were very different from direct prohibition since they gave the working class an opportunity to reflect upon the reasons why an application for out-relief would not be successful. Ideally the conditions would make the working classes reflect upon their own short-comings; their failure to practise thrift, their deficient sense of family obligations, their dirty and unsavoury homes. At the same time, the conditions of relief were an assurance that virtue would not go unrewarded . . . the virtuous would be rewarded with an out-relief dole.
> (K. Williams, 1981, pp. 98–9)

However, despite such grand ambitions, 'the educative ends of the crusade [against out-relief] were never approached by exemplary "strict" rules', instead, 'the crusade turned into a rather different kind of event' (*ibid*. p. 101). The strategy cannot be said to have failed for an increasingly deterrent Poor Law undoubtedly generated significant 'knowledge-effects' of its own. Maybe this knowledge did not cause the poor and needy to reflect upon their own inadequacies in quite the ways that had originally been envisaged but it certainly informed them of the kind of treatment they might expect from the state. In this respect the strategy might be said to have registered a crude kind of 'success'. In the five years after 1871 the total number of paupers fell by approximately one-third and the number of indoor paupers by about eleven per cent, but instead of the relatively sophisticated strategy of educative disentitlement, the authorities pursued 'dispauperisation by any and every means' (*ibid*. p. 101).

Henceforth, this 'crude logic of practical dispauperisation' constituted the basis of relief strategy under the Poor Law for almost the whole of the two decades after 1874. The strategy relied heavily upon the expansion of charitable activity during this period but never actually developed the sophisticated 'strict public regulations' originally envisaged. The 'crusade against pauperism' worked through a crudely orchestrated repressive deterrence; it attacked the living standards and condemned the lifestyles of the poorest at the same time as it stigmatised and ostracised those who found it necessary to apply for relief. Even so, outdoor relief continued, of necessity, to be widespread. The real impact of the campaign against pauperism, and the political climate it helped cultivate, lay in the opportunity it provided for enhancing the punitive, disciplinary and investigative functions of Poor Law institutions and their officials. At the same time, the strategy pushed the Poor Law authorities into closer working relationships with both the charitable and philanthropic societies and with the police, as they sought to pursue the vagrant and the 'workshy' with greater vigour and prevent the escalation of fraudulent relief claims (Stedman Jones, 1971, p. 272).

Nevertheless, even whilst the workhouse became a more repressive instrument with regard to the able-bodied, it still remained very much a receptacle for the aged and infirm poor and for the 'feeble-minded' and disabled. Classification became, therefore, an increasingly important component in the functioning of the workhouse in particular and of the Poor Law as a whole. As the end of the century approached, the inmate population of workhouses found themselves being segregated into more and more separate categories and accommodated within a greater diversity of Poor Law (or, increasingly, local authority) institutions within which, at first rather haltingly, forms of 'treatment' or 'rehabilitation' were attempted (K. Williams, 1981). The emergence of these specifically rehabilitative approaches has on occasion been heralded as the beginning of a relaxation of Poor Law discipline (Webb and Webb, 1909; De Schweinitz, 1943; Crowther, 1978 and 1981). Yet the drift into disciplinary and punitive measures for some was coterminous with and complementary to the introduction of selective and treatment-centred approaches for others. It seems that there was not so much a general relaxation in the mode of disciplining the poor as a transformation in its form and the emergence of markedly more selective disciplinary mechanisms.

In the years after the 1870s a number of the petty and unnecessary restrictions and privations of workhouse life were removed, but this hardly implies that it became noticeably more comfortable or attractive. In any event, discipline should not merely be equated with the privileges and privations of workhouse life (for example the right to wear one's own clothing, or to smoke, or the rule insisting that all inmates be out of bed by 6.30 every morning). Rather, discipline must be seen *as a system, in its entirety*. There is a tendency within historical studies of the institution to identify the rigour of the regime itself with its practical disciplinary effects. Both Crowther and Williams tend to fall into this trap, seeing the classified and segregated workhouse of the 1880s as a more congenial and less disciplinary institution than its forerunners earlier in the century. While the later institutions may well have been less overtly punitive they were no less disciplinary, indeed, quite the contrary. To fail to understand this is to fail to recognise that classification itself is a mode of discipline, one which has produced a whole spectrum of differing degrees of confinement under which inmates might be placed or moved depending upon their condition, character or behaviour. These systems of classification foreshadow the technology of normalisation which became fully operative in the twentieth century. It was in marking out deviations from stipulated social norms within programmes of treatment or rehabilitation that these classifications derived their significance. Classification involved segregating individuals by reference to certain ideological standards of respectability, sociability and success, whose ultimate reference was the prevailing social order and hierarchy, class discipline and the labour market.

The development of rigorous systems of discipline within society at large guaranteed by a primarily statutory series of provisions, was to come later. In the process of extending this classificatory discipline to society as a whole, the essentially criminal classifications of the poor developed in the 1840s and 1850s were replaced. New, socio-pathological assessments of the classes, pioneered to a large extent, by the Charity Organisation Society, the Eugenics Movement and later, by Booth and the 'new' Liberals, the Webbs and the Fabians eventually succeeded them (Searle, 1976; N. Rose, 1978 and 1985; Garland, 1985). It is fair to say, nevertheless, that the workhouse (and also the prison) remained a component of a grand system of discipline, the hub of disciplinary relations, even though the empirical form of this discipline was gradually changing. The discipline has to be understood in terms of its discourses, in terms of the objectives they constituted and the strategies thus evolved, not in terms of its precise applications. Thus, the discipline of the workhouse gained in efficacy as it became less brutal, and obtrusive, and more refined and systematic. However, it was not only within the workhouse that increasing pressure towards the disciplinary organisation of social relations was to be found. We also have to appreciate the disciplinary turn taken by the charities and philanthropic organisations in their delivery of relief to those deemed sufficiently worthy.

Social pathology and the poor

Charitable casework was organised around social promotion and the development of specific opportunities and incentives. Thrift, duty and self-help, the watchwords of Samuel Smiles, were now given a pseudo-scientific backing (fuelled, no doubt as a result of a crude translation of Darwinism into social thought) and attached to new administrative methods and techniques of intervention. Together they served as the banners under which 'progressive' social reform came to be organised.

> By the end of the 1860s, the theory of the survival of the fittest had become a doctrine which many enthusiasts applied to human economy as well as the biologic world . . . translated into a method of dealing with poverty, this meant the less relief the better. To be destitute to the point of having to ask for relief was to be guilty of a defect in character – in short, to be in need of reform.
>
> (Bosanquet, 1902)

Under more rigorous casework of the 1880s the 'science' of character was an even stronger driving force for change within philanthropy – the demands of scrutiny, inquiry, interrogation and observation became increasingly important as the means of assessing progress or improvement. 'Character', manifesting itself as a capacity for self-control and thrift, was in this way situated as the key to the charitable enterprise. In short, character was the very focus of the 'charitological obsession' (MacDonald, 1893; Fido, 1977; Jones, 1983). As the character of the pauper 'improved', he or she ceased to be a pauper; his or her capacity for self-control grew and he or she acquired more enduring habits of industry or domesticity. The objective of charitable casework was the moral mobility of the pauper, because, it was believed, this would lead to forms of social advancement, moral piety and his or her acceptance of the prevailing social order. Improvement, or success, in these endeavours was marked by the pauper's movement upwards through the degrees in the 'character assessment charts' of the charitable agency.

This emphasis upon individual character in casework and rehabilitation seems to be equivalent to the implicit faith of the early nineteenth-century penitentiary administrators in their array of punishments directed at the 'soul' – which, as Foucault and Ignatieff have shown, became the very 'prison' of the body (Foucault, 1977; Ignatieff, 1978). The metaphor applies with equal force in respect of relief casework for, as Helen Bosanquet reminded charitable visitors when advising them of ways of dealing with the poor, 'the soul literally is, or is built up of, all its experience' (Cormack, 1945). For the pauper or relief applicant then, character dictated the status of the human being. This was a view confirmed somewhat later, in 1917, by Mary Richmond. She was a pioneer of 'diagnostic' casework, bringing to casework and social investigation an elementary practical psychology which served as a precise vehicle for a detailed intervention into the lives of individuals.

Richmond refined the disparate investigative techniques prevailing in casework and pauper visitation in the latter decades of the nineteenth century and synthesised them into a single diagnostic technique. On the basis of this work the little-known science of 'characterology' was born. The new 'science' was little short of universal in its ambitions, as suggested in Richmond's remark that 'social work . . . takes no special point of view; it takes the whole human point of view' (Richmond, 1917, p.35).

This, however, is only the investigatory discipline in its more advanced stage. Social diagnosis promised a technique far more wide-ranging than the simple scrutiny of relief applicants and we need to consider the evolution of these techniques as they ushered in a new form of disciplinary social policy to complement the harsher and more directly punitive policies of the state's Poor Law. As I have already pointed out, however, any attempt to make a neat demarcation between public and private agencies was frustrated from the outset by the collapse of a 'sophisticated' strategy of educative disentitlement within the Poor Law into a crude imperative of 'dispauperisation'. Nevertheless, this formed the real context in which the charities operated and, in the absence of any clearer principle, they could always fall back upon their older, more 'moral' predelictions – not so much complementing the Poor Law as 'creaming-off' a few of the virtuous (Loch, 1883; Harris, 1972).

Thus, the division between the 'deserving' and the 'undeserving' became deeply etched into the history of poor relief. And whilst I do not intend to challenge here the obvious significance of moral ideologies in the history of social policy, (see, for instance, Golding and Middleton, 1982) the partial dissipation of an explicit moral discourse (ideologies and practices) in the developing relief work of the philanthropic organisations after the 1870s can be ignored only at some theoretical cost.

In the first place, a relief strategy based upon principles of treatment and rehabilitation – that is to say, a strategy of normalisation – would find itself unnecessarily restricted as a technique of population management if it confined its operations solely to those deemed morally worthy. In the second place, a relief strategy which ruled out the supposedly 'immoral', frequently ruled out most of those in need of assistance too. In the third place, a relief strategy based upon moral divisions frequently met some substantial opposition in working-class communities (Harris, 1972, p. 107). In so far as relief work frequently sought the co-operation of the working class, then such opposition posed clear problems. Finally, after the mid 1880s and certainly after 1890, 'the

Charity Organisation Society had been forced to renounce the criterion of "desert" as a basic principle of casework' (*ibid*).

C. S. Loch had often held that 'charity had to discriminate', that the very purpose of charity was to make distinctions amongst categories of recipients. But, as Fido has suggested, one of the initial functions of discrimination in relief practice was to curtail demand in order to safeguard the limited resources of the relief agency. In the later years of the century, however, opposition to the overzealous application of Charity Organisation Society (COS) principles and the specialisation taking place within casework brought to the fore new orientations within philanthropy. Charitable forms of relief, unlike the Poor Law, had always focused upon individuals, they promoted individual virtues and secured individual avenues of betterment, but hitherto they had always accepted the commonplace aetiology of pauperism as the result of the depraved morality of a class. Thus, in earlier conceptions, it was the class – the dangerous class – which was the source of the depravity. Later in the nineteenth century, however, a more sophisticated aetiology had developed. Social Darwinism had promoted an interest in heredity, whilst a growing environmentalist and quasi-social scientific discourse tended to locate the causes of pauperism and criminality in the background, the culture and lifestyle, of the pauper – albeit in association with inherited factors.

Casework also contributed to this growing aetiological sophistication, particularly through its rigorous investigation of the relief applicant. Caseworkers and relief workers sought to rehabilitate the pauper thoroughly, not merely to relieve distress on a temporary basis. Charity workers equated their interventions in the social and moral domains with the actions of a doctor in the medical ('Charity is the work of the social physician' C. S. Loch, 1883). Hence, charity workers had to isolate the causes of individual depravity in order to be able to apply the most effective to remedial treatments. Such orientations in charitable work led eventually to the diagnostic forms of casework which appeared in the first decades of the twentieth century. What the COS referred to as 'scientific charity', is the first embodiment of this.

Yet a diagnostic relief strategy based upon casework was necessarily individualistic. The specificity of the casework remedy, resting upon the isolation of the most salient causes of pauperism (or deviance) implied, in turn, the individualisation of the aetiology of pauperism (or deviance). Thus, when Loch proclaimed that, to be really beneficial, 'charity must adjust its means to the wants of the particular case' (Loch, 1883, pp. 7, 17), he was also acknowledging the new directions taken by relief strategy in the final decades of the nineteenth century.

But a relief strategy that was based on the objective of 'social rehabilitation' and that individualised cases so effectively, could no longer divide its potential clientele into the 'deserving' and the 'undeserving'. Instead it had to reflect differing grades of seriousness – the more or less urgent or difficult. Yet the COS never wholly abandoned its preoccupation with moral ideologies; in many respects these notions remained heavily implicit and henceforth moralism, individualism and diagnosis coexisted at the heart of the relief discipline. In 1883, although Loch was to argue that the COS should drop all reference to 'deserving' or 'undeserving' cases and concentrate instead upon those cases which were 'helpable', in practice this brought about very little change of approach. Loch's admonition to the 'thoughtless almoner' in 1883 did not produce a major change of emphasis in relief work, the transformations were rather more subtle. ' "Deserving" is the favourite word of the thoughtless almsgivers,' he argued, 'it implies a wrong test. Strictly used it is merciless; loosely used it is meaningless. Almoners should assist in order to cure' (*ibid.* p. 36).

The new terminology is interesting, but it can hardly be said to herald a new departure in practice or new moral preoccupations, for precisely those cases that were deemed 'curable' were so considered because of the moral virtue supposedly displayed by the applicants. Henceforth, it was *possible* to reform or assist only those who displayed the correct moral attitudes. And, in turn, the supposed 'curability' of the few served only to confirm the deep demoralisation of the pauperised remainder. However, by transcending, at least theoretically and discursively, the moral division between categories of relief applicants, the new emphasis upon social pathology and aetiological individualisation, casework and rehabilitation, treatment and norm signalled an end to the confinement of social deviance to the pauper class. In future the whole of the section of the population who could be called 'poor' – almost the whole of the working class, the class existing under the permanent and immediate threat of poverty – would become the potential clients of casework. The disciplinary potential of casework increased enormously, therefore, once it was allowed to articulate its own strategic objectives of social normalisation rather then being attached as a supplementary discipline, to the blunt and repressive instrument of the Poor Law.

The significance of these changes must not go unremarked. The relief strategy, which began as the means for assisting a group of the poor selected on the basis of individual character reformation, had now come to make a science out of charity and character within a scheme for 'attempting to fit the human being back into his place in society . . . for the real test is not whether individuals are deserving or underserving but whether the action taken will help the family to function again.' (Cormack, 1945, pp. 96, 111). Thus, social functioning, normalisation and, more and more, the family became the key factors in a new relief strategy pioneered through casework. These changes registered the end of social casework as a residual practice. No longer were its ministrations to be confined to an immoral minority; rather, 'casework' techniques came to be attached to a large number of other forms of social intervention, within which were deployed powerful sets of constraints and incentives – forms of opportunity and forms of surveillance, having the population as a whole as their material. A preventative, normalising casework had come of age. Whereas the philanthropy of the earlier decades of the century was entered into as a means of discriminating between potential applicants for assistance, the same was manifestly not true of the new philanthropic casework.

Although the initial investigation remained important and combating 'abuse' remained a high priority, a follow-up pattern of casework and visiting was crucial to perpetuating the superior influence of bourgeois morality. At the same time, individual casework was but one among many of the means by which Victorian society sought to construct relatively harmonious relations between the classes – relations accompanied by the proper modes of deference, patronage and respect. As casework developed, it became more and more effectively employed as a diagnostic technique seeking out the deeper individual problems of which poverty was simply an outward sign. By adapting older interrogatory disciplines to new settings, caseworkers were able to extract a kind of 'confession' from the poor. Set out in an accurate casepaper, such 'confessions' could reveal a great deal to the trained eye. Consequently, special devices, techniques and interview schedules were employed to assist in casework practice, for now 'the object of taking down a case is not merely to get a statement of the facts but, if possible, to enter the mind and thoughts of the applicant' (see Fido, 1977).

Casework ceased to be a means to an end and became instead part of an ongoing social relation. Supervision, observation and treatment were the ends, constant social diagnosis ensuring the maintenance of a correct balance. Charity was no longer a simple matter of 'asking and giving', Loch insisted, it must now strive for 'character transformation' (Loch, 1883). An integrated and diagnostic system of casework was thought capable of delivering not only the body of knowledge necessary to the task of social reform but also the techniques of character transformation. Subsequently, the extension of casework practice beyond the so-called 'residuum' offered the opportunity for simultaneously expanding the technique and bringing the whole of society within its scope. Significantly, whilst home visits had always represented a central focus for charitable activity, later it was the family and child care that provided the practical concerns marking the progressive reorientation of the discipline.

Towards the end of the nineteenth century, therefore, casework had become considerably more systematic and rigorous, but also more reflexive and relational, than its earlier counterpart, relief visiting. The practice had moved through a phase where, in 'discovering' the culpability of the poor, it had effectively individualised the aetiology of, and response to, pauperism and had begun to embark on a new course as a component of an emergent strategy of normalisation. Within the latter strategy, in concert with newly developing mechanisms of social insurance, techniques of intervention would reach out beyond the margins of pauperism and begin to erect statutory and collective forms of discipline around the working class as a whole. Inevitably, the capacity of casework to contribute to the social mobility and 'improvement' of members of the working class at the end of the nineteenth century rested heavily upon the real improvements registered in the social and economic conditions in Britain. In this context, quantitatively speaking, casework as such features only as a fairly marginal practice. However, its qualitative significance lay in the way it helped construct a new normative discourse, specify a range of desired conditions and relationships (notably the 'modern' patriarchal family) and finally, install one amongst a growing number of supervisory practices around the individual and private space, the family and domestic space and the society and social space. Amongst other practices, then, casework represents one of the expanding avenues of surveillance that came to comprise the particular discipline of social policy within a disciplinary society. Yet just as the working class itself was being recomposed and as casework practices were expanding and diversifying, so certain important changes began to register within the remaining, marginalised, 'residuum'.

Controlling the new 'residuum'

The developments outlined above are particularly interesting, not merely because they relate closely to that diminution of the nineteenth-century 'dangerous and criminal classes' (of which the pauper and the vagrant had been part) described in Chapter 3, but also because they testify to equivalent shifts, within other areas of social policy, by which relatively small groups of the 'deviant' are isolated and then subjected to harsh, even punitive, policy measures. Indeed, as Crowther has suggested, 'in a world where poverty was diminishing, pauperism could seem even more blameable' (Crowther, 1981, p. 56).

The social processes culminating in the isolation of a distinct category of 'hardened criminal', 'vagrant' or 'recidivist pauper' are entirely bound up with the more developed systems of classification and segregation of the inmates of institutions or the recipients of assistance which were gathering apace in the later decades of the nineteenth century. Within the Poor Law in particular, the final decades of the century saw a considerable expansion of systems of classification. Increasingly, the sick, the old and infirm, widows, children and persons of unsound mind were subdivided and separated not only within institutions but especially outside them; individualisation and normalisation frequently brought with them an increasingly preventative – or welfare – orientation.

The preventative character of welfare strategies became more efficient when these strategies were employed in conjunction with a number of long-standing trends that were coming to the fore. In the first place there was the expansion of manufacturing industry and relatively improved opportunities for the urban working classes – especially those in skilled trades. In the second place there was the increased stratification of the working class and the decasualisation of certain manual trades. Then came the opening up of new patterns of consumption with the development of mass retailing outlets – all of which were reflected in new social aspirations, especially amongst the more affluent and 'respectable' sections of the working class. Finally, there were the political, legal and constitutional developments, particularly the enfranchisement of the majority of the working-class males, the growth of the Labour and Trades Union movements and the extension of their civil and legal immunities. These changes in turn were reflected by the continuing development of a labourist lobby for social reform which was based upon criteria of 'right', 'needs' and social protection rather than the punitive philosophy of the Poor Law.

It was in the context of developments of this kind that the shift towards preventative relief strategies came about. Although these changes can be said to reflect an increasingly complex series of social divisions, they also express the emergence of a new and increasingly collectivist form of social order (Hall and Schwarz, 1985). Certainly there are good grounds for suggesting that the new order is more complex than that of half a century earlier, but important disciplinary elements of this new order – which it is appropriate to call preventative – can be identified. De Schweinitz points in this direction with the observation that, 'since 1349 the law had been applied almost exclusively to coerce the poor. . . . The spirit of the legislation had been negative. Now, government was being used, even though ineffectively, in a different way' (De Schweinitz, 1943, p. 160). The observation may be imprecise but it does suggest that the social order was now being orchestrated in a new way. And central to these new modes of social ordering were the techniques of disciplinary social intervention perfected in the interplay of public and charitable strategies for the management of poverty and pauperism.

The confining order of the nineteenth-century social structure began to give way to the relatively more flexible society made possible by capitalism and industrialism. In line with these new developments, but following a logic partly its own, relief strategy (perhaps now more appropriately termed welfare strategy) was also breaking free of the restrictive mould of the Poor Law. A combination of casework, insurance and 'self-help' multiplied a concern with social promotion across society, questions of consumption and 'lifestyle' took on a wider social significance.

On all sides, therefore, we have avenues of social promotion, classification and diversity, increased intervention and specialisation – yet all set against the dedramatisation of class and employment relationships and the universalisation of preventative welfare practices, practices that were no longer directed at the pauperised section of society specifically, but at the working class as a whole. Yet an important corollary to these developments frequently remains overlooked. Despite the positive and promotional opportunities made available by socio-economic developments and, hard on their heels, forms of welfare intervention broadening a disciplinary series of social relations (supervisions and simple restrictions) across the whole of the working class, the coercive core of these new policies remained, until 1929 at least, primarily fixed upon those classic institutions of social exclusion and correction, the workhouse and the prison. However, in the final years of the Poor Law the discipline within welfare strategies had begun to adopt differing forms as, *inter alia*, the labour camp ideal and the means test replaced the workhouse (but not the prison) transforming questions of social exclusion into the rather more administrative question if disentitlement.

But relations of social discipline have several dimensions. The preventative systems of welfare, sustained through promotional incentives and opportunities and orientated towards broad objectives of social order and collective well-being, were complemented by corrective systems embodying harsh discipline and punitive control. Existing outside these positive and integrative forms of welfare, the new 'residuum', characterised as representing the worst elements of society, became the object of more coercive policy measures. Even though the substantive orientation of policy had shifted from the coercion of the Poor Law era and even though the first elements of a more positive and integrationist welfare strategy were coming into being, systems of explicit discipline still served as the basis upon which the entire welfare edifice was founded.

The techniques and the strategic objectives of a disciplinary system of social policy were impelled beyond the confines of the Poor Law and the pauper class and became orientated towards conditions of well-being and states of welfare within society at large. Yet as each avenue of mobility leading away from pauperism was opened up and as each classification of relief recipients moved further away from the Poor Law, the ostracism, disentitlement and penalisation of the remaindered minority – 'the residuum' – grew. The disciplinary focus of social policy had, by now transcended the confines of the workhouse regime and began to find applications across the entire field of class relations. New forms of social intervention, which came to comprise the strategy of preventative social welfare, had placed the disciplining of the working class upon the first rungs of a primarily administrative ladder. Nevertheless, the basic forms of discipline upon which the whole structure rested were very familiar and easily observable in the institutions which remained to house the vagrant, workshy or criminal.

5

A new politics of needs: from moralism to normalisation

In the previous chapter I indicated that there was a growing division in the social responses to pauperism in the final decades of the nineteenth century. New employment relations and forms of domestic life, new patterns of social mobility and forms of state social policy certainly gave new substance to these strategies. Even so, the continued existence of explicitly penal sanctions in the new 'social' interventions of the state suggest that the new welfare strategies had a markedly disciplinary core. In particular, the disciplinary structure of the new strategy of preventive welfare is evident in the punitive exclusion from assistance, or the detention and confinement, of those considered vagrant, workshy, or otherwise 'undeserving'.

In the light of this, while remaining cognisant of the increasing bifurcation of disciplinary and welfare strategies, in the present chapter I shall be primarily concerned with charting that continuous core of discipline which has characterised social policy as a whole. It is less a question of specific penalties, hardships or obligations (though these are undoubtedly important) than a matter of their overall strategic significance, the objectives they seek and the discourses within which these are couched. In this respect, the bifurcation of disciplinary strategies regarding the treatment of certain groups serves as a means by which broader patterns of class and gender relations are themselves sustained. The maintenance of certain avenues of social mobility to selected groups is, in the manner of Tawney's 'tadpole philosophy', an important vindication of the unequal social structure as a whole and a valuable means for controlling the less privileged residuum (Tawney, 1938).

There can be few more authoritative restatements of this disciplinary preoccupation than that conveyed by James Davey (a chief inspector for the Poor Law Division of the Local Government Board) during the deliberations of the Royal Commission on the Poor Laws during 1905–9 – one of the great turning points of welfare strategy – concerning the principles of future poor relief. Davey urged that poor relief should retain the spirit of less-eligibility which, for him, comprised 'first . . . the loss of personal reputation (what is understood as the stigma of pauperism); secondly, the loss of personal freedom which is secured by detention in a workhouse; and thirdly, the loss of political freedom by suffering disenfranchisement' (Royal Commission *Report* Appendix, vol. 1, 1909).

As it transpired, of course, neither the Majority nor the Minority Reports of the Royal Commission advocated anything like a whole-hearted return to the principles of 1834. Although, in turn, both reports argued the necessity for developing the 'treatment' side of relief practice, yet there was substantial disagreement about the organisation of these treatment facilities and their endorsement by forms of penalty and deterrence. These differences reflected major disagreements regarding the scope and direction of state welfare division and led, ultimately, to the splitting of the Commission. I shall situate these debates regarding the future of treatment, welfare and discipline within the new and emerging welfare strategies and discourses of the early twentieth century. Before doing so, however, I must complement the discussion, begun in Chapter 4, of the increasingly sophisticated forms of casework and treatment, with a brief overview of the residualisation of a small class of the poor, vagrant, allegedly 'workshy' and 'refractory' and of the intensification of the disciplinary procedures to which they were subjected.

Labour, discipline and compulsion

As I have shown in previous chapters, the history of the Poor Law is a history of the organisation of disciplinary power. This became very explicit within the reformed Poor Law after 1834. But, as the century wore on, the apparent significance of this discipline – a discipline which came to affect the entire social sphere – to an increasingly promotional and preventive social policy, appears somewhat diminished. To reassert the prevailing disciplinary core of social policy I must return, briefly, to the 1870s, and the campaign against outdoor relief. The decade signals an important turning point, for it began with an attempt to mark out the respective responsibilities of the state and private philanthropy concerning the poor. Philanthropy was to cream off the better class of pauper whilst the Poor Law was to be left with the remaining, rather less 'deserving' cases. This division of responsibility implied a complementary relationship. The increasing severity of the Poor Law is only fully comprehensible in the light of the refinement of rehabilitative techniques by philanthropy, a development which, in turn, legitimated the greater use of force against the residuum of the 'undeserving poor', the 'demoralised and semi-criminal' (see Booth, 1902).

Perhaps the most explicit attempt to restore the deterrent character of the Poor Law at a time when the Charity Organisation Society was beginning to develop an increasingly casework-centred approach, concerns the Local Government Board's experiment with a specifically punitive 'test' workhouse at Poplar. Reviewing the 'deterrent workhouse' policy in his 1895 work, *The Better Administration of The Poor Laws*, William Chance offered an almost complete vindication of the COS position. The Poor Law should arrange its activities in order to assist in the best possible way the rehabilitative efforts of the charities, he claimed. Drawing liberally upon the Annual Reports of the Local Government Board, Chance found a great deal to approve of in the importance the LGB claimed to attach to 'classification' – 'a necessary condition for the maintainance of the discipline which lies at the root of any effective administration of indoor relief' (*LGB, Third Annual Report*, 1874).

For De Schweinitz, the regime at the Poplar 'test' workhouse was nothing short of 'penal – with long hours of work at stone breaking, oakum picking, wood cutting and corn grinding' (De Schweinitz, 1943, p. 159). As the Webbs argued, the objective was to establish 'a stricter and more deterrent discipline' for the able-bodied. (Webb and Webb, 1910, p. 160). In a sense, it could be said that the regime at the new 'test' workhouse was to become decidely more 'anti-social'. And indeed, where the punitive and deterrent features of a policy gain increasing prominence, it is relatively simple to discern aspects of an 'anti-social policy' but, as I shall show later, there is much more to an anti-social policy than that which is merely *explicitly* punitive.

Ten years after the establishment of the first 'test' workhouse, the Local Government Board found itself able to record significant progress in the area of pauper discipline and deterrence. Improved classification within workhouses had led to substantial administrative gains, for 'the removal of the sick to distinct buildings made it possible to restore due discipline among the able bodied' (*LGB Thirteenth Annual Report, 1884*). Concluding his discussion of these matters, Chance confirmed his view that 'by means of the workhouse test alone can real destitution be discovered, and fraud, imposition and lying be defeated' (Chance, 1895, p. 113). Of course, such remarks underline both the bifurcation of strategies for the treatment of pauperism and the complementary nature of the twin arms of the strategy itself. Yet the issue of the 'test' workhouse raised other difficult disciplinary problems. In particular the question of compulsory detention in the workhouse. As the Local Government Board saw it:

> much evil has arisen . . . and the discipline of the workhouse has been seriously impaired by the frequent exercise of the power which the inmates have hitherto possessed of discharging themselves from the workhouse at short and uncertain notice, claiming readmission as might best suit their inclination and convenience.
>
> (LGB Circular, 18 November 1871, in Chance, 1895)

The supposed 'evil' was, in part, remedied by statute in 1871 through the Pauper Inmates: Discharge and Regulation Act, further controls being made available to the workhouse authorities in 1882 by the Casual Poor Act. However, there remained those who were still unsatisfied and it was argued that legislation should extend the period for the compulsory detention of paupers for up to a week (*LGB Sixteenth Annual Report*). Particular examples could, it seems, always be produced to substantiate the case for increased powers of compulsory detention. For instance, during 1889, one man discharged himself from the Fulham workhouse ninety-three times, his lengthiest period of absence occurring as a result of a twenty-one-day prison sentence.

For my purposes, the issue illustrates one of the fundamental problems of the deterrent workhouse, for in many respects, compulsory detention ran quite contrary to the underlying philosophy of the Poor Law. The essence of the Poor Law had been encapsulated in that salutory act of reflection and calculation by the pauper him- or herself regarding the advantages and disadvantages of entering the workhouse. Nevertheless, gradually and for a variety of reasons – administrative simplification, rehabilitative and curative endeavours and, later, as explicit forms of penalty – forms of compulsory commitment and detention began to make their appearance. Compulsory detention remained a problem within Poor Law discourse for some time to come, and indeed, the question became an issue for the Majority and Minority groupings on the Poor Law Commission. In particular, subsequent proposals, to introduce disciplinary labour colonies for the poor and unemployed, took the issue of 'compulsion' to its limits.

The principle and most explicit 'objects' of the proposed compulsory powers were usually described as the 'vagrant', the 'incorrigible' and the 'recalcitrant' – in short, the 'residuum', those who were, allegedly, unable or unwilling to support themselves and their families (Loch, 1883; Webb and Webb, 1929; Harris, 1972; Crowther, 1981). Even so, the greater part of the concern about the unwarranted exercise of compulsory powers of detention (whether in the workhouse or, later, a penal labour colony) sprang from reformers' efforts to devise watertight distinctions between the 'genuinely poor' or 'merely unemployed' and the 'demoralised or semi-criminal' (to adopt Booth's phrase). The two arms of the disciplinary strategy came into focus once again. Few were concerned about the incarceration of the latter, but punitive treatment of the former, whose only crime was poverty, seemed to go against the received wisdom of liberal philanthropy. Furthermore, to incarcerate those who were merely poor might prove an impossible task (even if a rather restrictive definition of 'poverty' were employed), to say nothing of appearing somewhat incompatible with the working of the notionally 'free' economy and the limited role of the 'liberal' state. Even the 1834 Act had not envisaged locking up the poor, only 'paupers'; these distinctions were important, but the discourses within which they were established were not static. Joining in the growing discourse on 'treatment' and 'industrial rehabilitation' the Webbs, amongst others, although strongly opposed to the exercise of compulsion in the case of those merely poor or unemployed, argued persuasively for the development of a range of specialist treatment institutions – including labour colonies for the inculcation of industrial discipline and penal colonies for the 'workshy' and 'recalcitrant'. Under the guise of a discourse on 'treatment', therefore, a range of highly interventionist and coercive powers blossomed.

In rejecting an 'institutional' solution to problems of unemployment and poverty in favour of an approach emphasising the reorganisation of the labour market, the Webbs' views approximated closely to those of Beveridge. For instance, during the final decade of the nineteenth century Beveridge had strongly supported the introduction of a system of labour exchanges as a first move towards rationalising the labour market (Harris, 1972 and 1977). The labour colony, especially the penal labour colony, never did assume the prominence as an instrument of social policy that its most vociferous proponents had advocated. Nevertheless, around the turn of the century, there were numerous proposals for the introduction of industrial, labour, or farm, colonies intended to serve both as agencies of remoralisation and rehabilitation and as regimes of discipline and punishment (Colledge and Field, 1983).

In an obvious sense, the labour colony ideal synthesised many important elements of labour discipline. The combination of less-eligibility, relief work and the labour test with the rigours of workhouse detention suited many proponents of Poor Law reform and, in Poplar, where the first 'test' workhouse for the able-bodied had been established, one of the first labour colony schemes was introduced (Crowther, 1981, pp.

79, 240; Harris, 1972, pp. 189–92). Support for labour colonies emerged from a whole range of political persuasions during the last two decades of the nineteenth century. A variety of arguments surfaced, favouring different types of colony providing anything from rehabilitation to repression, and designed to combat any number of real or imagined socio-economic problems, from rural depopulation to physical deterioration. As Colledge and Field note, radicals, socialists and Fabians all supported the idea (Colledge and Field, 1983, p. 154). But it was Charles Booth and the Salvation Army's General Booth who envisaged the most extensive labour colony schemes. The latter's book, *In Darkest England and the Way Out* (Booth, 1890), contained a blueprint for a programme of progressive rehabilitation taking the downtrodden pauper, in stages, further and further away from the demoralising taint of the city and out into the regenerating air of the countryside. The Salvation Army did go so far as to establish a farm colony at Hadleigh, in Essex.

Charles Booth's plan, however, was much more in keeping with his own rather more 'moralistic problem definition' (K. Williams, 1981), and consisted of the proposal to segregate his entire 'Class B' (the 'very poor', 'casuals and loafers') into some form of disciplinary and remedial labour colony, whilst some more penal and punitive treatment was envisaged for 'Class A' (the 'demoralised and semi-criminal'). The scheme was nothing if not ambitious, and would have encompassed as much as 10 per cent of the working population (Brown, 1968; Stedman Jones, 1971, pp. 306–8; K. Williams, 1981, pp. 327–8). At the same time, similar proposals were advanced by Alfred Marshall and Samuel Barnett. Both insisted that the camps were to be progressive and rehabilitative and, above all, that they were to be entered voluntarily. The principle was not new; throughout the nineteenth century, entry to the workhouse had also been formally 'voluntary'. State slavery was politically unacceptable. As Stedman Jones noted:

> the only form compulsion could assume would be that of making life otherwise impossible. The casual poor would be forced to accept a condition of semi-servitude because of the difficulty of finding a fresh opening in an ever-hardening world.
>
> (Stedman Jones, 1971, p. 307).

The shape of things to come, perhaps.

Debates about discipline

The debate on compulsory powers in Poor Law institutions and an associated range of camps and colonies, became particularly focused during the deliberations of the Royal Commission established in 1905. Adequate accounts of the work of the Royal Commission can be found elsewhere, (Beveridge, 1909; De Schweinitz, 1943; B. Webb, 1948; P. Clarke, 1978) my attention will focus specifically upon the competing formulations of the role of compulsion and supervision within the Majority and Minority Reports and their respective articulation of disciplinary measures. The debate which unfolded soon became defined as 'the Webbs versus the Poor Law' (De Schweinitz, 1943, p. 185), although on the Commission itself, the four eventual signatories of the Minority Report were substantially outnumbered by the combined representatives of the Poor Law administration and the COS.

However, as even Beatrice Webb agreed, more united the Majority and Minority Reports than divided them (B. Webb, 1948, p. 321; Thane, 1982, p. 88). Nevertheless, there are significant differences of principle and numerous practical disagreements regarding the form of alternative methods for the organisation and delivery of 'preventative' services. As Clarke has noted, it appeared to sympathetic contemporaries that the Webbs were engaged in no less a project than 'working towards a different conception of the responsibility of the state in relation to poverty' (Clarke, 1978, p. 120). This produced a certain discontent amongst other members of the Commission. Significantly, however, *both* reports conformed closely to existing opinions in assuming, as Thane has suggested, 'the existence of a ne'er do well class at the base of society' for whom punitive labour colonies or similar institutions would be required (Thane, 1982, p. 90).

The Webbs certainly had a rather preconceived view of the Royal Commission's objectives; however, their attempt to characterise the respective strands of Poor Law opinion does highlight the points of agreement and disagreement between the different groups on the question of Poor Law reform. Even allowing for the partiality of their position, it is useful to have so authoritative a statement of the state of Poor Law discourse. In a book published one year after the appearance of the Minority Report, the Webbs attempted to describe the present 'level of development' of the Poor Laws. They believed that the law and administration had drifted far from the so-called 'principles of 1834' and sought to catalogue their own more contemporary 'principles of 1907' as a replacement. There were three of these: the principle of curative treatment, the principle of compulsion and the principle of universal provision (Webb and Webb, 1910, pp. 257–77).

The Majority Report came nowhere near to recognising these more modern principles of Poor Law discourse and practice, although it is clear that they were, implicitly at least, acknowledged as key features of the existing administration. The Majority Report retained a strongly moralistic aetiology, 'the causes of distress are not only economic and industrial; in their origin and character they are largely moral' (*Majority Report*, 1909, pp. 643–4). It followed that the primary need was for corrective techniques and institutions, which would exert their influence upon the morals of the poor. Thus, armed with a generic moral theory on the origins of distress, the Majority Report went on to recommend an equally general administrative response. It proposed a uniform system of Public Assistance Committees which would administer all relief and supervise the actions of all public and voluntary social service functions. Reflecting the views of the strong presence of COS personnel and supporters on the Royal Commission, it envisaged that the voluntary and charitable welfare sector would continue to perform a major, even expanding, role within relief (or welfare) administration. In Fraser's words, 'the Majority Report wished to make a swollen Poor Law into an all-purpose relief organisation' (D. Fraser, 1973, p. 149). The Webbs, on the other hand, referred somewhat caustically to the Majority Report's scheme as a proposal for a 'General Destitution Authority' and condemned the revival of the principle of deterrence (a new manifestation of 'less eligibility') within the Majority's Report (Webb and Webb, 1910, pp. 139–40 and 1929, p. 278).

The Webbs took particular exception to the fact that all the specialist institutions and responsibilities which had grown incrementally from the workhouse were to be staffed and administered by 'officers of a single, homogenous interchangeable service, deliberately focusing their attention upon the moral accompaniments assumed to be characteristic of destitute persons' (Webb and Webb, 1910). In 1909, discussing the Majority Report in the *Sociological Review*, Bosanquet commented that, 'the majority proceed upon the principle that where there is a failure of self-maintenance, there is a defect in the citizen character' (Bosanquet, 1909). This assumption of grave moral defects at the heart of all destitution, allied with the uniform remedy of moral training in an atmosphere of 'less eligibility' would, claimed the Webbs, inevitably mean that the stigma of nineteenth-century poor relief would be retained. Many of those whose need for assistance was greatest would still be deterred from applying for relief. In addition, the basic division between private and public relief agencies, stamped indelibly upon the Majority Report, would almost certainly perpetuate the ideology of 'deserving' and 'undeserving', a feature which even Loch had attempted to eradicate from the philosophy of philanthropy some twenty years earlier. Nevertheless, the signatories of the Majority Report were prepared to be quite candid in their defence of the double standard, saying, 'An essential principle to be observed in connection with [public] assistance to the able-bodied is that it shall be in some way less agreeable than the assistance given by the Voluntary Aid Committee' (Majority Report, 1909, p. 445).

The Webbs believed that two aspects of the Majority Report were fundamentally incompatible. On the one hand, the majority had proposed a major extension of relief and 'treatment' within the basic administrative model of the Poor Law, yet, on the other hand, they also envisaged bolstering up and refining the principle of deterrence. The Webbs considered it inevitable that an authority which was to deal only with cases of 'real destitution' would place a premium upon limitation – limitation of the numbers resorting to its assistance. It could not, reasonably, purport to offer any 'treatment' with a realistic prospect of 'cure', for it would only receive applicants for assistance as a very last resort, by which time they would be too far gone or, adopting the terminology of the Majority Report, they would be too 'demoralised' for social rehabilitation to be anything other than a palliative (Webb and Webb, 1910).

In an important argument, which casts significant light upon the Webbs criticisms of the Majority Report and yet also illuminates the expansive scheme of disciplinary social policies they envisaged, the Webbs drew attention to the fact that in a truly 'preventative' social policy the state must not wait for poverty and distress to reveal itself but must anticipate its appearance. This disciplinary and interventionist commitment on the part of the new Fabian social engineers recasts the relations of public and private in a vitally important fashion. The poor were no longer to be free to be poor; the claims of social order, political economy and social hygiene were to erase this small privilege. Thus, poverty was to become a new site for social and political intervention. I have already pointed out that during the later decades of the nineteenth century, poverty had come to be seen as a symptom of a defect of character, but now its significance changed again. Poverty ceased to be of interest for its own sake; it was less the suffering of the poor that motivated the new disciplinary social engineers than the hold that poverty gave them over the lives of the poor. The threat of poverty seemed to promise a 'key' with which access might be obtained – not only to the poor family, but also to the nearly poor family. Disciplinary mechanisms could thereby reach beyond the condition of poverty itself and gain a foothold in the lives of all working people, on the grounds of what they might become. The Webbs worked this argument through whilst developing their critique of the Majority Report.

So long as the conditions afforded by the Poor Law authority are 'deterrent', few will apply for this maintenance . . . even at the cost of foregoing *the treatment that they really need*. . . . As a Destitution Authority, it is inherently incapable of bringing pressure to bear on the lives and wills of these people, at the time when such pressure may be effective, namely, *long before they have become destitute*, at the time they are taking the first step towards the evil parasitism to which they will eventually succumb.

> (Webb and Webb, 1910, pp. 228–9, emphasis added)

Furthermore, they argued, no essentially deterrent 'Destitution Authority' would have the means to differentiate adequately between those who were voluntarily and those who were involuntarily idle, or, without a specialist team of fieldworkers, any proper means of recognising and assessing the 'needs' of families and individuals which those families or individuals did not articulate for themselves. Finally, it would be impossible to justify the extension of compulsory powers to any agency that sought, through a principle of deterrence, to 'pauperise and degrade', rather than improve and assist, persons who were unconvicted of any crime. Similar arguments were deployed against the Majority Report's proposal to extend compulsory powers of detention to cover those who had 'voluntarily' entered Poor Law institutions. If this were attempted, they argued, those most 'in need' of the treatments on offer would be scared off, 'the very patients [sic] to whom the "order for continuous treatment" would be most appropriate and most useful will refuse to come in' (*ibid.* p. 292).

Within the Webbs' proposals, it was 'need', rather than simply poverty, upon which the interventionist discourses of social policy came to settle. That is to say, 'need' expressed as a component of a normative discourse of social management. Whilst the twentieth century was to witness a great relativisation of concepts of poverty, the concept of need grew ever more obscure, more flexible, diverse and many-faceted. Poverty seemed to provide the state with a single point of access into the lives of the poorest, whereas 'need' offered several points of access and many levels and dimensions as it reflected a far richer conception of the human experience. Later still, desires and aspirations, were also to be added to the frame, their disciplinary potential hitherto unexplored – but this is to race ahead of myself.

In framing their own 'progressive' alternatives, the Webbs recounted the ever-increasing scale of administrative compulsion and regulation with which the Poor Law had become replete. They then began to outline their own comprehensive proposals for the reorientation of relief strategy, the dismantling of the Poor Law and its replacement by a preventative infrastructure of specialist services. In so doing, they attacked the arbitrary character of workhouse management and the untrained, unscientific and largely unsupervised activities of workhouse personnel. They went on to remark, in terms which for my purposes carry particular significance, that:

> No-one acquainted with the administration of prisons, or reformatories or foreign penal colonies will under-rate the difficulty of securing for the institution officers with the requisite characteristics for making discipline curative and reformatory. *The whole technique of dealing with adults who are criminal, disorderly or merely 'workshy' is yet in the making.*
> (Minority Report, 1909, p. 71, emphasis added)

The Minority Report's proposals for developing those 'techniques for dealing with adults' are one of my principal concerns. The techniques eventually proposed, whilst no longer purely punitive, betray an overriding concern with efficiency and normalisation that runs to the heart of modern conceptions of social discipline. So, somewhat paradoxically, and despite the Webbs' pointed criticisms of the deterrent Poor Law, it is not too difficult to see how their own proposals contributed to a new disciplinary strategy which further exacerbated the residualisation of the poorest. The whole of even the Webbs' most progressive writing was dogged by the spectre of the 'residuum', a class with few apparent morals and even less willpower thought likely to overrun the resources of even the most minutely improved scheme of assistance.

At the heart of the Webbs' social philosophy there lurked a profoundly moralistic preoccupation with respect to the proper conduct of life, a preoccupation which informed their attempts to reorganise the mechanisms of social intervention. Although acknowledging that the poor, deterred from entering the workhouse, might beg, steal and sponge in order to avoid starvation and that, in the circumstances, this represented a reasonable option for them to take, such essentially pragmatic observations were seldom reflected in their proposed remedies. As a result, within the broader context of their proposals for the national reorganisation of the labour market (a requirement considered a necessary prerequisite of any effective social policy) their proposals for the relief of poverty continued to emphasise an essentially individual 'treatment'. For the most 'difficult' cases (those living in the most depressed and degraded conditions and, therefore, in the greatest need) they proposed an even more intensive form of penal labour discipline (Minority Report, 1909, p. 96).

A new series of social divisions were being written into the functioning of the welfare institutions. The Webbs were advocating a combination of welfare strategies aiming at the remoralisation of the mass – a direct consequence of which was the fact that the residualisation of the poorest would become ever more pronounced (Webb and Webb, 1926). What is more, the Webbs compounded the problem of the marginality of the poor by recommending the intensification of the discipline to which the poorest were subjected – despite their own argument that an augmentation of disciplinary measures would render any system of rehabilitation and treatment self-defeating. For all their criticisms of the Poor Law system, the Webbs appear to have rejected its generalised strategy of repressive deterrence only to retain selective elements of its disciplinary technique within a new constellation of regulatory and administrative powers. Concluding their criticisms of the Majority Report's seeming penchant for the increasing use of general powers of compulsion within a refurbished Poor Law, the Webbs remarked that:

> It [is] useless for the state to run a penal establishment for the refractory and 'sturdy rogue' unless it also has the power of taking persons up and putting them there. But why, unless we can invent something better than a mere destitution authority, should we take this function out of the hands of the Police and Prison Authorities.
>
> (Minority Report, 1909, p. 62)

Yet, precisely 230 pages later in their report, in the midst of a series of proposals designed to secure the preventative orientation of future welfare policies, the Webbs (strictly, the Minority group of the Poor Law Commissioners) appear to advocate something sounding remarkably similar to the penal labour establishment just rejected. They would undoubtedly claim that their own proposals were much improved in that they amounted to far more than a mere 'destitution authority' and that they envisaged conferring new powers of committal upon these institutions. Yet this simply extended the disciplinary potential of such institutions. Under the guise of welfare and rehabilitation, coercive powers were to be extended to punitive and disciplinary institutions. The poor could no longer refuse the hospitality of the workhouse, preferring the 'freedom' of their poverty to the rigours of institutionalisation. Instead poverty, and later need, was to become an offence to 'the social'; it would require appropriate treatment. It was in the nature of an 'anti-social policy' that it would cater for needs and provide welfare only in this highly conditional fashion. Henceforth, in order to receive the meagre benevolence of the state a recipient also had to submit to its discipline. Furthermore, the needy might only refuse the state's overtures in welfare on pain of further disciplinary measures. Under the Webbs' stratagem, the interventionary powers of the new 'Fabian State' were to be nothing if not comprehensive (Barker, 1984).

Efficiency and the prevention of destitution

The Webbs' own proposals, defined in specific policy terms within the Minority Report, were the product of a long association with analyses of pauperism, state administration and critical reflection on the Poor Laws. This 'reflection' did not cease with the publication of the Report in 1909. The following year two books appeared in which the Webbs reiterated, expanded and defended their arguments. The first was a review of developments in English Poor Law Policy up to and including the debate on the 1909 Royal Commission, whilst the second outlined a bold agenda for putting into practice the new preventative ethos which the Webbs hoped would replace the older, more repressive, mentality of the Poor Law.

Yet despite the fact that this work represented the more liberal and 'progressive' wings of contemporary social and political opinion, its fairly uncompromising moral tone allied it closely to the social philosophy of the 'National Efficiency' lobby. And, unfortunately, the very attitudes which *The Prevention of Destitution* sought to inculcate within civil society, proved to be a fertile soil for the imperialist doctrines of National Efficiency, helping the search for remedies for the seeming national decline and, ultimately, legitimating a host of disciplinary measures which, looking to improve the efficiency of capital and labour alike, sought to bind the working-class interest in welfare to the economic interests of national and imperial capitalism. Of course, this would not be the only occasion upon which a strong link was forged between nationalism and welfare. In packaging their social remedies for the nation's consideration, the Webbs conveyed a dire warning to the governing classes.

> Our growing consciousness of the stress of international competition is reminding us that unless we take the necessary steps to rid ourselves of this disease [i.e. destitution] we shall fall still more behind and eventually succumb before younger and more energetic rivals. And there is another ground of urgency. The destitute themselves and the manual working class next above them . . . now possess votes, and are steadily acquiring political power; so that the governing classes find themselves more and more pressed to grapple with the problem, on pain of seeing the task taken out of their hands, to fall, perhaps, into those of men who may attempt to deal with it less in the real and highest interests of the community as a whole and in the long run, than for the immediate material benefit of the sufferers themselves.
>
> (Webb and Webb, 1910, pp. 5–6)

Nevertheless, it is difficult to appreciate fully the disciplinary and imperialist dimensions of the Webbs' agenda for social reform without giving some more detailed consideration to the particular proposals upon which it rested.

The Webbs took as their starting point the fact that 'there are today . . . more destitute persons being maintained at public expense outside the Poor Law than inside its scope' (*ibid.* p. 296). This observation prompted many commentators to acknowledge that the Poor Law had, in many senses, outgrown itself. The Webbs were keen to see the break up of the formal and restrictive mould of the Poor Law which, they claimed, had hampered the development of more progressive alternatives. They favoured the greater specialisation of relief policies as part of a preventative reorientation of welfare. Paradoxically, however, such specialisation ultimately served only to confirm the existence of a negative and residual orientation within social policy, anchoring perceptions of social welfare (treatments and interventions) almost exclusively to the pathologies of the social sphere and, in turn, to the failings of individuals. However, to the Webbs, proposals which offered an alternative to the confining atmosphere of Poor Law administration are likely to have appeared progressive. Twentieth-century society, they claimed, had no place for any public authority whose functions were restricted to the 'relief' of poverty; a more efficient and 'constructive' application of the social power was long overdue (*ibid.* p. 296).

The change of direction urged by the Webbs conformed to the pattern of incremental change which had characterised Poor Law development thus far, but they hoped to install three new principles (the 'Principles of 1907' referred to earlier) as the guiding force of social welfare policy. 'Prevention' was to be the focus of state activity and it was to be achieved by means of universal provision, compulsion and curative treatment. Prevention was not an end in itself, of course, it was valuable above all for its political and economic efficiency. When the Webbs advocated universalism it was a universalism of a particularly utilitarian variety.

> Prevention is the very basis of the Minority Report proposals. It . . . underlies all three 'principles of 1907'. The Local Authorities do not apply the principle of curative treatment wholly, or even mainly, for the pleasure or the advantage of the individual sufferer; what they have in mind is the prevention of future evils to the community. . . . If in one service or another the principle of universal prevention is adopted, it is because we have become convinced . . . that universal prevention is actually less expensive than any alternative.
>
> (*ibid.* pp. 298–9)

The new machinery for putting these principles into practice was to emerge from amongst the functions and services which had grown up around the Poor Law at local level. In future there was to be the (local) education authority, the (local) health authority, the (local) lunacy authority, the (local) pensions authority and, perhaps most significant of all, the (local and national) unemployment authority and the development of a national system of labour exchanges. These were the administrative arrangements with which the Webbs were to pursue the break up of the Poor Law. In keeping with the new principles, the new agencies were to have wide ranging responsibilities for supervision and intervention, a universal scope of application and compulsory powers.

> It is vital that the Local Health Authority should be empowered and required to search and ensure proper treatment for the incipient stages of all diseases. It is vital that the Local Lunacy Authority should be empowered and required to search out and ensure proper care and control for all persons certified as mentally defective. . . . It is vital that the Local Education Authority should be empowered and required to search out and ensure, quite irrespective of the family's destitution, whatever Parliament may prescribe as the National Minimum of nurture and training for all children. . . . It is becoming no less clear that some authority must register and deal with the man who is unemployed, long before extended unemployment has demoralised him and reduced his family to destitution.
>
> (*Ibid.* p. 301)

Around its poorest, therefore, it seems that the incipient Fabian state was planning to erect a whole host of disciplinary institutions with wide-ranging investigative powers and responsibilities. Welfare came with a certain price for the turn-of-the-century working class. Even those to whom its ambiguous 'benevolence' was to be extended urged caution (Yeo, 1979), whereas women, 'aliens' and the 'demoralised poor' – and other groups more predominantly controlled or excluded by the new arrangements of welfare – might have yet further grounds for concern.

The widespread conferment of compulsory powers is of no small significance, in a sense it confirms my underlying argument that the new relations of welfare must be understood, in the first place from what has been termed 'the perspective of the state' (Taylor-Gooby, 1981), and in the second in an intensely disciplinary light. Nevertheless, for my present purposes, the solitary 'national' administration amongst the Webbs' other, predominantly 'local' administrations, demands special attention. It constituted the central feature of their own proposals and, by virtue of the fact that its concern was with the unemployed, able-bodied labourer (the same focus as the Poor Law) and that it involved some of the most obvious and explicit disciplinary mechanisms, it must also constitute the central feature of my own analysis.

For the unemployed, it was a 'disciplinary supervision . . . a more humane, as well as more effective 'deterrence' that the Webbs had in mind. (Webb and Webb, 1910, p. 316). The policy was preventative in a national sense for it intervened directly in the labour market, whilst, at the individual level, social discipline was the principle 'treatment' on offer. For these reasons, the policy is more readily understood in terms of deterrence than in terms of prevention and welfare.

> The new National Authority for Unemployment . . . will be able to deter men from becoming unemployed not only by actually preventing many unnecessary breaches in continuity of employment, but also by putting the necessary pressure on the will of those who are 'born tired' or who have become 'unemployable' either to accept and retain the situations that will be definitely offered to them, or else submit themselves to disciplinary training, with the Detention Colony in the background.
>
> (*ibid.* p. 317).

If any doubt lingers regarding the disciplinary formulation of this new labour market policy, then the Webbs' elaboration of their ideas for the National Unemployment Authority are especially instructive.

> If we had an Unemployment Authority responsible for either finding a man a job or placing him in training, we could for the first time strictly enforce upon every man and woman . . . failing to maintain themselves or their dependants, the obligation to make use of this organ of the state. . . . It would be unnecessary to enquire why he was out of work . . . he would simply be required to be at the Labour Exchange where he would either be provided with a job or found the means of improving his working capacity while he was waiting for a job. If it were discovered that there was a grave moral defect . . . he would have to submit himself, in a detention colony, to a treatment which would be at once curative and deterrent in the old Poor Law sense.
>
> (*ibid.* pp. 306–7)

The Webbs, in seeing the labour exchange as part of an essentially deterrent strategy of social provision, took a noticeably harsher view than many. Yet along with other advocates of the Minority Report, the Webbs argued that the system of labour exchanges would be unworkable without some form of compulsion. They had in mind the disciplinary compulsion afforded by the threat to commit the more 'reluctant' of the unemployed to the labour colony. This 'extreme' use of compulsory powers was rejected by many contemporaries although, in the insurantial scheme which eventually emerged after 1911, administrative sanctions, in the form of benefit disentitlements, were well to the fore.

We find, therefore, that despite the differences of emphasis and direction a large body of 'progressive' opinion tended to favour the application of compulsory powers against some or, usually, all of the unemployed (see Stedman Jones, 1971, pp. 332–3). The difference – and this was to become very significant – lay in the fact that some, following the Webbs, favoured an interventionist power of compulsion, whereas others, presuming on the installation of a system of unemployment insurance, favoured the attachment of conditions to receipt of unemployment payments. Whether by sticks, or carrots withheld, the state was to mount a panoply of disciplinary powers around its conception of working-class obligations within industry and the labour market. But of course the net of disciplinary measures did not end there – neither did the obligations. We have already seen how the Webbs sought to encapsulate within a profoundly disciplinary framework, both the responsibility to maintain oneself and one's dependents and the responsibility to adhere to the minimum standards of nurture and training prescribed by parliament 'quite irrespective of the family's destitution'.

The arguments favouring the exchanges touched upon many of the concerns which had preoccupied relief administrators throughout the nineteenth century. In an obvious sense, the labour exchange dealt directly with the problem of the able-bodied labourer, the precise object of virtually all disciplinary techniques under the Poor Law. Yet the labour exchange met this 'troublesome object', the unemployed man, in a very flexible relationship. The labour exchange (accompanied by a range of compulsory powers and the added sanction of disentitlement) could quite effectively discriminate between applicants for benefits according to a range of subtle criteria. Many of these criteria appeared to rest upon apparently 'moral' foundations. Those deemed 'virtuous', 'deserving' and in 'genuine' pursuit of employment might gain assistance, while others might find themselves penalised. Given such a comprehensive series of functions, the labour exchange would of necessity encounter, and need to find a solution for, the problem of the 'vagrant', that figure which had so troubled nineteenth-century relief administrators and policemen alike.

In the early decades of the nineteenth century, the vagrant came to occupy a position similar, in relation to morality and social order, to that occupied thirty years earlier by the pauper (Procacci, 1978). Indeed, the vagrant performed a similar ideological function. In its own 'ideological space' the figure and imputed character of the vagrant legitimated the intensification of disciplinary techniques within policies for dealing with poverty and unemployment and, at the same time, helped maintain the structure of incentives and sanctions for the rest of the workers, employed and unemployed, on the labour market. As a Fabian tract of 1905 had put it:

those who are a tax on the community for which they have never done a fair share of work and never will must be dealt with under some form of criminal law since society will soon recognise that to live without working is a crime. . . . The deliberately idle must be set to hard labour, and their social vice, if it may be, sweated out of them.

(Fabian Tract No. 126, quoted in Stedman Jones, 1971)

As Crowther, echoing the findings of both Beveridge and the Webbs, has shown, the correlation between high rates of unemployment and high levels of recorded vagrancy is very strong, thus supporting the implication that the great majority of these 'vagrants' were, in fact, in search of work (Crowther, 1981). But this piece of information, even if it had been available, unsullied by the preoccupations of the age, would have made the relief administrators' task no easier. A disciplinary regime would have deterred all bar the really needy; the really needy would, on the other hand, have hardly been helped by such a regime. The Minority Report seems to have hit the nail on the head: 'As long as the workman in search of a job has to wander, it is impossible to distinguish between him and the professional vagrant' (Minority Report, 1909, p. 265).

The almost 'automatic' operation of the National Labour Exchange was thought to hold a solution to this problem. Vagrancy could be eliminated at a stroke, compulsory notification of vacancies, compulsory registration of the unemployed, and new technology in the shape of the telephone would do away with the necessity of the 'search' for work. The organisation of future relief and unemployment policies would henceforth assume a rather more systematic character as assistance, training and rehabilitation policies were erected around the imperatives of the market economy, dovetailing the transition between occupations and regularising the supply of and demand for labour (Minority Report, 1909, pp. 280, 307; Beveridge, 1909, pp. 210–18). The capacity of the labour exchanges to assist the advancing institutionalisation of national labour market policies led the Webbs to refer to them as a huge 'human sorting house' (Minority Report, 1909, pp. 301–3). Unfortunately, at the same time that this state 'sorting house' appeared to acknowledge to some degree the human needs of labour it simultaneously subordinated them to the political and economic imperatives of industrial capitalism.

As the apex of a system of relief administration that promised so much, it is small wonder that the system of labour exchanges raised so many expectations. Indeed, a system which promised to reduce the enduring problem of relief distribution to a simple administrative decision, yet combined so synthetically the recycling of labour power, the detection of needs, the deterrence of imposture and the punishment or treatment of the 'disreputable' or 'unfit', was bound to appear attractive to social reformers. Henceforth, any man found wandering would be under a duty to

> report himself to the nearest branch of the National Labour Exchange, where he would find, without fail, either opportunity of working or else [other] suitable provision. If this were done it would be possible to make all the minor offences of vagrancy . . . occasions for instant and invariable commitment by the Justices, not for short sentences to the ordinary prison, which experience shows to be useless, but to one or other of the reformatory Detention Colonies which must form an integral part of the system of provision.
>
> (Minority Report, 1909, p. 266)

In this way, all consideration of the most effective operation of the labour exchange was qualified by the near universal belief in the existence of a 'residuum' of the idle, semi-criminal and unfit at the base of society, an existence that the successful operation of the labour exchange system would make increasingly apparent.

> We have to face the fact that, make what arrangements we will, there will be, at all times and under any organisation of society, a residuum of men who will be found in distress from want of employment . . . though the individuals may come and go, a residuum will always be there.
>
> (cited in Stedman Jones, 1971, p. 335; Gilbert, 1966, p. 251)

The unemployed residuum was presumed to contain all manner of strange characters: 'individuals of defective will, intelligence or training; of dissolute habits or irregularities of character; or of chronically weak physical health; together with all sorts of industrial 'misfits' and intermingled among them all, the constitutionally vagabond or "workshy" ' (Minority Report, 1909, p. 294). This distribution of characteristics helped give coherence to a range of seemingly inconsistent views suggesting, on the one hand, that the 'residuum' formed a 'class' of their own and, on the other, that they were no more than an agglomeration of defective individuals. Those seeing the 'residuum' as a class apart tended to advocate a response of fairly generalised deterrence, whereas those (including the Webbs) viewing the 'residuum' as a mass of demoralised individuals, developed their own more specific remedies. Deploying a wealth of essentially socio-pathological studies of heredity, behaviour and aetiology, they held the view that the especially debased condition of the destitute resulted from a rather more individual series of handicaps, deficiencies or weaknesses, whether these be physical or moral. Henceforth, those who accepted this latter interpretation were able to explain the existence of a 'residuum' irrespective of the state of the economy.

Policing the boundaries between employment and relief, rehabilitation or 'treatment', the administrative system would mobilise the contrived social relations of the labour market and help focus the administrative system's disciplinary power upon those who failed to conform to its restrictive norms. Those who, either by circumstance or by condition, were least able to derive much advantage from the statutory regulation of the labour market, or who actively resisted its particular interventions, became the authorities' most immediate targets. This confrontation between a generalised discipline, supplemented by particular forms of statutory regulation, and those who were unable to conform could only have one result. The imbalance between generalised discipline and individualised pathology tended to produce its own doubly-defective characters. A range of social characteristics was construed by the authorities as representative of certain inherently immoral, pathological conditions while those individuals attributed with such characteristics were considered the proper objects of assessment, classification and correction.

> [Assistance] must be merely preliminary to solving the particularly 'human problem' that each man presents . . . . What is to be discovered is why these particular individuals have been left stranded and unemployed; and how their individual efficiency can be increased . . . . The first thing to be done is to 'test' them . . . probing their capacity so as to find the points at which they are weak.
>
> (Minority Report, 1909, p. 299)

Moral guidance and industrial and physical training were the remedies proposed for these groups of the relatively 'unemployable'. The unemployed were singled out on the basis of their problematic relationship with the labour market and treated accordingly. All other relationships were subordinated to this privileged one, and all other explanations of forms of physical or mental deficiency were effectively marginalised. The means adopted for the rehabilitation and training of 'inadequates' clearly confirmed the prevalent ideological assumptions about the individual origins of physical and social pathology. On the whole, however, the Minority Poor Law commissioners seemed to have had their sights set upon the supposedly 'immoral' members of the 'residuum' as likely candidates for their penal colonies. A rather firmer line of 'treatment' was proposed for those whose apparent inadequacies seemed to stem from primarily 'moral' deficiencies.

> There are moral invalids as well as physical ones. The men who have lost situations through irregularity of conduct of one kind or another plainly need training in character, under the beneficent influence of continuous order and discipline . . . it is inevitable that the particular workers who

find themselves the rejected of all employers should be capable of improvement . . . which of us, indeed, is not capable of improvement by careful testing or training?

(Minority Report, 1909, p. 300)

In this way, therefore, the 'human sorting house' theme was further developed. In future, national labour market policy could be co-ordinated by a state department which relayed the pressures and conditions of the labour market directly to the whole of the working class – everyone was 'capable of improvement' after all – through its growing control over the mechanisms of relief. As Yeo has noted, more than simple administrative efficiency was achieved by the state's increasing absorbtion of the private voluntary and friendly societies (Yeo, 1979).

The authors of the Minority Report proposed the setting up of a National Unemployment Authority to deal with the able-bodied unemployed. This Authority would occupy a special position, standing between the labour market, the state and the unemployed, and its sources of disciplinary power would be fourfold.

In the first place, the Unemployment Authority's disciplinary power would derive from the structurally unequal relationship established between capital and labour within the labour market. In the second place, its power would rest upon its ability to exert differing degrees of pressure upon the unemployed, depending upon the wider supply of labour within the labour market; that is to say, the Authority would be able to translate industrial and economic policy goals into social administration and attune relief practice to the needs of industry. In the third place, the Authority's exercise of discipline would derive from its battery of penalties and sanctions – it would be empowered to withhold relief from the unemployed who refused to attend industrial training establishments or to order their compulsory commitment to detention colonies. Finally its power would stem from its well-established apparatus of individualisation. In sum, the National Unemployment Authority would offer a highly flexible and graduated means of relating the unemployed worker's situation to the underlying discipline of the labour market.

It is, however, just one of the advantages of training . . . that it can indefinitely be adjusted so as to apply to each . . . the exact stimulus required to call out his faculties. With what we may call the 'industrial malingerer' there will be other remedies. With the co-operation of the National Labour Exchange he can be given successive chances of employment; and, after a certain number of trials, his repeated return will be a cause for his judicial commitment to a detention colony.

(Minority Report, 1909, p. 104)

Where, in an earlier period, the 'juridico-discursive' prohibitions had organised a formal/legal repression of pauperism, begging and vagrancy, whilst still maintaining the broad framework of Common Law freedoms, the new forms of disciplinary intervention were to exercise social relations of an altogether different order. The new forms of power were to be as explicit in their forms of discipline as they were in their social targets and political objectives. An era of prohibitions was being replaced by an era of political and economic calculation in which the objectives and methods of social administration were intertwined, deriving their coherence from the political economy of British capitalism. In the new sphere of disciplinary statutory intervention, problems of policy and their solutions, forms of knowledge, political objectives and administrative techniques were all to be tightly bound together by the imperatives of national economic policy making and the need to manage the labour market and contain the working class.

The state apparatus advocated by the Webbs entailed the establishment of a fundamental continuity between law and administration, between questions of 'right' and questions of policy thereby entirely superceding the liberal framework of 'rights' governing the 'free' relations of civil society. Thus, not for the first time, welfare measures seemed to spawn an expanding range of 'anti-social' forms of administration and control. The Webbs' solution to the related problems of economic management and destitution, as expressed in the Minority Report of the Poor Law Commission, was to situate the social relations of the working class upon an almost exclusively disciplinary plane by instituting a separate and more punitive system of social regulation for the working class. The new code of regulations which was to police working-class life would be, in every sense, a form of second-class justice. It required far more exacting standards of public and private behaviour but offered much less in the way of safeguards or redress. It proposed to intervene more frequently in greater depth while assuming more discretionary responsibilities but seldom providing more by way of help, guidance or material resources. In short, the Webbs' 'plan' appears very much as an attempt to supervise and regulate the social existence of the working class, to modernise the discipline that had been embodied within the Poor Law, even intensifying its control over the 'deviant' or 'abnormal', and to subsume all this beneath the imperatives of national industrial and economic policy. Whilst it would certainly be wrong to attribute all such regulative development and its associated 'anti-social' consequences to a misguided welfare ideal, (paternalism, imperialism, nationalism and an incipient bureaucratic professionalism – to say nothing of considerations of capitalist efficiency and eugenics – could well account for much of that) we should, never-theless, be wary, as Titmuss insisted in 1964, of both the ends to which welfare is put and of the conditions upon which it is bestowed. An analysis of the 'Fabian statism' of the Webbs makes the wisdom of Titmuss's remark abundantly clear.

Throughout the nineteenth century while the situation of the pauper had been, in the literal meaning of the term, 'less-eligible,' even the Poor Law had retained, to a degree, the principle of voluntarism, the vestige of a formal legal freedom. In fact, as I pointed out, this 'free-dom' was the key to the very operation of the Poor Law. The Webbs wanted to change all this. Their proposals were the first coherent national administrative strategy in which a new social order had been so precisely outlined. Changing social and economic conditions gener-ated a host of new forms of power and new modes of social intervention deploying new objects and discourses. In turn, these produced their own forms of resistance, deviance and failure. New configurations of discipline exerted their normalising influence across the developing 'social sphere', and social administration (call it a discipline? A dis-course? A practice?) was born, distributing its incentives, benefits, visions of need, penalties and sanctions throughout the population at large. Henceforth, social administration and a new public administrative law (a recent invention, barely half a century old) would make a deep impression upon the lives of working-class people.

> So long as he commits no crime, and neglects none of his social obligations; so long as he does not fail to get lodging, food and clothing for himself and his family; so long as his children are not found lacking medical attention when ill, or underfed at school; so long, indeed, as his family ask nor require any form of public assistance, he will be free to live as he likes. But directly any of these things happen, it will be a condition that the husband and the father, if certified as able-bodied, shall be in attendance at the Training Establishment to which he is assigned. If he is recalcitrant he will be judicially committed to a detention colony.
> (Minority Report, 1909, p. 305, see also pp. 329, 344)

The poor, it seems, were to be free to conform, if they could.

The wide variety of conditions which were to serve as the occasion for specific interventions rather undermines the Webbs' earlier disavowal of the principles of deterrence. The proposals, in their entirety, envisaged nothing less than the erection of a disciplinary continuum wherein the acceptance of social norms and roles, the achievement of standards and the demonstration of social competences were all to be underwritten by the requirement of total compliance. Thus the 'law of the poor' was to impose a rigid disciplinary regime indeed. It sought to link requests for assistance to a more intensive supervision, interpreting the mere need for assistance in an unfavourable light. Minimum standards were to be imposed, often upon those least able to achieve them, submission being always encouraged, failure being rewarded by judicial sanction.

Yet the detention colony was not to be a prison or convict settlement, 'though it will only be entered upon conviction by a judicial authority.' It was to remain under the responsibility of the Unemployment Authority and the men committed there, 'should not be regarded as criminals'. By insisting upon this arrangement, the authors of the Minority Report were clinging to the belief that the detention colony could provide rehabilitation, despite overwhelming evidence to the contrary stemming from the nineteenth century's experience of workhouse and the prisons. 'Inmates are sent there to be treated for, and if possible cured of, a morbid state of mind which makes them incapable of fulfilling a useful place in the industrial world' (Minority Report, 1909, p. 308). Persons might leave detention colonies and be returned to ordinary training establishments, 'on probation', but repeated failure or recalcitrance (the categories begin to merge), 'would be criminal offences leading to sentences of penal servitude in a convict settlement' (*Ibid.*). Inmates would not be criminals, and the colony would not be a prison, but the more we discover of the Webbs' plans, the more it seems to resemble one. The ostensibly rehabilitative emphasis of the proposals rapidly gave way to a two-pronged assault upon the 'freedom' of the working class – the simultaneous imposition of standards of competence in the fulfillment of normative social obligations and the punishment of failure or resistance.

The working man was to be free of the restraints of the National Authority, 'so long as he abstained from crime (including vagrancy and mendicity), and maintained himself and his family *without receiving or needing Public Assistance in any form*' (emphasis added). On the other hand, compulsion would come into play the moment any working men failed 'to fulfill any of their social obligations', or were 'found houseless, or requiring Public Assistance for themselves or their families.' Furthermore, men were to be committed by magistrates 'and compulsorily detained and kept to work', if convicted of 'any such offences as Vagrancy, Mendicity, Neglect to maintain family or apply for Public Assistance for their maintenance if destitute, repeated recalcitrance or breach of discipline in a Training Establishment' (Minority Report, 1909, pp. 329, 244). In so comprehensive a list of sanctions, whether to police the exercise of duties and responsibilities, or shepherd the population towards an appropriate relationship with the newly-establishing realm of 'public rights', or simply attend upon the mere existence of unmet 'needs', notions of the 'social' and the 'penal' merge and overlap. It is not that they form separate 'jurisdictions' (despite the Webbs' disclaimers) rather, that they represent an essentially continuous distribution with a single series of objectives in view – the disciplinary organisation of the 'social sphere'.

Yet whilst the Webbs had hoped to contrive a highly systematic and largely 'self-acting' administration, their proposals still rested to a large extent upon the exercise of deterrence and prohibition – preserving 'the ontology of poverty in a rationalised system of state confinement of the recalcitrant', as Kay and Mott have put it (Kay and Mott, 1983, p. 108). The Webbs were working towards an essentially institutional means for the reformation of the working class at precisely the time that 'Beveridge was coming to the conclusion that such a method was unnecessary and that insurance rather than labour reformatories should be the administrative counterpart of a system of labour exchanges' (Harris, 1972, p. 256). Whilst the Webbs believed that a system of unemployment relief operating on the basis of a national system of labour exchanges would be 'unworkable without compulsion', Beveridge and Churchill saw the 'voluntary' operation of the exchanges as the key to a system of insurance which promised to be considerably more 'self-acting' than anything so far conceived of.

Yet the Webbs' proposals were not simply by-passed and there were substantial similarities and overlaps between these and the proposals which eventually surfaced in the Liberal legislative programme of 1906–11. The Webbs had sought to introduce the most sophisticated principles of social administration into the machinery of government. The disciplinary continuum they hoped to establish was not entirely a mechanism of repression, but a transitional point between the Poor Law and political techniques not yet fully evolved. Their scheme was a positive form of administration in its own right, refining forms of discipline and contributing to a new science of social administration which interwove new techniques, forms of knowledge and objects within the new social relations emerging between the classes and between society and the state.

Secondly, as we have seen, Beveridge, like many of his contemporaries, entertained notions about the 'almost inevitable' existence of a 'residuum' at the base of society, and approved of the use of penal labour colonies for its reformation, or at least containment. Harris has suggested that Beveridge always considered the detention colonies as, 'the least important and most peripheral aspect of [his] scheme for the unemployed' (Harris, 1972, pp. 134–5 and 1977, pp. 118–20), but this is less important. Like prisons in the penal system or means-testing in the social security system, the detention colonies had a strategic significance above and beyond their actual utilisation. Both the Webbs and Beveridge had in mind proposals which would discipline the working classes as a whole and the poorest in particular.

The crucial factor distinguishing the Webbs' proposals from those of Beveridge and Churchill was insurance. Insurance helped change the character of labour discipline to incorporate 'civil society' as a whole. But above all, it promised to be a self-acting mechanism which would link the economy, the labour market and the 'social' demands of subsistence with an administrative technique that substituted policy (calculation, actuarial budgeting and procedure – i.e. means) for politics (confrontation, choice, and responsibility – i.e. ends) and which would help transform need into a specifically disciplinary principle.

Morals, mathematics and insurance

Neither of the two Reports of the Poor Law Commission had recommended the introduction of compulsory unemployment insurance. As Beveridge saw it, both sets of proposals favouring only systems of subsidies to existing trade union or friendly society schemes, patently failed to tackle the problem of the 'residuum'. For, as he went on to point out, 'very few trade unionists . . . were found among the applicants to Distress Committees' (Beveridge, 1930, p. 264).

As I have suggested, virtually all contributors to the debate on poverty and unemployment seemed to accept the existence of a 'residuum'. The problem seemed to be, therefore, that of designing a scheme which would address the needs of industry and labour and cater for the needs of the temporarily unemployed whilst acting as a spur to the 'malingerer' (the new persona thrust forward by the new discourse on social insurance assuming many of the characteristics hitherto ascribed to the idle, thriftless and recalcitrant) and yet also embody the implicit notion of work as a duty (Collie, 1913). All this might seem a pretty tall order for any scheme of disciplinary social policy. Nevertheless, the parameters of a new insurantial strategy were admirably sketched out by Llewellyn-Smith in 1910. Problems of political order and sound social administration were simply reconstituted as technical questions by the application of actuarial principles.

> The crucial question from a practical point of view is therefore, whether it is possible to devise a scheme of insurance which, while nominally covering unemployment due to all causes other than those which can be definitely excluded, shall *automatically discriminate* as between the classes of unemployment for which insurance is or is not an appropriate remedy . . . (1) The scheme must be compulsory; otherwise the bad personal risks against which we must always be on our guard would be

certain to predominate . . . (2) The scheme must be contributory, for only by exacting rigorously as a necessary qualification for benefit that a sufficient number of weeks' contributions shall have been paid by each recipient can we hope to put limits on the exceptionally bad risks.

(Llewellyn-Smith, 1910)

For their part, the Webbs took a very poor view of the proposals for compulsory insurance. Their criticisms covered, the potential cost, the possible scale of the 'malingerer' problem and, strangely enough, the question of compulsion. Their remarks make it clear how far their own stated preference for systems of prevention, deterrence and treatment, inclined them to reject the whole idea. Convinced of the positive qualities of a statist and institutional collectivism, the Webbs were blind to the disciplinary potential opened up by the new, more 'liberal', techniques of social insurance.

Whilst many of the Webbs' contemporaries shared similar concerns about the dangers of widespread malingering, not all were so convinced that the problem could not be solved within a scheme of insurance. Churchill, in particular, was keen to point out how insurance could help foster common mutual interests between employers, employees and the state. And he was willing to go much further, claiming that the concept of social insurance encapsulated, 'the immediate future of democratic politics', capable of transforming the worker into a citizen. The essence of Churchill's assumption rested upon the premise that if the working class could be given a 'stake' in the nation, in the form of insurance credits, this would constitute an investment in the institutions of society, enhancing 'social security' in a uniquely double-edged fashion by tempering the impatient radicalism of the working class (Jones and Novak, 1979). In any event, in case the insurance system should fail to tap the reservoir of altruism and common interests, or workers should seek to exploit the insurance scheme, there were to be safeguards; benefits were to be kept sufficiently low in order to 'imply a sensible and even severe difference between being in work or out of work' (Churchill, 1909, quoted in Harris, 1977, p. 171).

Few appeared to share Churchill's confidence that the disciplinary effects of the system of National Insurance could be safely left to the impersonal and automatic operation of the insurance fund itself – to 'mathematics' rather than to 'morals and a corps of investigators', as Churchill tended to characterise the issue. In 1909, he had written in support of the mathematical and actuarial conception of social discipline effected through a system of social insurance.

The best and truest safeguards are those which unite the self-interest of the individual with the interest of the fund. The spirit of the Insurance scheme is not to weaken the impulse of self-preservation, but to strengthen it by affording it the means of struggle, and the fear of running through benefits, or passing out of the Insurance Scheme altogether, must be constantly operative.

(Churchill, 1909, quoted in Gilbert, 1966, pp. 271–2)

Within the National Insurance scheme, the fraudulent, the malingerer, the workshy and the otherwise recalcitrant would effectively discipline themselves. The ideal of a (relatively) self-acting system of discipline resting upon no human agency seemed close at hand. Through the institutions of the labour exchange, National Insurance and the national labour market, the working man was, in a sense, installed within a closely circumscribed zone of formal 'freedom' from which to determine his own socio-economic destiny. He alone would draw upon himself the respective benefits, incentives and sanctions of National Insurance and the labour market and, knowing the consequences, he alone would make the choices. In this sense, and with an automated system of social discipline operating through the National Insurance scheme's mechanism of 'graduated disentitlement' (by which benefits were diminished progressively as the period of claiming continued) the working man was placed, as subject and object, at the centre of an 'automatic' series of benefits and sanctions, the precise combination of which he was, himself, so Churchill argued, the principle author.

Such a reorientation of the mechanisms of unemployment relief and of the relation between the labour market and the 'right' to subsistence would render the consequences of a host of 'abuses' all the more immediate in their impact upon the malingering workman. It was in this sense that, as Beveridge was to argue, 'all relief was to be educational' (Beveridge, 1930, p. 234). As the conditions for the receipt of relief became understood – together with the consequences of prolonged overreliance – members of the working class were given a kind of vicarious responsibility for their own self-discipline. They were no longer to be the relatively passive objects of a form of disciplinary control, but henceforth, would be implicated as active subjects in the reproduction of a new kind of power over themselves. Perhaps it goes without saying, but these developments were intimately connected with the extension of the franchise and the advent of a new 'democratic' political order. Working-class involvement in government expanded according to a political logic peculiar to 'the social', yet simultaneously the disciplinary relations of 'the social' began to bite ever more firmly upon their working-class hosts. The new 'social-contract' exchanged welfare and a share in government for the acceptance of social discipline.

Churchill hoped that his National Insurance scheme could be arranged so that any man found 'malingering' would gradually lose benefit while out of work or, alternatively, find it expensive to reinstate an entitlement on his return to work. He was anxious that moral judgements be avoided, 'I do not like mixing up moralities and mathematics', believing that the most effectual operation of the scheme could be achieved only by impersonal means. (Churchill, 1909). A graduated and cumulative disentitlement, abiding by 'clear, ruthless, mathematical rules' was envisaged. Each individual might be prodded back to work when his benefit fell to a sufficiently low level. The novelty of the whole scheme was, after all, that if a workman were to malinger, 'he malingers against himself' (Churchill, quoted in Deacon, 1976). In the manner of a truly disciplinary society, members of the working class were to be both subjects and objects of a power relation; the executors of their own discipline.

It made sense that the reference group for the insurance strategy should be the working population as a whole. Each labourer had his own peculiarities and idiosyncrasies which might defy the operation of a more personalised discipline, but insurance worked in accordance with averages and norms. Deviance and individuality became knowable and calculable and, therefore, capable of containment within the insurance mechanism through the manipulation of averages and the application of laws of probability. The insurantial strategy sought to interrelate individuality and collectivity in such a way that normative regulations could be derived from, and defined in relation to, the entire insured population. In this way, the foundations of discipline were, in a sense, entirely collective and yet formed of the consequences of individual transgressions. Equally, it was as individuals (and families) that the population would encounter these disciplinary regulations.

The techniques of insurance prepared the ground for the partial transformation of social administration into a mathematical science in which all social relations, all deviance and differentiation, as well as all norms became the property of an administrative discourse. In future, margins of deviance (malingering, unemployment, strikes, fraud and sickness) would be anticipated and thereby rendered calculable. They would be accommodated within administrative technique and would no longer require the exercise of a special or ad hoc disciplinary measure. Perhaps this confirms, once and for all, the positive and productive character of deviance as a relay for the exercise of disciplinary power. Forms of 'deviance' within the labour market became entirely useful for they could be accommodated by future actuarial calculation and used to help redefine the parameters dictating the margins of assistance and penalty within the National Insurance scheme. For Churchill, this could all add up to a very flexible and relational system of discipline indeed. Thus,

> a disposition to overindulge in alcohol, a hot temper, a bad manner . . . a new process of manufacture, a contraction in trade, are all alike factors in the risk. . . . We seek to substitute for the pressure of the forces of nature, operating by chance on individuals, the pressures of the laws of insurance, operating through averages with modifying and mitigating effects in individual cases.
>
> (Churchill, 1909)

Yet for all the neat synthesis of disciplinary and incentive effects promised by the insurantial strategy, on closer examination, the scheme's basis of social discipline appears rather crude. Certainly the insurantial techniques provided a highly subtle and self-perpetuating vehicle for the transmission of disciplinary effects; this is not in dispute, but the socio-political objectives upon which the insurantial techniques were founded were not too far removed from those aspired to by the designers of the New Poor Law. As a result, the elements of insurantial technique: graduated disentitlement, individualisation and the low levels of benefit, still tended to reproduce a number of the deterrent features of the nineteenth-century Poor Law within the National Insurance scheme.

Despite its subtle individualisation effects, the new insurantial discipline lacked the highly personalised features of supervision, compulsion and control, rehabilitation and treatment that many such as the Webbs had long advocated. Churchill's vision of the insurantial techniques appeared to prioritise the specifically actuarial forms of mass fiscal control over and above the specifically disciplinary activities of the labour exchange. Thus, while the new discipline might have been quite effective in 'encouraging' the will to work, it was less use in actually securing these objectives. It was precisely to those workmen whose attitude to work was considered the most problematic, that the insurance system offered the least in the way of specific compulsion or practical assistance.

The people who fell through the 'net of entitlements' were those considered by the authorities as the most 'unemployable' or most 'demoralised' – the 'hardened malingerers'. Such characters would have been forced into begging, or theft, or eventually onto the Poor Law. For while the system of insurance employed highly effective principles of discipline *at the level of populations*, at the level of the *individual*, in relation to questions of rehabilitation, poverty and deviance, it offered few specific answers. Nor did the system permit the development of any understanding of aetiology. The knowledge base of insurance was a macro-social science of population administration, and so when confronted with a particular case the authorities had few means at their disposal for modifying the system to suit individual circumstances. In effect, lacking a knowledge of the poor *as individuals*, and even, like Churchill, explicitly repudiating the idea that such information should be a concern of the insurance scheme at all, the administrators of social insurance found themselves unable to discriminate – even though the whole system rested upon the *de facto* exclusion of a number of the 'most difficult' cases from the scheme. To those 'most difficult' cases, insurance was as much an irrelevance as a means to well-being in 1911 as 'Self-Help' had been in the 1870s. The absurdity was, of course, that it was precisely the most residual groups which had been the major focus of a great deal of official and unofficial concern regarding the causes and consequences of poverty and unemployment. Forms of social insurance could ease the burden of hardship falling upon particular groups in particular circumstances, but they were hardly 'preventative' in the ways envisaged by the Webbs. On this the Webbs were correct to criticise. An insurance system could never *treat*, cure or rehabilitate effectively. Neither could it really prevent a number from eventually exhausting their benefits – especially in bad years. On this question, the Webbs and Beveridge were in accord, both saw a role for the labour exchange in policing the poorest and acting as the fulcrum for a range of broadly preventative interventions into the lives of the 'residuum'. By virtue of the fact that it came into contact with all the unemployment insurance applicants, the labour exchange could identify those claimants with special needs or problems, or those whose motivation to work appeared questionable. As Beveridge noted, the labour exchange opened up a means of 'dispauperisation' more humane, less costly and more effective than simple deterrence in that it endeavoured to make the finding of work easy instead of merely making relief harder to obtain or endure. He saw it necessary to expand upon this conception of the role of the labour exchange, adding that,

> it is not suggested that the whole principle of 'deterrence' can be dispensed with in regard to the able-bodied. That principle serves not only to drive men to work, but also to make personal provision for their unemployment, sickness etc. It is, however, suggested that the Labour Exchange test may ultimately be made the basis of a relief system, whether or not it is supported also by a modified deterrence.
>
> (Beveridge, 1930, p. 216)

The groups who bore the brunt of the Insurance scheme's disciplinary force were typically those excluded from it. Their condition was often considered to have an exemplary quality, to provide a lesson in thrift and morality to the 'respectable' and employed classes. Yet as forms of rehabilitation began to dissect and categorise the 'residuum' still further, insurance became less and less effective as the solitary key to labour regulation and social discipline. The condition of the 'residuum' came to be seen as too remote from the condition of those merely unemployed and in any event, those groups forming the 'residuum' found themselves being increasingly treated as criminals and subjected to a range of criminal and socio-pathological interventions. In the turbulent years after the First World War, therefore, social commentators and policy-makers came to take the view that the introduction of restrictions upon entitlement to unemployment and health insurance was necessary in order to safeguard the actuarial foundation of the insurance fund, to arrest the spread of 'demoralisation' and to provide a more direct and effective framework of disciplinary regulation for the management of the labour market. The solution, therefore, seemed to lie in enhancing the investigative powers of the labour exchanges (see Harris, 1977, pp. 171–6).

It had never been questioned that conditions of entitlement were indispensable to a National Insurance scheme, although Churchill lost his fight to keep these restricted to actuarial conditions. Despite Churchill's advocacy to the contrary, the National Insurance scheme was supplemented by a series of conditions which placed restrictions upon the conduct of applicants in order to support and protect the principles of industrial discipline. Notably, the installation of sex and nationality as qualifying conditions seemed to pass with little remark – women were initially eligible to reduced levels of entitlement and later similar restrictions applied to 'alien' men; 'alien' women, however, were largely ignored (see Cohen, 1985).

The scheme was to be utilised, alongside the system of labour exchanges, as the instrument of a highly interventionist statutory labour market policy attuning the population to the needs of industry. As Beveridge made clear, 'the problem of unemployment is the adjustment of the supply of labour and the demand for labour. The supply of labour in a country is, in the widest sense, *the supply of population*' (Beveridge, 1930, pp. 4, 215–6). In this light, the new insurance regulations have to be understood as forms of social policy engaged in a practical reconstitution of the population itself. The new regulations marked a fairly massive expansion of state administration and of its executive authority. They certainly provided state personnel with more extensive control over the operation of the insurance scheme but, more importantly, they extended the hold of public authority over the conditions of working-class life. The regulations restricting entitlement in certain cases, or demanding the fulfilment of specific conditions in others, involved a clear compromise of the 'right' to benefit. This was not, however, the first example of the blurring of law and administration for, under the Poor Law, this process had advanced quite rapidly. Yet the regulations introduced into the system of insurance were significant for the way in which they erected a detailed framework of executive regulation and administrative action around the 'formally free' situation of the working man in the labour market.

Hence the Insurance scheme (and later the apparatuses of Public Assistance, National Assistance and Social Security) and the supplemental batteries of regulations, conditions of entitlement, compulsions, restrictions and sanctions, formed a highly disciplinary (and decidedly 'anti-social') matrix of obligations, requirements and conditions within which working-class people had to live.

Thus, it is possible to talk about the intensification of disciplinary relations across a population. Of course, this was not only experienced in respect of obligations to work. The multiple pressures faced by women, for instance, focused predominantly upon the family – and specifically upon the ideal of 'motherhood'. These issues will be developed later, but even at this point it is important to reaffirm the fact that the disciplinary relations of modern society do not all run in the same direction, on the contrary, they are contradictory, conflict-ridden and uneven. Nor do they emanate from a single centre, though certainly the state is heavily involved. As I have said, I am not describing the 'disciplined' society. Yet the disciplinary mechanisms are purposive; they have functions, and they do have an overwhelming integrity. I am concerned, above all, to describe a situation in modern industrial society in which the principal modes of domination take a disciplinary form, that is to say, a relational form whereby human beings are inextricably implicated within the strategies and mechanisms of their own subjection.

Tests and regulations

At face value, the combined series of conditions of entitlement and the grounds for disqualification from benefit may seem innocuous enough (especially when compared with today's standards). Nevertheless, these early forms of disciplinary regulation operating within and beyond the focal point provided by the labour exchange, do have an enduring significance – especially after March 1921 and the introduction of the 'genuinely-seeking-work' test, and 1922 when the first means tests were introduced.

In the years after the First World War, the unemployment insurance principle came under pressure from rapidly rising and longer-term unemployment. In this light, the 'genuinely seeking work' test can be said to mark a change of emphasis rather than an entirely new approach. The requirement of 'genuineness' may have appeared a token ideological safeguard in the face of the final, almost inevitable, abandonment of the actuarial basis of the 1911 scheme. But it was to have far-reaching implications.

In response to the large number of unemployed exhausting their entitlement to benefit, the Government extended the period of entitlement by the 'Out of Work Donation', a non-contributory addition introduced almost immediately after the end of the War. Many saw this extension of the period of entitlement as likely to reduce the incentive to find work because it lessened the fear of exhausting benefit. As a result, it was deemed necessary to bolster up the checks and controls upon 'malingering'. The abandonment of the insurance principle, even for a short period, led the government to seek some alternative means of reinforcing the discipline of the labour market and, as I shall show, of the family.

Deacon has argued (Deacon, 1976), that the introduction of the new test marked an implicit shift in the burden of proof regarding unemployment. It also marked the failure of the national labour exchange ideal. Only about one-fifth of all vacancies were actually notified to the labour exchanges, making it difficult for the authorities to prove that an unemployed person had turned down suitable work. Thus the extension of the period of entitlement by the 'Out of Work Donation' provided an opportunity to shift the responsibility to prove 'genuine' unemployment onto the shoulders of the unemployed themselves. Later, when the criterion *'genuinely seeking* work' was transformed into the *'availability for* work' test, their responsibility grew that much more burdensome. For 'availability' referred to a state of mind, incapable of precise demonstration, inconclusive in tests, but it had the effect of emphatically shifting the burden of responsibility for unemployment. This transfer in the onus of proof further obfuscated the division between 'legality' and 'policy' in social intervention and led to a considerable tightening up in the administration of benefit; in the year after the introduction of the new test, rates of benefit refusal almost tripled (*ibid.*). One particularly dramatic, although perhaps less immediately apparent, effect of the test was the widespread exclusion of married women from benefit. As Thane has argued, women 'were assumed to have less need for a full income than a man and were less likely to protest at its withdrawal' (Thane, 1982, p. 174).

Beveridge also saw the 'genuinely-seeking-work' rule as part of an attempt to supplement the disrupted mathematical discipline of insurance with an expanded administrative supervision. Yet the special circumstances of the war and 'traditional' assumptions about the exit of women from the labour market in peace-time had their own impact on the insurance scheme. 'The Ministry of Labour became convinced that the "donation" was being widely abused and the chief offenders were believed to be married women who had worked in munitions factories during the War'. These women had built up an entitlement to benefit, though it was presumed that they were no longer members of the labour force (Deacon, 1976, p. 24). Beveridge advanced such arguments with even greater force and, given that only twelve years later he was to draw up the report, *Social Insurance and Allied Services* (The Beveridge Report), which was to prove crucial to the foundation of the Welfare State, his remarks carry an enduring significance. The value of the 'genuinely-seeking-work' test lay, he argued,

> not in keeping out the workshy and unemployable . . . but in the weapon of offensive defence it afforded against claims by women who on marriage had practically retired from industry and were not wanted by employers, but tried, not unnaturally to get something for nothing [*sic*] out of the fund.
> (Beveridge, 1930, p. 280 f.n.)

More than any previous measure, the 'genuinely-seeking-work' test inserted a series of disciplinary regulations designed to manage the labour market into the very heart of the working-class household. Men had to bow to the needs and demands of the labour market, whereas women, now summarily expelled from the world of work, were expected to answer the needs and demands of the family and conform to an ideal of motherhood cemented into place during the previous three to four decades by discourses promoting domestic hygiene, social imperialism, and child welfare (Davin, 1978; Donzelot, 1980; Lewis, 1980). The autonomous 'liberalism' of Churchill's system of insurance had been usurped by regulative principles of a particular force and direction. Hence, if we are correct to see the 'modern' social order installed in the early twentieth century as having the family as one of its major foundations and 'familialism' one of its central principles, then this is both an institution set in a profoundly disciplinary cast and a discourse with markedly 'anti-social' overtones.

The invention of 'availability testing' – a single rule with diverging implications for male and female unemployed – signified the hoisting of a fictional standard to the legislative framework provided by labour-market policy and presaged an immense proliferation of administrative intervention into the social sphere as the state apparatus sought to utilise its new instruments, deploy new normative discourses and estab-lish new socio-economic relationships. In this sense, the introduction of the 'genuinely-seeking-work' test inaugurated a process rather similar to that pertaining between the Poor Law and philanthropy at the end of the nineteenth century, whereby the extension of assistance to some was 'complemented' by increased severity for others. Thus, in 1921, when benefit rates were to be increased, it was suggested that, 'we must strengthen the regulations and there must be closer attention to the administration of the payment of benefits on lines that make it impossible to encourage idleness' (quoted in Deacon, 1976). Such a trade-off in political imperatives seems a well-nigh universal feature of the relations of welfare as Deacon's own conclusion suggests.

> It was [politically] impossible to transfer the long-term unemployed to the Poor Law and it thus became a question of retaining extended benefit while minimising its harmful effects. Strict administration was seen as a means of achieving these objectives, particularly since the Labour Movement remained preoccupied with the level and duration of benefits and did not regard their administration as an important issue until later in the decade. If the seeking-work test was not prompted by malice, it was 'tightened up' with a callous disregard for the hardships and injustices which resulted.
>
> (Deacon, 1976, p. 91)

The testing of 'availability' and the second of the new conditions, the testing of means, contributed to a major intensification of state intervention into working-class life. State administration was beginning to have a significant impact upon social existence. Gradually, administration was reorganising society and reconstructing the conditions under which social life took place. A particularly important example of this is provided by the means test.

Although a major feature of the politics of social security, with between one-quarter and one-third of the population dependent upon some form of means-tested benefit, the means test itself has seldom received the kind of attention it deserves. That is to say, social administration has traditionally interpreted the means test from the point of view of *distribution*. The test is seen almost exclusively as an element in a distributional system and its important role in reinforcing a particular form of disciplinary class relations is largely overlooked.

An earlier 'test of resources' had been introduced in 1908 to police the administration of the Pension Act. An accompanying battery of conditions sought to ensure that the meagre benefits offered by the Act did not go to the 'undeserving' or less reputable elderly – for instance, ex-prisoners, drunks, 'aliens' and their wives, and persons guilty of 'habitual failure to work' (Deacon and Bradshaw, 1983). Similar considerations applied to those (not all) claimants required to submit to a means test for their 'transitional' unemployment benefits at the end of the First World War. Nevertheless, social historians and policy commentators have tended to opt for the obvious when explaining the introduction of the means test in 1922: 'it was primarily an economic measure', says Deacon. 'A means test was introduced . . . as a further cost-cutting measure', says Thane (Deacon, 1976, p. 76; Thane, 1982, p. 174).

Yet the means test introduced a particularly intrusive and individualised form of disciplinary relationship between the state and the applicant for benefit. It imposed quite a different kind of relationship to that prevailing under a system of insurance. Under the latter, the state administered aggregate factors whereas, in order to operate the means test, the state was required to intervene and reciprocate in every case, employing investigators to check the details and verify the statements of all applicants. The labour-intensive nature of this activity required complex administrative marshalling and rendered the process very costly. Indeed, it had been thought, prior to 1922, that the expensive and involved procedures of investigation would render the means test quite impractical. In the light of this, we must search for other explanations of the means test. Objectives other than cost, or the efficient distribution of relief (especially as the means test is a particularly inefficient method of distribution), seem to be more important causes of the British social security system's predisposition for means tests. The means test appears rather less directly concerned with the politics of redistribution and more with the statutory regulation of poverty.

I have already said that 'investigation' and 'testing' of family households was nothing new; home visits for essentially similar purposes had been widespread throughout the nineteenth century. The formalisation of such testing under the auspices of the state made little difference to these investigatory activities themselves, the major changes were in connection with the extended scale of their operations and their new utility, not as a prelude to rehabilitation, but as a means of discipline and disentitlement.

If one steps back to review the history of means-testing, one is apt to be struck by a strange paradox, perhaps a paradox of the kind that seems to have occurred to Foucault in his analysis of the perpetual failure of the prison to reform those incarcerated – despite the very best endeavours of the penal reformers. In the case of the means test a similar history of failure can be declared; means-tested social security has seldom come anywhere near *eliminating* poverty. More properly, it should be understood as a technique for redistributing, reapportioning, reorganising and reproducing poverty itself – that is, reconstituting poverty as a political relation. In this light, a hidden history of the means test can be allowed to appear. It is a history in which one is struck more by the means test's contribution to the regulation of social and familial relations – its role as political technique – than by its immediate significance as a method for allocating 'resources'. The means test can then be seen as a political technique, the culmination of a number of both statutory and non-statutory forms of supervision and investigation, and the ascription of politically appropriate levels of subsistence.

The means test 'tested' the resources of individuals, families or households, matching them against a catalogue of recognised 'requirements' producing a snapshot, or margin, of 'need'. The test officially endorsed a particular pattern of relationships, responsibilities and expectations, whilst sanctioning and condemning others. Similarly, the means test's recognition of certain '*needs*' was to alter fundamentally the nature of that concept, by attaching to a feature of subsistence, deprivation or even desire, the authority of official sanction. Henceforth, needs began to be *attributed* to people and to families, in a normative sense, as state social policy advanced along the lines of social intervention that instruments such as the means test (and perhaps also compulsory education, sanitary inspection, social work and health visiting) had forged with working-class families.

This combination of the identification of new forms of 'need' and the attachment of financial penalties or incentives to certain types of relationship ensured that the means test was rather more than a simple technique for the allocation of resources. Indeed, once redefined, the means test appears as a particularly important piece of political technology. It can be seen to have constructed a series of highly functional and economically-orientated disciplinary social relations at the heart of working-class existence. Consider also its role in the development of knowledge about living standards and a supposed aetiology of poverty – as well as its authorisation of so many forms of 'social intervention' – and we are left with a highly significant political instrument.

In these respects, the means test, the requirement of 'availability for work' and the rigorous conditions of entitlement to benefit, are at one. Together, they signal the intensification of industrial-capitalist disciplinary forms within 'modern society' and imprint these disciplinary relations ever deeper into the heart of social existence and lifestyles. It is, of course, no accident that the nationalisation of the labour market and the first specification of the instruments and objectives of a national economic policy, (Tomlinson, 1981), emerged at precisely the time that the disciplinary basis of social class relations was undergoing such a major refinement. In fact, these developments are intrinsically related. In particular, they are related within the social and political transformations that both prompted and which accompanied the demise of the

Poor Law and led to its replacement by a scheme of National Insurance. In the process, the working classes were introduced to formal political membership of society by the extension of the franchise, yet simultaneously subordinated, *en masse*, to the national economic imperatives of industrial capitalism.

As I have sought to show, it is important to examine the role that state 'social' policy has played in the construction of this modern era, not least because the emergence of 'the social' is coterminous with the rise of modern industrial capitalism itself. However, many of the characteristics and requirements of modern industrial capitalism are at best corrosive of democratic and egalitarian principles or profoundly 'anti-social' in themselves. Furthermore, the new statuses attained by working-class men and by women derive in large measure from the new relations established by the modern states with their 'citizenry'. Yet, as we have seen, these new relations of citizenship were established upon a uniquely disciplinary footing. Whilst Marxists are, often rightly, cautious of 'bourgeois rights', (Campbell, 1983), one does not have to dispose entirely of T. H. Marshall's analysis of 'citizenship' along with his 'reformist bathwater', but the extent and significance of systems of power and discipline, operationalised as 'social' policy, must be acknowledged, especially when they have so often served to dominate and constrain rather than liberate and enlighten. It is this central core of a statist 'anti-social' policy, masquerading as welfare, that I have been seeking to illuminate. In the following chapter, I turn to consider the further development of such welfare discourses and related disciplinary strategies in the era of the Welfare State.

6

In the shadows of state welfare

The real politics of social security

The Poor Law and National Insurance established different political dynamics and set different disciplinary relations in play. The Poor Law had contained poverty. It confined poverty, along with all its moral and economic symbolism, to the poor alone. Yet whilst the Poor Law attempted to use the condition of the poor as the basis for a deterrent system of relief aimed at the whole working class, the lives of the latter were often more directly governed by the relationships of the labour market itself, by contracts of employment, the hierarchy of industrial relations or the patriarchy of the family. The repression of the poor certainly assisted in the deployment of disciplinary principles and techniques throughout society, but the direct, repressive, force of the Poor Law system was felt primarily by the poor – or, more correctly, paupers – themselves.

The same cannot be said of the disciplinary relations established through the mechanisms of social insurance, the attempted establishment of the National Labour Exchange system and the new, essentially disciplinary, modes of identifying 'need' and policing entitlement. Rather, centralised administration and the growth of the insured population installed a sphere of unlimited state intervention. The disciplinary features of state social policy became increasingly co-extensive with the social relations of modern industry and the normative idealism of the family. 'The whole class had notice of poverty served upon it', remarked Kay and Mott, 'every worker became a potential pauper' (Kay and Mott, 1983, p. 108; see also Langan, 1985). And it would be no less true to add that women had the duties of motherhood enthusiastically thrust upon them, *en masse*, by the emergent 'social' state (Donzelot, 1980; Lewis, 1980).

The inter-war years, therefore, saw the culmination of a process of transformation in the exercise of disciplinary power centring upon new forms of collectivist state intervention and the distribution of resources to meet new, normative, conceptions of 'social' need and new political aspirations. Yet, paradoxically, the very years which saw the evolution of the most advanced criteria of 'social citizenship' conferred upon the people at large, were the same years which saw the state effectively deploying the most extensive administrative mechanisms for limiting the effect of these new 'rights'. Perhaps there is an important lesson here. Yet while new techniques of division and disentitlement appeared to derive their particular force and coherence from the economic climate within which they were deployed and the social conditions upon which they were imposed, this is only part of the story. The deep recession of the inter-war years certainly provided an economic rationale within which forms of practical disentitlement blossomed, but we must look further and deeper to understand the social and political context.

Conceiving the politics of welfare simply as an issue of entitlement/-disentitlement – in terms of access to and exclusion from benefits and services – is a corollary of a certain economistic reading of the normative orientation of social policy around forms of 'need'. This rather limited and traditional view of the politics of welfare reduces questions of social security administration to a static and almost one-dimensional plane. Static, because disentitlement is looked upon as a single specific act, a finite application of an essentially juridical power, rather than an ongoing, near-permanent and certainly pervasive, process of supervision, scrutiny and monitoring. One-dimensional, because the policy is interpreted almost wholly from the perspective of the state meeting designated 'social needs'. Such conceptions of social policy appear to endow it with but one direction and one beneficiary. The consequence of this conception of the exercise of state social policy is that our attention is diverted away from the fundamental disciplinary relationship itself towards the particular item – benefit, service or other resource – being distributed.

Viewing the politics of welfare in this way, we often fail to recognise, in the distribution and redistribution of simple resources, the circulation of power relations, the reproduction of patterns of hierarchy and subordination and the more broadly 'political' question of inequality. Even the turn-of-the-century philanthropist knew better. After all, for philanthropy, the 'gift' itself was nothing, the relationship between giver and receiver everything. The irony is, of course, that even a more extensive distribution of benefits simultaneously involves the creation of more extensive networks of distributive discipline. These issues, standing on the threshold of the Beveridge Report and its advocacy for the expansion of state welfare, are important.

In earlier chapters, I emphasised the importance of viewing discipline in terms of systems of power relations. These power relations, arranged around essentially normative and behavioural standards, deeply implicate the subjects of discipline within their daily operations. The reappraisal of 'welfare strategy' based upon insights derived from a disciplinary perspective raises important questions for our present conception of a 'distributive' social policy. Despite the fact that the very significance of social administration invariably rests upon its intended reorganisation of social relations through a forceful but regular application of normalising techniques, these characteristics of the subject (the discipline?) have been largely overlooked. The establishment of forms of entitlement and disentitlement, or the determination of criteria of sufficiency or deprivation, are typically criticised from the standpoint of distributive justice – as if they were capable of 'fair' applications divorced from their role within a broader political economy of power. While questions of needs, rights and entitlement have become, in recent years, one of the main focal points in disputes about social security – indeed, they are the very principles which make the whole administrative discourse palatable – it is important not to overlook the vital question of social discipline. For it is in terms of state regulation and social discipline rather than the meeting of needs, and political and economic order rather than rights and entitlement, that the immediate future of social security seems to lie. Of course, in making these dynamics of social security explicit, we do no more than return to that rather older conception of social security prevalent before the idealism of 'the social' seemed to have turned it inside out. In this older discourse, security referred more directly to 'order' and the protection of the status quo. The security envisaged was the security of property, security against the poor as opposed to the security of the poor (see Annette, 1979; Squires, 1981). A conception of security which is, once again, making its presence felt.

Beveridge and the social state

Yet all this seems a long distance from the largely positive reception given the Beveridge Report, *Social Insurance and Allied Services*, in 1942 (Beveridge, 1942), its author's warm embrace of patriarchy and imperialism notwithstanding (see, *inter alia*, Williams, 1989). Even so,

only a dozen years earlier, Beveridge had been an enthusiastic sup-
porter of proposals to punish 'malingerers' and the 'workshy' with
corrective discipline in penal labour colonies (Harris, 1977, pp. 354–6).
Even in the progressive reformism of post-war social security, discipline
was never very far away.

It is important to preface a discussion of the Beveridge Report with
these few remarks in order to make it clear that the publication of the
Report and the subsequent inauguration of the post-war Welfare State
were essentially disciplinary events. The language of the Beveridge
Report, and of Keynesian political economy as a whole, is the language
of a new form of state with new political technologies at its disposal.
Political involvement in employment, trade, marketing, prices and
incomes, taxation, housing, health and education via the range of 'social
enactments' new to the twentieth century were indicative of the passing
of an immense 'social transformation' (Fraser, 1978; Donzelot, 1979).
This transformation involved a fundamental shift in the modes of operation and legitimation of the state. State power no longer rested upon
the vestiges of constitutional or legal privilege, henceforth political
legitimation would be more and more dependent upon the capacity of
the state to satisfy social and political demands and meet new socio-
political objectives (Pasquino, 1981; Held, 1984). The new 'social' and
'distributive' logic of the Welfare State was not a reflection of benevolent humanism, as Beveridge's own language might imply, but an
inherent political characteristic of social democracy brought about by
the rise of a new normalising discipline. This discipline formed the core
of all welfare strategies and promoted a new politics of needs and a
resurgent discourse of rights. It fostered new ambitions and new aspirations, envisaging men and women being driven by a hope for the best
rather than a fear of the worst. It seemed to offer incentives for success
rather than penalties for failure – although, ironically, from a disciplinary point of view, they would amount to much the same thing, simply
means to an end.

In referring to this 'revolutionary moment', when 'landmarks of every
kind' were being abolished, Beveridge seemed to grasp the 'social'
significance of these changes taking place (Beveridge, 1942, para. 7).
The cataclysmic language can be forgiven, and the one-dimensional
stress upon distributive social provision ('meeting need', 'satisfying
want') is no more than characteristic of the new discourse of 'the social',
but even at a glance, it can be seen that there is an absence of underlying
disciplinary principle. Also absent is any real sense of the legacy of
punitive measures hitherto adopted by the British state (often supported
by substantial sections of British society) in response to problems of
pauperism and poverty. As Golding has noted, the British have had

considerable difficulty on many occasions in distinguishing poverty from crime (Golding, 1982). We need to examine the Beveridge proposals a little more closely.

I have already identified a number of the organising components and relations of the new Welfare State. Distributive justice and incentives feature strongly and from these we can derive our contemporary pre-occupations with needs and rights. In turn, these are largely unintelligible except within a discourse articulating modes of individuality – new ways of life, aspirations and desires – with collective and centralised forms of discipline. More importantly, implicit to the whole Beveridgean scheme, are fundamental notions of normalisation. None of this is to suggest that hierarchy, inequality, social division, poverty, patriarchy or injustice were henceforth banished from the ideological terrain of the Welfare State. Indeed, far from it for, as I have shown, 'the social' is well able to accommodate principles from a contradictory register and quite at home with the more repressive and authoritarian forms of policy and administration. (In fact, one of the more protracted and still unresolved conflicts running throughout 'the social' concerns precisely the degree to which it harbours a logic primarily punitive, divisive and exploitative, or one that is egalitarian, integrative and co-operative.)

Both Keynes and Beveridge sought a major reassessment of the political economy of welfare. However, the matrix of principles and ideals forming the modern discourse on 'social' security proved a fabricated and somewhat deceptive environment. As Golding and Middleton have noted, the Beveridge Report did not emerge into an ideological vacuum, on the contrary, 'the imagery of poverty and welfare with which the new utopia was to be constructed were deeply engraved into popular expectations'. In particular, by way of a reinterpretation of the spirit of normative idealism which Beveridge seemed to be hoping to harness, they argue,

> Three key ideas formed the tripod on which public understanding of poverty and welfare rested. These were efficiency, morality and pathology: efficiency of the labour market and the economy; morality of the work ethic and self-sufficiency; and the pathology of individual inadequacy as the cause of poverty.
>
> (Golding and Middleton, 1982, p. 48)

Whereas the ostensible focus of the Beveridge Report lay upon the meeting of need and the elimination of deprivation – the attack on the 'five giants' – the important question has less to do with the actual benefits and resources distributed than with the privileged norms and relationships deployed within that distribution. It is less a question of the articulation of a new ideal of citizenship than of the sanctioning of certain incentives and aspirations, less a question of rights and justice than the rearrangement of disciplinary networks around individuals and families, and above all, less a question of 'need' than of the power relation which need establishes, the role that it is made to play, the way that it serves as a means of gaining access to the person. Perhaps more than any other concept within the 'social' discourse, therefore, 'need' refashions the boundaries between public and private, individuality and collectivity.

These then are the points of entry into the social discourse of Beveridge. In a sense, they chart the lines which must guide any political appraisal of the disciplinary Welfare State. Where Beveridge speaks in terms of ideals of citizenship we need to look for the accompanying implicit forms of social division, where he considers ideals of welfare we must expect disciplined relationships, where he speaks of rights and incentives we need to seek out their opposites, disentitlements and disincentives, in order to ask what roles they are all performing and what objectives they seek. Finally, where he addresses the question of social need we must identify the corresponding forms of social pathology and unearth the modes of normalisation which underly them both. In short, where, Beveridge explicitly draws upon a 'social' discourse, we should look carefully for its counterpart, the 'anti-social', lying close by.

The political economy of incentives

It is appropriate to begin by considering the combination of disciplinary and incentive principles which guided Beveridge's approach to social security. Key sections of the 1942 Report are written from the perspective of a 'positive', often 'economically utilitarian', discourse of incentives – as, for that matter, are its companion volumes, *Full Employment in a Free Society* (1944) and *Voluntary Action* (1948) – but they are no less disciplinary principles for all that. As Beveridge put it, in a famous passage near the very beginning of his Report, 'the State in organising security should not stifle incentive, opportunity, responsibility; in establishing a national minimum, it should leave room and encouragement for voluntary action by each individual to provide more than that minimum for himself and his family' (Beveridge, 1942, pp. 7–8, para. 9, see also para. 302). In extracts like this, the Beveridge report interlinks three themes; security, incentives and the future. Combined, they form the elements of a blueprint for a positive, integrative, form of social order 'directed at a population which does not have to struggle for its survival but only for its betterment, for improvement in category and individual promotion.' (Donzelot, 1979, p. 82). This represents the positive discourse of incentives at its most natural and most simple. Personal ideals are directly solicited; the individual should strive for more – for himself. Ambition is thereby individualised and the family is invoked as the site for these, apparently 'natural' aspirations.

One of the crucial contradictions of the political economy of incentives emerges here. For Beveridge, incentives represented a positive, 'economic', and broadly egalitarian means of discipline. As he saw it, an efficient system of incentives would be a far more effective means of disciplining the mass workforces of modern welfare capitalism. Furthermore, Beveridge assumed, in the progressive social order of the Welfare State, the incentive structure of welfare capitalism could not be underpinned by an essentially regulative containment of the poor and unemployed. As he argued in 1944, in matters of unemployment and industrial discipline, 'detailed legislation is neither needed nor useful' (Beveridge, 1944). Yet despite this optimism, the continued existence of marked inequalities and a perpetual fear about damaging incentives to work, meant that it was precisely towards 'detailed legislation' that subsequent governments turned in their search for solutions to the problems of the labour market and apparent social indiscipline.

Furthermore, despite Beveridge's idealism, the 'incentives question' has often virtually besieged the politics of social security. Incentives to work (or to work harder, longer, or in less tolerable conditions) are invariably understood as a vital part of any arrangement of social security. This language of incentives and the notion of the 'social' or 'family' wage, to which it is closely allied, reflects what Lea has termed the 'monetization of social control', whereby incentive mechanisms guide the individual towards acceptance of certain privileged socioeconomic objectives or relationships, forming an effective network of sanctions around the aspirations of individuals. 'Monetization', Lea argues, 'is the basis of the consolidation of reformism as the mass ideology of the labour movement' (Lea, 1979, p. 87). It is important to make this connection and acknowledge the significance played here by incentive principles, precisely because it is this very same reformist discourse within which the Beveridge Report is couched and which contemporary ideologies of welfare perpetuate.

As I have suggested, incentive principles underly a good deal of the 1942 Beveridge Report (also his subsequent reports) and, although rather less explicitly utopian than the ideal of 'hope', which Beveridge thought should direct men's actions in the welfare society, they formed a none the less positive framework for social order – 'the distinguishing marks of a free society' (Beveridge, 1948, p. 10). Incentive principles feature significantly in the 1942 Report in two specific contexts; the first, concerning the proposals for voluntary insurance, the 'Encouragement of Thrift' and the 'social' revitalisation of the economy and, the second, in respect of the proposals for children's allowances and the protection of work incentives.

Social capitalism?

The Beveridge plan sought to provide compulsory social insurance to a subsistence level, 'for primary needs and general risks'. But it was by no means considered a ceiling upon savings and personal insurance. For Beveridge, the 'reluctant collectivist', however, the role of the state in relation to individual choices about voluntary insurance presented a problem. As he recognised, decisions about savings and voluntary insurance undoubtedly corresponded to people's own personal preferences and their perceptions about their own 'real needs'. At the same time he detected a broader problem, 'material progress depends upon technical progress which depends upon investment and ultimately upon savings' (Beveridge, 1942, p. 143, para. 376). Hitherto the sources of investment had been derived from the surplus income of the wealthy, or (much the same thing) from profits. Yet, he ventured:

> if and in so far as, after the war incomes are distributed more equally than at present or the share of wages of the total product is increased, it is important that part of the additional resources going to wage-earners and others of limited means should be saved by them instead of being spent.
>
> (*ibid*. p. 143, para. 376)

Increase of personal means, he argued, carried with it 'a corresponding increase of obligations'. It seemed reasonable, therefore, that the state should facilitate and encourage such saving either by regulation or by financial assistance. An expansion of thrift appeared to bring immeasurable individual moral virtues, it seemed also to be the 'socially' responsible thing to do. Above all, however, it seemed likely 'to be an essential measure of economic policy' (*ibid*. p. 143, para. 376). It seems that Beveridge believed that, in the new social climate of the 'welfare society', the state could act as a virtual broker for public altruism, harnessing and directing individual incentives as a motive force for social change towards greater material prosperity for all. These themes were developed more thoroughly in *Voluntary Action* in 1948.

The preoccupations of *Voluntary Action* were twofold. The first, concern was with 'the motive of personal thrift, of saving to have one's money at one's own command, saving for personal independence'. The second with, 'the business motive; the pursuit of a livelihood or of gain for oneself in meeting the needs of one's fellow citizens' (Beveridge, 1948, p. 321). Beveridge emphatically believed that 'the business motive' could be put to good 'social' purpose. The aspirations of individual citizens, in particular their propensity to save and invest and their desire for higher standards of living, could be equated with 'private enterprise' and its pursuit of profitability and channelled so as to serve the nobler aims of society. Building societies and friendly societies were thought to epitomise these ideals, representing, 'private enterprise, not in business but in the service of mankind, not for gain but under the driving power of social conscience'. But, he continued, 'the business motive is a good servant but a bad master, and a society which gives itself up to the dominance of the business motive is a bad society' (*ibid.* pp. 322–3). Beveridge believed that the betterment of the individual was to lead to the betterment of all. His conception of 'voluntary action' was vital, therefore, to his ideal of the free society, not a society of unregulated capitalism by any means, but a society in which altruism and mutualism prevailed providing a 'counterweight to selfishness' (Williams and Williams, 1987, p. 21).

Beveridge's view of the role and scope of 'voluntary action' was by no means restricted to monetary considerations, but a number of his assumptions seem indicative of the limits and inadequacies of his vision in this sphere. On the one hand, the creeping egalitarianism, or greater distributional justice, in matters of income and wealth, presumed by Beveridge to become a characteristic feature of the post-war world, hardly materialised (Titmuss, 1962; Atkinson, 1974; Le Grand, 1982; Rentoul, 1987). On the other hand, as Williams and Williams have noted, the forms of saving adopted by the middle classes seldom appeared to display the selfless altruism aspired to by Beveridge and yet, although ostensibly private, were frequently in receipt of substantial tax concessions. Beveridge overlooked the broader social and political implications of what Titmuss came to term the 'social division of welfare'. 'If an unregulated private welfare system expanded in Britain after 1945 that was partly because Beveridge, who never recognised its existence, never made any proposals for regulating private welfare' (Williams and Williams, 1987, p. 148). Hence, despite a fine rhetoric about mutualism and collective 'social' responsibilities, Beveridge never made it very clear how the forces of altruism were actually to be marshalled, or the resources assembled, other than as a merely moral crusade. In the event, mutualism and collectivism were unable to match the vitality of private enterprise and, as Williams and Williams observed, the friendly societies assumed a marginal role as a convenient tax shelter for the personal savings of the wealthy. Ironically, 'the institutions of working-class mutualism [came to] have an after-life as adjuncts to middle-class individualism' (Williams and Williams, 1987, pp. 150–1). And, as Cutler *et al.* remark:

> the story since 1945 is a simple one. Other 'selfish' forms of saving expanded to fill the space which, in Beveridge's fantasy, was to be occupied by altruistic mutuality . . . the largest and fastest growing [being] occupational pensions . . . . All this is not only an embarrassment for liberal ideologues, but a practical problem for us all because . . . at every point private pensions have regressive repercussions for the distribution of income as they accelerate inequality.
>
> (Cutler *et al.*, 1986, pp. 44 and 61)

And yet, in a nutshell, this typifies precisely the broader dilemma of 'the social' which has so far been our concern. In the demise of mutualism and altruism – the failure of a discourse of positive incentives to embrace collective ideals – 'the social' is to some extent reconstituted. The 'welfare society' envisaged by Beveridge became the 'irresponsible society' sketched by Titmuss in 1959 (Titmuss, 1963). New, personal and privatised motives insinuate themselves into the 'business fabric' once deemed (it must be said, rather idealistically) complementary to the Welfare State. Individualism and inequality have taken over where, collectivism and social justice were thought to prevail. The shabby minimum given, often begrudgingly, by the state compares poorly with the glittering prizes enticingly held out by the private sector. In turn, private incentives foster private desires and aspirations. The positive political economy of incentives swings into reverse, underpinning not freedom and independence but the rather more coercive relations of monetary discipline; a dependent, beleaguered consumerism and a competitive individualism out of control. The 'anti-social' has, in a sense, colonised 'the social'. Here and there, only the occasional name hints at a collective, benevolent or philanthropic past – 'Friends Provident', the 'Prudential', 'Commercial Union', 'Scottish Widows', etc. Perhaps these are still 'social' institutions, performing a 'social' purpose, but it is not the 'social' of Beveridge, still less of Titmuss.

In many respects, these 'local' dimensions to the incentives question connect neatly to the broader, macro-economic, environment. Expressed in the discourse of marginalist economics and public choice theory, incentive principles reflect the prominent ideology of 'business confidence' which for many years has constrained the development of a more progressive social policy. In 1956, the danger of damaging business incentives weighed heavily upon Crosland's vision of the future when he wrote that 'the problem of profit is the central economic dilemma facing contemporary social-democracy' (Crosland, 1964,

p. 300). He has certainly not been the last to draw such conclusions. Nevertheless, in the context provided by the broad political economy of incentives, the more specific discourse of work incentives flourished.

Work incentives

This brings me to the second area of the 1942 Report, where the incentives discourse becomes clearly focused; to some extent it concerns the provision of allowances for children. Three issues are involved here: first, the need to maintain an income differential between periods of working and non-working; second, Beveridge's desire to ensure that the means-tested assistance benefits, 'be felt to be something less desirable than insurance benefit' (Beveridge, 1942, p. 141, para. 369); third, Beveridge's normative commitment to the family.

The problem of work incentives is made explicit in Beveridge's discussion of the potential offered by a scheme of children's allowances.

> It is dangerous to allow benefit during unemployment or disability to equal or exceed earnings during work. But without earnings for children, during earning and not-earning alike, this danger cannot be avoided . . . the gap between income during earning and during interruption of earning should be as large as possible for every man.
>
> (*ibid*. p. 154, para. 412)

The perception of many socialists – but by no means all – was, of course, quite different. For them, the issue was not to be settled by keeping benefits low enough to ensure a continued incentive to work, but rather by ensuring that wages were high enough in the first place (see Clarke *et al.*, 1987, pp. 110–13). However, there were profound problems in a single-minded advocacy in favour of wages as a solution to poverty, not least that it tended to reinforce the ideological significance of the male breadwinner. Yet, in subsequent years, the debate concerning poverty and low pay, work incentives and the poverty trap, largely adhered to the themes established by Beveridge in 1942 (see Hemming, 1984).

Beveridge addressed these questions in 1944 in *Full Employment in a Free Society*, noting that 'there are some who will say that full employment, combined with unemployment insurance, will remove the incentive of effort which depends on fear of starvation.' But he countered this claim with the argument that, 'for civilized human beings ambition and desire for service are adequate incentives. It may be that cattle must be driven by fear. Men can and should be led by hope' (Beveridge, 1944, p. 250). This, above all, is Beveridge's self-acknowledged 'contribution to a wider social policy'. It is, no doubt, an ambitious ideal. But, as I have already said, without any institutional means for relating individual aspirations and ambitions to collective forms of welfare (other than the rather passive solidarities of National Insurance), this positive economy of incentives had little opportunity to develop. On the one hand, these incentive mechanisms (and the aspirations to which they gave rise) could become distorted by the competitive individualism of the market place. On the other, they might simply degenerate into their opposites, a disciplinary series of specific disincentives attached to certain behaviours, activities or relationships of which the state might disapprove – a development that Beveridge himself anticipated. For example, entitlement to the 'less desirable' assistance benefits should, he argued, be made 'subject to any condition as to behaviour which may seem likely to hasten restoration of earning power', with the threat of 'penal treatment' for non-compliance in the background (Beveridge, 1942, pp. 141–2, paras. 369 and 373).

Traces of discipline and deterrence

Such remarks help draw our attention back to the explicitly disciplinary foundations of the Beveridge-inspired Welfare State. The ideal of the positive economy of incentives is an important founding principle of the Welfare State, but it is not the only one. We would do well to take note of Beveridge's sense of the disciplinary foundations of social security and the (apparently lingering) traces of deterrence upon which the new Welfare State was based. For, as Novak has argued in an attempt to link the language of incentives with the language of discipline, in a society 'where poverty remains the principle incentive, the relief of poverty cannot abolish poverty . . . it has to reinforce the discipline which its provisions against the consequences of poverty and unemployment relieves' (Novak, 1975, p. 261; see also Novak, 1988). Addressing just this question of discipline in social security, Beveridge wrote:

> At the basis of any scheme of social security . . . there must be provision for a limited class of men who through weakness or badness of character fail to comply. In the last resort the man who fails to comply with the conditions for obtaining benefit or assistance and leaves his family without resources must be subject to penal treatment.
>
> (Beveridge, 1942, p. 147, para. 373)

The statement contains a great deal. Discipline is posited as essential in any scheme of welfare, indeed it serves as its very foundation. It will deal with the wilful 'deviant' as well as the pathologically incapable who fail to comply with established social norms – either those spelt out in the 'conditions of entitlement', or in relation to the family. Furthermore, not punishment, but 'treatment' is proposed. Remedial and rehabilitative, 'treatment' will not exclude the deviant or deficient; 'the social' does not work like this, rather, they are drawn back into the relationships of 'the social' and made to perform according to its patterned expectations. Finally, in a phrase which recalls certain structuralist debates on the role of the state, 'in the last resort' the essential disciplinary preconditions prevail and the pretence of social security is swept away. All along, it has been the imperatives of industrial discipline, profitability and political order – in other words, social security of an older type – which have been paramount.

Nevertheless, despite this essentially disciplinary foundation, the Beveridge Report appeared otherwise to present the issue of disciplinary control as a rather more marginal consideration. This can undoubtedly be explained by the fact that Beveridge's strategy complemented the ascendancy of a political economy of incentives founded upon Keynesian macro-economic ideas and the promise of full employment. As I shall show, however, the issue of discipline did not remain on the periphery for long. For instance, in 1944, Beveridge felt compelled to devote a chapter of *Full Employment in a Free Society* to what he called the 'internal implications' of full employment. Foremost was the problem of industrial discipline. 'Some people', he suggested, 'anticipate that if a policy of full employment becomes effective, industrial discipline and efficiency resting upon discipline will be destroyed or diminished' (Beveridge, 1944, p. 194, see also p. 22). He drew upon a remark from the *Bankers Magazine* to illustrate his point.

> Is there not a tendency in much of this modern planning – not forgetting the Beveridge plan – to overlook the fact that, human nature being what it is, the workers of the future, capitalists and wage earners alike, will require the old spur of rewards and punishment (good profits and good wages, fears of losses and bankruptcy, and, yes, fears of unemployment and poverty) to ensure the necessary drive in this world of internal and international competition.
>
> (*Bankers Magazine*, October 1943, quoted in Beveridge, 1944)

An editorial in *The Times* was no less explicit in its depiction of the consequences that full employment and the introduction of social security benefits might have on the incentive to work. 'Unemployment', it argued, 'was no mere accidental blemish upon a private enterprise economy.' On the contrary, it was part of the essential mechanism of the system with an important function to fulfil. 'The first function of unemployment . . . [was] that it maintained the authority of master over man . . . . The absence of a fear of unemployment might . . . have a disruptive effect upon factory discipline' (*The Times*, 22 January 1943, quoted in Beveridge, 1944).

To some extent, Beveridge accepted such sentiments; problems of industrial discipline had, in the past, 'become more prominent in times of good trade'. The Board of Trade endorsed this view with the observation that 'unpunctuality . . . was found to be considerably greater . . . in times of active trade than in years of depression.' Furthermore, such evidence as was available from the record of disallowances and suspensions of benefit in the case of 'employees dismissed for misconduct', or cases of 'voluntary unemployment' seemed to suggest a pattern fluctuating in accordance with the 'trade cycle' (Beveridge, 1944, pp. 195–7). Thus, despite his desire to install a predominantly positive framework of incentives around the labour market, it appeared that some form of rather more direct coercion might be necessary to deal with those men of 'unsteady character', or the 'unreliable'. Nevertheless, he continued to claim that, on the whole, the insurance scheme, could adequately penalise those characters dismissed on grounds of misconduct and still discourage the 'workshy'. In any event, without full employment and the offer of a job, an individual's willingness to work could not be effectively tested. In general, therefore, Beveridge believed that the level of benefits, the conditions of entitlement and the inconvenience of changing employment, would, 'in all normal cases, continue to be a motive for steady work and good performance' (*ibid.* p. 197). Incentives there would undoubtedly be, but a layer of implicit disciplinary sanctions – in Beveridge's terms, 'some residual element of deterrence' – lay not far beneath them (see Harris, 1977, p. 391).

Beveridge's arguments regarding the protection of incentives appear to have prevailed but only in so far as the 'national minimum' guaranteed by the state was drawn at a sufficiently low level. As Townsend has noted, in persuading the Conservatives of the merits of the idea of a national minimum,

> Keynes and Beveridge . . . tended to draw the minimum at a low level, for they wanted individuals to have room for manoeuvre to add to State provision by their own efforts. There had to be no disincentive to individual enterprise, no strict limits imposed on the freedom of employers, the big corporations or the insurance interests.
>
> (Townsend, 1975)

The incentives problem had effectively hijacked the discourse of social security. More than just Conservatives came to deploy the rhetoric of work incentives in the years after Beveridge. Even Socialists seemed mesmerised by the spectre of disincentives to work or to invest, fearing that 'excessive' state intervention might stifle the vitality of the nation. For instance, in 1956 Crosland argued that, 'the distribution of personal income has become significantly more equal', that, 'primary poverty has been largely eliminated', that, 'the Beveridge revolution has been carried through', and, above all, that, 'we have now reached the point where further redistribution would make little difference to the standard of living of the masses; to make the rich less rich would not make the poor significantly less poor' (Crosland, 1964, pp. 14, 59, 123). However, it was in the pages of *Socialist Commentary* in 1955, that the Left seemed to take up the rhetoric of disincentives most completely:

> We have pushed progressive taxation so far in this country that we are clearly in the neighbourhood of its limits, not only in the sense that the incomes of the rich are, after taxation, comparatively small; but also in the sense that we are destroying the incentive to take risks.
> (Lewis, 1955 quoted in Saville, 1965)

Approximately ten years later, the Labour government's response to the so-called 'rediscovery of poverty' was overshadowed by a prevailing fear of undermining incentives to work. In the midst of a selective uprating of benefit levels a 'wage stop' principle was reintroduced to ensure that claimants could not be better off out of work. Labour were to abolish the 'wage stop' principle in 1975, but not before they had fallen prey to the incentives argument once more, in 1968, and introduced the notorious 'four-week rule' as a means of pressurising the long-term unemployed into jobs (See George, 1968; Meacher, 1974).

Thus, the 'burden theory' of welfare took shape. To advocates of this theory, rather than being a contribution to freedom and social justice, something about the Welfare State appeared to endanger the very foundations of social and economic life. Hostile principles were infiltrating social security discourse, the positive economy of incentives installed by Beveridge turned out to be a two-dimensional mechanism. As a disciplinary means of shaping and structuring the aspirations of the mass of the population, incentives proved suitable foundations for a positive, almost consensual, conception of social order, but turned upon the poorest, they had quite a different impact. For those able to take advantage of them, incentives formed a suitable complement to competitive individualism, for those unable to do so, they merely reinforced a sense of failure. The structure of incentives employed the needs of the poorest as virtual weapons against them; poverty became a prison, encircling and strangling the lives of some of the most deprived people. It was not as an incentive system, therefore, that the poorest encountered social security but rather as its opposite, a poverty trap.

Despite Beveridge's plan, therefore, social security did not abolish want, it merely recycled poverty. Unfortunately, it was the poverty-trap itself not the broader political economy of inequality which came to preoccupy the policy sciences. In some respects this was understandable, the poverty trap represented the point at which the worst inequities were concentrated, where disincentives were at their most severe. But as I have said, when viewed through the lens of social reformism, the poverty trap was simply an upturned image of the incentive problem. Paradoxically, therefore, the especial emphasis conferred upon the poverty trap within the discourse of social administration served only to reaffirm the broader discourse of incentives within which social security itself had become 'trapped'.

Piven and Cloward have suggested that the political significance of this negative application of incentive principles through social security rests upon its ability to reinforce the disciplinary relations operating throughout the 'social sphere' as a whole. They claim that the welfare system has made an important contribution to bolstering the incentive structure of capitalism and has enhanced the market's power to direct and control labour (Piven and Cloward, 1974, pp.32–3). The incentives discourse has to be seen as a relatively coherent whole complementing the political and economic relations of welfare capitalism. The social security system effectively relays a series of disciplinary relations beyond the normal range attained by the market. Yet appreciating the significance of the disciplinary Welfare State involves understanding the essentially double-edged character of the political techniques emanating from the incentives discourse. Incentives were always a means of labour discipline, their virtue lay in the fact that they left their subjects in apparent control of their lives; for others, however, they became the means by which the most explicit form of control – control through poverty – became imposed. Unlike earlier forms of societal organisation, welfare capitalism did not rest upon the confinement and isolation of the poor. Both Keynes and Beveridge were aware of this important characteristic of modern society; indeed Beveridge had sought to avoid recourse to 'detailed legislation' in managing unemployment and poverty. Ironically, however, this seemed precisely the direction in which the deficiencies of the incentive principle led.

Two further sets of relations played a role in ushering the state towards the adoption of a more directly interventionist stance concerning the management of poverty. The incentive principle was not the only feature of Beveridge's social policy to conceal a profoundly 'anti-social' antithesis. The normative discourse on 'need' had always been most important for the interventionist power it conferred. Its mirror-image, social pathology, performed a similar role but without suggesting anything like the degree of progressive autonomy implied by 'need'. Likewise, 'rights' were quickly beseiged by their opposites, that is to say, suggestions of illegality (accusations of 'fraud and abuse') and mechanisms of disentitlement, thus emphasising the essentially peripheral role played by rights as components of the modes of normalisation operating within Beveridge's discourse.

As I shall show, these two dynamics tended to sustain and reinforce each other and, in turn, both reaffirmed an increasingly negative political economy of incentives. Something of the virulence with which concerns about the alleged 'abuses' of social security developed in the postwar period is suggested by the widespread belief, already examined, that social security was, in itself, very largely an 'abuse' of the free relations of the market economy. If 'welfare' was a burden upon the economy in general terms then, in individual cases, it was almost certainly fostering disincentives to work. Alternatively, when individuals were thought to have claimed or received more than they required to meet their most basic needs, they were deemed to have 'abused' the humanitarian ideals which were presumed to underlie the Welfare State. In a sense, this reading of the 'abuse' issue recalls the Victorian age's concern with the 'clever pauper' who was said to 'abuse' the charity of philanthropic agencies. A similar preoccupation with such 'abuses', at once both general and specific, can be discerned in the works of many recent 'New Right' commentators on social policy (see for example Boyson, 1971; Joseph and Sumption 1979; Parker, 1982; Minford, 1987). In turn, this ascendancy of a moral vocabulary of 'abuse' served to legitimate the introduction of further measures to control access to entitlement, thereby increasingly compromising the language of rights within which the discourse of social security was, at least notionally, set.

If we turn to the forms of social pathology populating the Welfare State, we can identify a similar link with the broader political economy of incentives. Socio-pathological discourses implied that poverty was best understood as an individual, rather than a structural, feature of modern capitalist societies. The evidence of social pathology tended to overturn a collectivist emphasis on 'social need' by transforming it into a feature of individual character. Standing in relation to some normative principle, 'need' implied a simple deficiency that might be overcome. Social pathology suggested that it could not. Greater effort in response to suitable incentives, or self-help and self-discipline, might be enough to overcome mere 'needs', but social pathology pointed to something deeper, that is to say, 'needs' beyond the individual's powers to remedy.

In a sense, we can say that social pathology reconstituted the horizon of recognised needs. By injecting an implicitly voluntarist principle, differentiating between those needs that individuals might solve for themselves and those for which state help would be required, the discourse on social pathology entirely recast notions of need. Henceforth, there would be 'real needs', beyond the scope of individual solution, and those needs for which individuals have, supposedly, only themselves to blame. In this liberal-individualist reformulation of 'true' and 'false' needs, we have a fascinating reversal of the more orthodox materialist conceptions of need. Once installed, this critical ideological distinction began to mount its own assault upon the discourse of social security, growing support for increasingly 'selective' social security policies being one of its most obvious manifestations after the mid–1960s (see Joseph, 1966; Boyson, 1971; Stevenson, 1973).

I have already pointed out that Beveridge's social policy was rife with contradictions, but he could hardly have been aware that they would eventually come to exert themselves with such a vengeance. With the demise of the political idealism upon which the principle of universal state welfare rested – attributable, in part, to the emerging contradictions already identified within the Beveridge formula – and with the weakening performance of the British economy, the incentive principle locked firmly into reverse. In fundamental ways this transformed the relationship between 'needs', 'rights' and 'welfare' within social security discourse. I shall now consider these ideological dynamics as they evolved in the post-war period. They are crucial to an understanding of the proliferation of disciplinary and regulative mechanisms within the apparatuses of social security – that is to say, the processes by which a profoundly 'anti-social policy' has grown and developed.

The question of 'abuse'

Taken together, the effect of the three reverse dynamics implicit within social security discourse was to suggest, not only that the sphere of 'genuine need' was much smaller than Beveridge had implied but that, for those 'real needs' which remained, the language of rights was entirely inappropriate. Furthermore, it was assumed that attempts to broaden the definition of 'allowable need', or extend the framework of rights, would be likely to undermine work incentives and destabilise the family with, in turn, serious consequences for the economy and for society. If we examine the political dynamics within social security discourse we will recognise the increasing emphasis given to questions of 'abuse' and, more importantly, we will be able to appreciate the implications of this preoccupation.

Two areas, above all, exemplify the disciplinary relations set in motion with the modern discourse on social security. Both concern the growing preoccupation with social security 'abuse'. They involve, respectively, the patrolling of the labour market and the policing of the family.

Patrolling the labour market

To some extent the low political saliency of the 'abuse' issue in social security in the immediate post-war period can be discerned from the limited number of claimants prosecuted for 'fraud' or 'false statement' under the provisions of the social security acts, or the relatively limited scale of the Board's pursuit of 'liable relatives'. Only 605 prosecutions are recorded for 1948. The figures remain at a similarly low level throughout the 1950s, only crossing the thousand-mark in the early 1960s. The figures provide a striking contrast to statistics produced in the 1980s. To take two simple examples: in 1981 a survey team commissioned by the Department of Employment and the Department of Social Security estimated that 'around 8 per cent of claimants are working whilst claiming benefit' (Rayner Report, DE/DHSS, p.63). By 1989, eight years later, the estimated figure, produced in conjunction with what had now become an annual report on measures to combat illegal claiming, had risen to 10 per cent (see the *Guardian*, 2 August 1989, p.4). Over the same period an increasing preoccupation with alleged 'abuses' came to affect the social security system as a whole, with the effect that levels of claims control activity increased substantially.

Although 'abuse' itself had not been a predominant or explicit feature of the new arrangements for social security, the National Assistance Board (NAB) inherited from the Poor Law a lingering preoccupation with questions of labour discipline, with rehabilitation and with 'less eligibility'. In particular concerns about possible, 'abuse' fell primarily upon the means-tested assistance benefits. Being a means-tested benefit, national assistance almost inevitably involved a more intrusive and explicitly interventionist mode of administration than the insurance-based or 'universal' benefits. In Chapter 5, I began to unearth something of the 'hidden history' of the means test. In the following pages, one of the major legacies of the means test as a political technique will become clearer. Frank Field has noted that 'if you operate a means test, you have to "police" it . . . this leads to a whole series of bizarre checks and balances operated throughout the whole system of means-tested assistance' (Field, 1975). While means-testing certainly exacerbated the stigma of poverty, the policing of the means test intensified the pressures to which the poorest were subject. Hitherto, poverty had implied exclusion, now it also meant surveillance and encirclement in a web of disciplinary relationships; privileged relationships and enforced dependencies.

When, in 1948, the NAB came to accept the need for discipline and strict administration in resettlement centres, it did so partly in order to dispel the idea that the 'workshy', and persons 'without a settled way of life', could live an easy life at public expense. 'Experience has shown that the maintenance of a firm discipline in Centres [is] essential to check abuse' (NAB *Annual Report*, 1948, p. 29).

In the early years of national assistance, 'abuse' seemed to stand in a close relation to social pathology. Subsequent annual reports of the Board remarked upon 'the restlessness and mental indiscipline to be found among men in Reception Centres'. Furthermore, whilst instances of drunkenness, laziness and general 'workshyness' drew particular comment, it was felt that such characteristics 'often disguised other more personal factors' (NAB *Annual Report*, 1949, pp. 29–30). Although such issues had a direct bearing upon the Board's rehabilitative responsibilities it was initially felt inappropriate to seek to solve problems of a personal character through prosecution. The same attitude was reaffirmed in 1950, but the Board went on to suggest that prosecution might be an option in the case of those men who had been provided with several opportunities to re-establish themselves but had abused them all. Considering the problems it faced in reaching decisions in 'difficult' cases, the NAB outlined its rationale for social intervention in terms which drew heavily upon the discourses of social pathology and notions of social discipline.

> Most people would describe [such men] as malingerers or workshy and consider no further explanation necessary. It may be, however, that there is a psychological explanation for their conduct, and that it is the product of a condition which could be treated and cured. But if there is a cure it requires the cooperation of the man, and such men as these will generally not cooperate. . . . The officers of Reception Centres . . . persevere in the attempt to help and influence even the man who has abused what they have done for him before, but the stage comes when nothing seems left to try but punishment or the threat of it. There is at least a chance that prison will bring the man to a better sense of responsibility.
>
> (NAB *Annual Report*, 1950, p.24)

Despite this peripheral reference to punishment 'in the last resort' (rather like Beveridge's own formula), throughout the early 1950s, the

National Assistance Board's annual reports typically expressed rather more concern about the pathologically 'workshy' than the fraudulent, even though the two categories often seemed to merge. By 1952, some limited progress seems to have been made in distinguishing the 'would-be fraudulent' from the 'inadequate'. The Board began to use its powers, under section 10 of the 1948 National Assistance Act, to direct the 'workshy' to undergo a course of corrective training at a re-establishment centre. In its own broadly 'rehabilitative' terms, re-establishment hardly appeared very successful but it did, on occasion, seem to perform a reasonably deterrent function – men tended to discontinue their benefit claims rather than attend the centres (see NAB *Annual Report*, 1952, p.13).

The distinction between the 'inadequate' and the 'abusive' was further clarified by a tightening-up of the criteria of 'availability'. Noting that, 'parliament intended that criminal proceedings should be reserved for serious cases in which other remedies were unsuitable or had been tried and failed' (*ibid.*), the Board attempted to impose a stricter conception of 'availability for work'. The new definition was supported by the threat of suspension of benefit, or even a prosecution under section 51 of the 1948 National Assistance Act (persistent failure to maintain self and/or dependants), in the last instance. An 'availability test' entailed questioning intentionality – the state of a claimant's mind. However, even though the Board was significantly less severe in these assessments than its predecessors of the 1920s and 1930s had been, it confidently asserted that during 1951 and 1952 several thousand recipients of assistance were 'out of work by their own choice'. Nevertheless, despite the apparent evidence of widespread 'abuse', a principle became established that, in order for a prosecution to be brought, men should have refused several reasonable offers of work. The principle stands in sharp contrast to the rather more draconian measures of the present day, but we should not let this contrast blind us to the relatively subtle changes occurring in conceptions of abuse in the 1950s.

In 1952 several thousand workshy individuals were a cause of concern but little more. The Board referred to them as 'a few undeserving applicants'. In itself, this was nothing new, but it placed these 'undeserving characters' in a relationship that was, in later years, to take on a powerful significance. The 'undeserving' were, the Board alleged, taking advantage 'of the provisions made for people in genuine need' (*ibid.* p. 15). The language is still essentially social-democratic in form; for instance, questions of 'need' are still paramount, but the 'need' principle is now substantially qualified. This had two consequences. The first was that it led to a critical diminution of the significance of the idea of 'need' itself. The unwarranted claims of the 'undeserving' seemed to be corroding the very integrity of the idea of 'need'. Even though 'need' had never been a self-evident fact in any arrangement of social policy, in the normative 'social' discourses embraced by the Welfare State, it did possess a certain autonomy. However, as the NAB ventured a distinction between 'genuine need' and (presumably) 'false need' this autonomy was lost. The second was that, partly as a result of this loss of autonomy, the relationship between 'need' and entitlement was redefined. 'Need' simply became one more factor in the determination of entitlement. The process of determination itself became all-important – just as the Board was beginning to develop rather more stringent measures to control entitlement. As if to emphasise the point, the following year, in the 1953 annual report, the Board described the appointment of the first contingent of 'special investigators' to work specifically in the field of 'fraud and abuse'.

In 1954, the NAB continued to detail the action it had begun to take both to control abuse and to pressurise those whose inclination to seek work was not considered sufficiently strong. Early in the year, a review of the 'voluntarily unemployed' was undertaken. The results appeared in later years, they seemed to lead to the drawing of a more sophisticated distinction between the 'workshy' and the 'abusive'. The evidence did not support the view that 'workshyness' was widespread – quite the contrary. But in one important respect the report was quite unequivocal, a 'hard core' of the 'voluntarily unemployed' and potentially fraudulent could now be identified with increasing precision (NAB *Annual Report*, 1956, p.15). In later years the Board went on to attempt to demonstrate this, although the crucial distinctions between 'workshy' and 'abusive' often seemed to break down in practice. The new procedures for patrolling the labour market were undoubtedly more successful in enhancing the disciplinary character of the social security system, but this was not their only effect. As the Board became more diligent in its pursuit of the 'workshy', whether deviant or pathological, 'fraudulent' or 'inadequate', the size and significance of both groups – the 'hard core' as a whole – appeared to grow.

Policing the family

However, it was not only in the area of employment relations that the discipline of social security came to focus, for the family also became a particular site for concern. Although the Beveridge Report had declared a firm commitment to the principles of the patriarchal family, two problematic issues began to emerge. As the post-war decades wore on, 'failure to maintain dependants' and 'undisclosed cohabitation' generated more and more attention. In 1948, the National Assistance Board had assumed responsibility for some 41,600 single women and their children. In the 1950s and 1960s the number rose markedly, but despite the increasing incidence of illegitimacy and family break-up, a concern about the phenomenon of 'fictitious desertion' seemed to motivate attempts to apply financial pressure on single parents through the medium of social security.

In 1948, the problem of the 'absent liable relative' seemed only a peripheral concern, but by the following year, following a 100 per cent increase in the number of claims made by separated wives and unmarried mothers, 'enforcement of liability' assumed the status of a problem. In particular, the loss to public funds resulting from this 'abuse' led the Board to consider what further action it might take to tackle the issue. By 1950 the Board was pleased to report that, 'with increasing experience . . . officers had more success in tracing defaulting liable relatives' (NAB *Annual Report*, 1950, p.18). Subsequent years reveal a steadily rising number of prosecutions for 'failure to maintain' and also the emergence of an apparent 'hard core' who seemed 'so set in their determination never to support their wives that they will go to prison, if need be over and over again, rather than pay' (NAB *Annual Report*, 1951, p.19). Such developments reflect similar processes occurring with respect to the patrolling of the labour market.

In the following year, 1952, the law was changed to enable wives to give evidence against husbands charged with the offence of 'failure to maintain'. The effect of the change was to return the law to the position it had occupied under the Poor Law. Although enacted as a means by which to pursue deserting husbands, the new regulation applied a lever primarily against the wife. Deserted wives and single parents were 'encouraged' to divulge information to enable the administration to trace former partners so that it (or the women themselves) might prosecute or take action to recover maintenance due from 'alleged fathers'. Women who were reluctant to co-operate with 'liable relative officers' might prejudice their entitlement to benefit. The Board was adamant that women and children could not be left to starve, 'in the hope of effecting a reconciliation' (NAB *Annual Report*, 1953, p.20), but the language used is not wholly convincing. Only when the Board's officers were convinced that 'the separation looks like continuing' did they appear to 'feel obliged' to grant sufficient assistance. In its actions in such cases the NAB manifested a tendency to take a particularly harsh line with those who failed to conform to certain established behavioural norms. Indeed, in a more general sense, social policy has shown itself especially susceptible to scandalous relationships. In particular the myth of 'fictitious desertion' has played no small part in legitimating a more intensive 'policing' of single parents. Of course, such remarks apply with equal weight to the phenomenon of 'undisclosed cohabitation', a scandalous relationship which has prompted some of the most intrusive and stigmatising interventions adopted by social security investigators (see Field and Grieve, 1971; Clayton, 1981; Squires, 1984).

The number of individuals against whom liable-relative proceedings were instituted continued to rise throughout the second half of the 1950s and the whole of the 1960s, although the practice of subjecting women to a testing interview drew increasing criticism. In 1974, evidence from the Health Visitors' Association, corroborated by evidence from the Women's National Commission, presented to the Finer Commission on One-Parent Families stated that, 'undue pressure is brought to bear at a time when the mother is already under considerable stress' (Finer Report, vol. 1, pp. 138–41). Such criticisms led to the adoption of new rules designed to protect mothers from harassment by liable-relative officers but, by 1981, these rules were apparently being ignored. The pressure on single parents was maintained, seemingly because, 'it is officially suspected that this is the area in which there is most fraud' (Healy, 1981). As if to confirm this impression, a government statement on 'fraud savings' in 1981 suggested that liable-relative work was the most cost-effective of all the government's initiatives against social security 'abuse' (Patrick Jenkin, 6 May 1981 in *Hansard*, vol. 4, cols 79–80). Subsequent guidelines issued for the use of liable relative investigators when conducting interviews with single parents suggest that the patriarchal commitments of the British social security system have spawned a powerful disciplinary legacy policing the family with an intensity not dissimilar to that focused upon the labour market (see Squires, 1984 for a fuller analysis).

This brief sketch of efforts to 'police' what are seen as familial obligations complements Barrett and McIntosh's important analysis of *The Anti-social Family* (Barrett and McIntosh, 1982). In this work, the authors describe the oppressive patriarchal relationships which constitute familialism as a political discourse and pervade both systems of welfare and the modern 'family form'. The punitive turn taken by liable-relative work in the 1980s is often presented – by its critics as well as its defenders – as driven by a primarily economic motive, yet the moral and patriarchal claims made by prominent representatives of the New Right in favour of financial sanctions against single parents, strongly suggest that cost-effectiveness is far from being the only consideration. Minford, in particular, speaks of 'discouraging' illegitimacy and 'punishing' the violations of single parents, though he is not alone in this respect (Minford, 1987, pp. 81–2).

Protecting public funds

The descriptions just presented of the social security administration's rising preoccupation with two prominent forms of alleged 'abuse' are enough to confirm the ideological significance of the issue in the matrix of concerns surrounding the discourse of social security. However, we need to link this emerging concern with 'abuse' to the wider range of ideological dynamics at play within the discourse.

In the 1957 annual report of the National Assistance Board, for instance, a significant rescheduling of priorities can be detected. In this year, not only was the 'prevention of abuse' given special consideration in its own right for the first time but, also, the Board expanded the notion of 'abuse' to embrace a range of behaviour, attitudes and conditions that had hitherto only been considered separately. Thus, 'fraud,' 'wilful idleness', 'voluntary unemployment', 'restricted availability' and 'failure to maintain' were all brought under the single head of 'abuse'. The many-faceted character of 'abuse' gave the impression that the problem was almost endemic to the social security system.

Compared with present-day discussions, the treatment of the question of 'abuse' in 1957 seems almost an exercise in tolerance. By and large the Board's approach was consensual and moderate, but the question of 'abuse' was now on the agenda. In the longer term, its emergence was instrumental in subverting the very principle of social security. I have already pointed out how the powerful language of 'need' had begun to be transformed by essentially administrative procedures intent on restricting entitlements, now, however, welfare itself was in danger of being undermined. The ascendancy of the apparent problem of 'abuse' seemed to vindicate the arguments of those who had claimed that social security was a disincentive to work; it helped shift the focus away from difficult questions of poverty and social justice onto the rather simpler plane of dishonesty, 'desert' and right and wrong. Benefits were made to appear too generous and their administration too lax, the theory of the welfare 'burden' seemed justified.

In a crucial paragraph, the Board drew attention to its duties to the needy and the consequences that would befall should it fail them, but these vital duties were balanced by 'the Board's duty to safeguard public funds' (NAB *Annual Report*, 1957, p. 25). This was the first occasion on which the Board's responsibilities had been articulated in this fashion and, although at first sight the statement may seem fairly uncontroversial, it takes on a greater significance when considered in a broader political and economic context. Keynesian political economy, the broad framework within which the Beveridge Report had been sited, construed public expenditure in a positive light; the whole Beveridge package, for social policy, for full employment, and for voluntary action, had consisted of a positive framework of incentives. Now they were being shoved into reverse – 'safeguarding public funds' or protecting public expenditure was emerging as a priority. The problem of containing 'abuse' was assuming greater significance than the problem of meeting 'need' – or promoting the takeup of benefits. But maybe this is a little premature, after all, 'poverty' itself was rediscovered in the 1960s – but so was the 'scrounger'. No, in small, perhaps even trifling, ways the discourse of social security was turning. 'Abuse' had entered the frame, it proved to be the thin end of a very large wedge.

Having established the new 'duties of the Board', the increasingly 'defensive' and disciplinary social security administration went on to establish that the system was especially prone to forms of 'abuse'. The Board remarked how, 'National Assistance, like other systems of payments to meet need . . . can be the target of unscrupulous persons.' It argued that its officers were encouraged to be vigilant against abusers, but 'without imposing delay, hardship or indignity on the far greater number of honest and respectable persons'. It noted, however, that it was not easy to be helpful and watchful at the same time. Nevertheless, the public were assured that 'the Board believe that the officers have, on the whole, succeeded remarkably well in maintaining the right balance' (*ibid.*). By 1964, however, a rather more cautionary note was sounded. 'It is not easy to strike a balance between providing proper safeguards against offence and ensuring that urgent need is met without delay or undue formality' (NAB *Annual Report*, 1964, p.49).

This notion of 'balance' is interesting. In a legal sense a notion of 'balance' is often used when describing the relationship between parties to a dispute. In social policy we are sometimes presented with an alleged 'balance' between welfare and control. But the notion is both deceptive and inadequate. Deceptive because it implies some consensual arrangement of policy, inadequate because no balance is actually struck. In social security systems the concept can only refer to differing styles of administration; the relative deterrence of the claims control process, or the severity with which entitlements are assessed.

For a long time criminologists considered social security 'abuse' an essentially 'victimless' offence, no one specifically lost out when offenders remained undetected. In more recent times, the emergence of a specifically monetarist economic philosophy, underscored by Milton Friedman's dictum that 'there's no such thing as a free lunch', has implied that there is no such thing as a victimless fraud either. As a result, it has become increasingly easy to justify exceptional policy measures to safeguard the supposedly beleagured public purse. Yet if the 'balance' between prompt assessment of entitlements – meeting needs and upholding rights – and cross-checking 'abuses', is redrawn to emphasise the latter, claimants may suffer in very direct and immediate ways. If the policing of the poverty line becomes oppressive, few but the poorest will ever know about it. This is a very one-sided conception of balance.

In 1965, the National Assistance Board went some way towards acknowledging that harsh administration could lead to injustices, but still framed the issue in terms of a 'balance'. 'It will still be necessary to strike a fair balance', the Annual Report argued, 'between vigour and determination in the prevention of abuse and the avoidance of harshness in administration which could result in honest people preferring not to claim their entitlement' (NAB *Final Report*, 1965, p.x).

We ought not to leave this consideration of the framing of the 'abuse' question without noting the early form taken by that fictional paragon of virtue, later to become so important in the ideological discourse of social security, namely, the 'genuine claimant', that member of the 'general body of perfectly honest and straightforward' or 'honest and respectable' persons against whom all 'abusers' were defined. In 1957 it was considered improper to impose 'delay, hardship or indignity' upon this respectable majority of claimants. By 1964, however, it was acknowledged that it was difficult to contain abuse effectively without doing so. Times change. By the 1970s, the administration appeared to have become rather less discerning. 'It is inevitable that steps taken to prevent and detect abuse will involve some delays in dealing with claims and the subjection of honest claimants to some measure of cross questioning and investigation of their private lives' (Fisher Report, 1973, p. 10). Such delays and interrogations were deemed 'a price which has to be paid to avoid a greater evil'. In terms of the dynamics at work within the social security discourse, these admissions were critical. The rhetoric of 'abuse' was compromising the nominal 'rights' installed by the Beveridge 'revolution' and eating into the crucial language of 'needs' upon which so many of the assumptions of social security rested. Of course, this was precisely Enoch Powell's objective when he remarked, in 1972, that 'the translation of a need into a right is the most widespread and dangerous of modern heresies' (Powell, 1972, p. 12). For Beveridge, the 'great evil' had been want, though there were five 'giants' in all. The modern discourse on social security appeared to have installed a sixth, 'abuse', and it had somehow jumped to the head of the queue. The reverse dynamics unleashed by the contradictions and tensions of the Beveridge compromise were beginning to take effect.

From poverty to social pathology

The question of 'abuse' interacted with the negative economy of incentives developing in the post-war period producing a powerful blend of ideological concerns. In so doing, it undermined key features of the discourse of social security – especially the normative principle of 'need' and the ideal of welfare rights. The same was true of the emerging discourse of social pathology. Indeed, the advance of social pathology marked an assault upon the ideological significance of poverty in a capitalist society. Yet social pathology did not just minimise, or even individualise, the problem of poverty, rather it proceeded to deny it. Broad social processes were not considered responsible for particular manifestations of deprivation, instead these had to be sought in the make-up of the individual, in the functioning of the family or perhaps even in the character of the community.

In the supposedly affluent society of the post-war period the most tangible links between class structure and poverty, and poverty and crime were thought by many to have been broken. Even socialists were not immune from this assumption. In the absence of a neat callibration of 'social problems' along the supposed lines of class, a new series of 'explanations' of poverty and deprivation could rise more easily to the forefront. If the class structure no longer seemed to predict the incidence of poverty reliably, causes had to be sought in individual and situational factors. I do not have sufficient space here to review the emergence and full significance of this new discourse, (see Holman, 1978), but I must consider its impact upon notions of needs and rights in an increasingly disciplinary and defensive politics of social security.

Some advance notice of the new discourse can be found in Beveridge's confident assumption that the scope of means-tested national assistance would be fairly limited once full employment was achieved and the national insurance scheme operating. Henceforth, only individuals with particular needs would find themselves in poverty. These isolated individuals, or 'casualties of the welfare state' as they became known on occasion (Harvey, 1960), were looked upon as 'social inadequates' who failed to 'fit in'. It seemed that they were becoming rather more numerous, 'as the technical apparatus of life becomes more complex' (Longford, 1964).

In many respects the discourse on social pathology can be seen as a fairly direct descendant of the individualistic accounts of deviance and social deprivation pioneered in the 'total institutions' of the nineteenth century, only later emerging into the social field in the forms of social casework advanced by philanthropists. The combination of methods of classification and diagnosis led to the development of markedly more sophisticated analyses of deviance or deprivation emphasising individual characteristics, situational factors and defective social relations as the primary causes of poverty (see Cormack, 1945). A study written in the 1930s, 'The Social Problem Group', typical of a good deal of this work, presented a series of analyses which suggested that personal inadequacies and deficiencies rather than poverty were the principle causes of social disadvantage. Indeed, poverty seemed to be a factor of rather marginal relevance (Blacker, 1936).

This connection between social pathology and forms of supposed social inadequacy found widespread application in the 1950s and early 1960s concerning the question of the 'problem family'. Such families were frequently deemed 'problematic' as much by reference to personal or relational criteria as by reference to their poverty (see Philp and Timms, 1962; Hastings and Jay, 1965). The notion of the 'problem family', typically, stood upon the implied culpability of women as inadequate mothers (Holman, 1974, 1978; Ehrenreich and English, 1977). In turn, this notion provided a basis for launching many forms of disciplinary social intervention into the home, effectively policing the performance of women in their motherhood role. Not poverty, but 'inadequacy' was constituted as the problem, a description which effectively redefined the needs of the (female) parent. The general point is admirably made in Barbara Wootton's characterisation of the socio-pathological orientation of 1950s social work. Noting that 'much prominence has been given to the supposed disappearance of poverty from the list of urgent problems confronting the so-called "Welfare State" ', she went on to cite Penelope Hall's depiction of the apparently changing character of social problems:

> in the past, problems of poverty . . . were so pressing that reformers concentrated on them, whereas the most urgent problems which confront sociologists, social administrators and social workers today are such symptoms of a sick society as the increasing number of marriage breakdowns, the spread of juvenile delinquency, and the dissatisfactions and frustrations of the worker in spite of improved pay and conditions – that is, problems of psychological maladjustment rather than material need.
>
> (Hall, quoted in Wootton, 1959, p. 269)

It seemed, therefore, the mother's 'real needs' could not be met by material resources alone or, if they were, at least a rather more selective distribution was suggested. Instead, and above all else, social rehabilitation and a careful supervision of the mother's performance would be necessary. Furthermore, even the need for financial assistance could be taken as a sign of some deeper deficiency – for instance, the 1949 annual report of the National Assistance Board drew attention to the number of supposed 'problem families' receiving its assistance. Accordingly, the Board's officers were encouraged to co-operate with other workers 'in the field of maladjustment . . . by bringing to their notice the families who are in need of moral rehabilitation' (NAB *Annual Report*, 1949, p. 18). As I have already said, need provided a point of entry to the person or the family, it signalled the possibility of a deeper malaise. 'Material dissatisfactions [were interpreted] as pegs upon which to hang dissatisfactions with one's self or one's relationships' (Wootton, 1959, pp. 294–5). Ironically, therefore, in the very process of losing its privileged status as the foremost explanation for deprivation 'unmet need' came to play an increasingly important role as the means by which a network of disciplinary interventions was expanded. The significance of the supposed 'rediscovery of poverty' in the mid–1960s has to be seen in this light. The 'rediscovery' – or perhaps 'liberation' might be a better term – of poverty proved both functional and necessary. The revelation that large numbers of working-class families lived in conditions of marked deprivation and hardship, each household a separate case-study of misfortune, disadvantage and failure, unleashed a range of ascriptive pathological disciplines upon them. As poverty was relativised, so the disciplinary arena was extended. For the poorest, in the 'affluent society' of the 1960s, the alternative to the 'permissive family' was the disciplined family.

It was not simply in terms of a shifting politics of the family, however, that the pathological discourses and their entourage of disciplinary relations undermined the ideological significance of material 'need' and eroded the 'rights' and privileges of the social sphere (privacy and patriarchy). If we examine the inroads made by socio-pathological discourses in the fields of employment and labour discipline, we shall see that some equally significant developments were occurring here too.

Perhaps the most obvious descendants of the early twentieth-century socio-pathological discourses, and therefore the first characters upon whom the post-war socio-pathological disciplines obtained significant purchase, were those individuals typically described by the National Assistance Board as 'persons without a settled way of living'. These characters, formerly known as 'vagrants', 'tramps', 'ex-prisoners' or, collectively, as 'the residuum', were marked out for the NAB by virtue of 'some peculiarity of personality or a varying degree of mental unbalance'. Alternatively, it was their inability, 'to follow a normal way of life', or their tendency to 'drink heavily or have objectionable personal habits', which distinguished them (NAB *Annual Report*, 1960, p. 33). On another occasion, they were described as, 'men who have been unable to grapple with some personal problem or overcome a defect of character, or who are escaping from the responsibilities and disciplines of a settled life' (NAB *Annual Report*, 1962, p. 50). The Board's 1963 annual report made particular (and unusual) reference to the 'resettlement' of women, the occasion being the closure of the only centre catering exclusively for women. Otherwise, the 'resettlement' of women attracted relatively little comment. As I have said, the pathologies of women were typically confined, along with the women themselves, to the domestic sphere.

The problems posed by the pathological individuals who appeared to rely upon the social security system had preoccupied the NAB for some considerable time. Section two of the 1948 Act required the Board to 'promote' the well-being of persons in the exercise of its responsibilities. This duty appears to have been interpreted broadly. In 1949, the Board's reports began to feature a number of so-called 'welfare and rehabilitation cases'. The cases were accompanied by a commentary, drawn from a largely socio-pathological discourse detailing, in turn, the nature of the families' and individuals' problems and the action taken to resolve them. Taken together, the cases – all of which were 'success stories' – and the activities described in relation to those 'persons without a settled way of living', chart the limited, but generally 'positive', tone of the Board's work in the early years. An emphasis on 'welfare' and a particular vision of 'need' still prevailed.

Although perceived as a small minority, these 'welfare and rehabilitation' cases were still a problem and, even during the 1950s, a relatively growing problem. In 1955, amidst a context of full employment, it seemed that the continued existence of a 'hard core' of pathological individuals, many of whom seemed permanently dependent upon assistance benefits, had to be explained by reference to causes other than poverty.

> As the number of persons receiving assistance on account of unemployment declines, those who are handicapped and difficult to place in employment form an increasing proportion. This difficulty applies especially to those whose handicap takes the form of a mental instability of one kind or another, which is reflected in an unprepossessing appearance, eccentric conduct or an attitude of resentment to the world at large.
>
> (NAB *Annual Report*, 1955, p. 29)

The report continued, stressing the careful handling necessary to overcome such difficulties, which arose from a combination of serious personal handicaps and 'an unsatisfactory attitude towards employment'. Officers were reminded that, before invoking the penal sanctions provided by the 1948 Act, they should endeavour to use all their persuasive powers on any persons, who are 'to all appearances mentally and physically fit for work [but who] show signs of settling down to a life on assistance'.

Towards the end of the 1950s the NAB embarked upon a number of programmes designed to increase the pressure upon the long-term unemployed. As Deacon has argued, such initiatives reflect a growing concern about the problem of 'voluntary unemployment' at a time of particular sensitivity about any rises in the unemployment figures (Deacon, 1981). And of course, behind many such concerns lay a preoccupation with work incentives and the view that the Welfare State ought not to become too comfortable.

In the late 1950s, the 'voluntarily unemployed' and the 'workshy' were still considered a 'hard core' minority, and an explicitly socio-pathological language features prominently in descriptions of them. Nevertheless, by 1960, political pressures appear to have precipitated some rather more direct action against such men, 'whose continued unemployment is basically due to the absence of the will to work, if not a positive desire to avoid it'. However, the 1960 Report continued:

> men who are content with a life of idleness at the public expense are far from being a homogenous group and present several problems which are seldom capable of simple solution. They include men who make the most of some minor disability as an excuse for not working and others who have acquired a reputation for unreliability, possibly aggravated by a prison record. . . . The earlier that a man's inclination to idleness and the reason for it can be identified, the greater the chance of success in returning him to a working life. But diagnosis and treatment present very considerable difficulties.
>
> (NAB *Annual Report*, 1960, p. 27)

The work-incentives issue surfaced prominently in many of these discussions of the 'voluntarily unemployed'. Yet very often, those whose attitude to work was considered the most problematic were either unskilled, or suffering from certain disabilities – precisely the groups most likely to be found amongst the lowest paid. However, little attention was given to these underlying problems of poverty and low pay. Instead, the disciplinary pressure was maintained and, throughout the 1960s, many attempts were made to 'encourage' the pathologically 'workshy' into forms of employment. Yet even whilst the Board's officers were exhorted to be vigilant in preventing 'abuses' by the 'workshy', a broadly pathological language continued to be the principal frame of reference within which they were discussed and explained. The disciplinary discourses overlapped. The pathologically 'workshy' and 'voluntarily unemployed' were both morally (and legally) culpable yet, apparently, also subject to 'needs' more individually pressing than poverty – needs that it would be inappropriate to seek to solve through general redistribution. A more selective approach seemed to be called for.

As the 1960s wore on, the rising concern about 'abuse' seemed to precipitate more determined action with regard to the 'workshy' and 'voluntarily unemployed'. In the 1930s public assistance officers had been officially encouraged to keep a lookout for 'malingerers'; in the 1970s and 1980s 'fraud awareness' was to be the theme, but in the 1960s, NAB officers were given 'human relations training' in order to help them recognise the specific handicaps of the long-term unemployed and help them deal with their 'anti-social attitudes'. The Board denied that the object of the training was to encourage its officers 'to try to become amateur psychologists', but insisted that by gaining an understanding of the claimants' underlying problems the officers might be better equipped to do their jobs (NAB *Annual Report*, 1964, pp. 40–1).

In this guise, the human relations training appeared to be informed by many of the socio-pathological assumptions hitherto evident in the Board's 'rehabilitation' work. The long-term unemployed were seen as especially appropriate candidates for this form of assessment and a familiar repertoire of causes and symptoms, dignified by the title of 'evidence', is enlisted in support of the new 'unemployment review' techniques.

> Persons with employment difficulties often present problems in human relations. There is abundant evidence to show that long-term unemployment and frequent changes of job often cause, or are caused by, emotional problems. This is not to suggest that everyone with a poor work record has such problems, or that the Board's officers should feel debarred from taking a firm line with the man who has a disposition to avoid regular work when he is apparently quite capable of it. But officers have to be alive to the possibility that there may be . . . instability underlying such attitudes to work.
>
> (*ibid*. pp. 104–5)

In its final annual report, the Board recounted evidence from a range of surveys undertaken into the character of the long-term unemployed. It seemed keen to refute the opinion, becoming prevalent amongst a general public 'hearing about occasional flagrant cases of wilful idleness', that most of the long-term unemployed were 'workshys or layabouts sponging off the Welfare State'. However, the categories it employed were often ambiguous. Unemployment and deprivation certainly interacted with damaging psychological conditions, domestic stress, neglect and personality disorders, to produce a complex range of problematic symptoms, but the discourse of social pathology placed the underlying causes of unemployment upon the individual. 'Often unemployment is only one of a number of symptoms of a general inability to face up to life; other social and domestic problems are common among these men' (NAB *Annual Report*, 1965, p.vii).

Finally, the Board went on to summarise its work with the long-term unemployed in a fine vindication of its 'welfare role'. The diligent work of the NAB welfare officers, armed with their socio-pathological insights, their casework and their human-relations training, were, it claimed, making 'a valuable contribution to the alleviation of human misery'. And then, as if to justify the activity further, it added, 'it is at the same time yielding worthwhile savings in public expenditure' (*ibid.* p. vi). Subsequently, as we shall see, 'savings in public expenditure' became a particularly prominent yardstick in the politics of social security.

The 1966 Ministry of Social Security Act replaced the National Assistance Board with the Supplementary Benefits Commission, a body which, initially, continued to respond to problems of 'voluntary' and long-term unemployment along the lines established by its predecessor. Later the Commission began to develop more specialist responses to what it considered its more 'difficult' cases. In particular, motivated by the growing political pressure with respect to the question of 'abuse' as well as a concern to reduce the numbers of long-term unemployed, it embarked upon an expansion of 'unemployment review' activity. As Stevenson has acknowledged, this particular work originated in attempts to prevent 'abuse', even though the administration 'has long realised that a fair proportion of the so-called "workshy" have a variety of disabling psychological and social problems' (Stevenson, 1973, p. 78).

The fact that 'unemployment review' should perform both 'welfare' and 'control' functions so congruently, seems to underline the ideological significance of the socio-pathological discourses within the politics of social security. Poverty and unemployment were but symptoms; if claimants were abusive, fraudulent or unemployable, the causes of the difficulties in each case had to be traced back to the individual. From this perspective, clearer 'welfare rights' were no answer, 'inadequate' claimants were thought unlikely to be able to handle their affairs anyway and fraudulent claimants would simply see new rights as new temptations. Not 'rights' but individual discretion exercised by skilled officers was needed. And an appropriate package of care, control and financial support had to be tailored to the needs of each case. There was no ideological question of 'balance' involved, just a new mode of administration – disciplined surveillance. This was the solution to poverty suggested by social pathology.

The Supplementary Benefits Commission developed its more 'specialised' response to the pathologies of poverty with the appointment of a 'social work advisor' in 1968. At the time, unemployment was still rising as were concerns about 'abuse' and the 'workshy'. In an ill-founded attempt to allay public fears – fears substantially inflated by sections of the press – about 'spongers and layabouts' living an easy life at public expense, the Department of Health and Social Security initiated a number of 'abuse campaigns'. In the same month, the 'four-week rule' was introduced, ostensibly as a means of reviewing the job prospects and aspirations of the unemployed, but actually as a means of urging them off the unemployment register (Crossman, 1977, pp. 134–5, 148–9).

In this context, there occurred a change of emphasis in the 'unemployment review' function. As circumstances dictated, it assumed less and less a 'welfare' role and more a 'detective' role. According to Stevenson:

> In a period of full employment men receiving Supplementary Benefit are, in a sense, stigmatised from the outset as failures, [whereas] large scale unemployment blurs the distinctions and the least adequate in our society can camouflage themselves in the queue alongside the others.
>
> (Stevenson, 1973, p. 17)

Of course, if the supposed 'inadequate', the 'abusers', and the 'fraudulent' are presumed hidden amongst the mass, then the techniques of individualised surveillance and discipline must be applied to the mass with equal vigour in order to discover them. In which case, 'the Supplementary Benefits Commission is trapped between its responsibility to protect the public purse and to have regard for welfare' (*ibid*. p. 33). Stevenson went on to underline how the individualisation of care and control was necessary in the treatment of such 'difficult' claimants, 'some of whom must be described as the most inadequate in our society, some of whom are fraudulent, and some of whom are offensive' (*ibid*. p. 37).

This portrait of the pathological individualism of social security claimants was taken further still by Knight and West. They argued that:

> Taking more than average advantage of welfare payments, and neglecting welfare contributions are features which tend to be transmitted from father to son. In both older and younger generations of males the criminal minority contributes less while taking more than average from the welfare state. In so far as this reflects a social attitude communicated from father to son, it could be relevant to the transmission of associated delinquent tendencies. Judging from their claims to supplementary benefit, criminal groups have a high incidence of needy individuals.
>
> (Knight and West, 1977)

Such a conclusion connects criminality and deprivation, and 'abuse' and 'voluntary unemployment', with the personal inadequacies which poverty and 'need' are said to conceal. Consistent with socio-pathological perspectives, deviant traits are seen as either inheritable or attributable to deficient familial relationships. Furthermore, the whole dismal picture is connected to an implicitly negative vision of incentives, both in terms of incentives to work, and the broader economy of 'social' incentives which the Welfare State was once thought to promote. The emergence of such an assessment in 1977 was certainly no coincidence. In the context of steeply rising unemployment, and following one of the most pronounced bouts of 'scroungerphobia' ever encountered in post-war Britain, the New Right's analysis of the 'welfare burden' achieved increasing political prominence (see, for instance, Popay, 1977; Luckhaus, 1980; Golding and Middleton, 1982; A. Clarke, 1983).

I have tried to demonstrate that concerns about the long-term unemployed, about the 'workshy', the 'inadequate', the 'abusers' and the fraudulent are the product of a coherent matrix of ideological themes. Together, the issue of social security 'abuse' and the discourses of social pathology, formed a web of interlocking ideas which, in very detailed and practical ways, came to restructure a number of broad political debates central to the politics of welfare. From a proposal for eliminating want, meeting needs, promoting rights, and achieving a whole range of broadly 'social' aspirations through the positive economy of incentives which Beveridge hoped his plan might mobilise, a rather more 'anti-social' climate has emerged. Undoubtedly this transformation was partly engendered by the very tensions and contradictions in the Beveridge blueprint itself – to say nothing of the way it was implemented.

Yet these tensions and contradictions required something to activate them. Critics found the Achilles' heel of the post-war Welfare State in the 'abuse' question and the underlying belief that social security impeded work incentives. Furthermore, working through the very fabric of this Welfare State, its institutions, principles and political objectives, were a range of discourses with a powerfully 'anti-social' orientation to human well-being. These disciplinary discourses, originating in the nineteenth century's attempts to manage its problems of social, economic and political order and turned to use in its most austere institutions – prisons, factories, workhouses – found a new disciplinary licence in the new social order of welfare capitalism. Social democracy became host to the disciplinary Welfare State, overturning the positive dynamics of the, albeit limited, Beveridge 'revolution'. In the process, the political significance of poverty as the very basis of a structure of inequality and oppression was lost as poverty became individualised and reconstituted as personal dysfunction. The progressive dimensions of 'need' were distorted and reversed into their older, normative and pathological forms, while the nascent, positive and potentially liberating, concepts of 'right' were aborted. For the moment, the old disciplines had prevailed. 'Anti-social' policy.

7

Free markets, active citizens and 'anti-social' policies

Enterprise, ideology and modern needs

Despite its scepticism about specifically 'social' policies, one of the interesting, and undoubtedly significant, characteristics of the modern New Right has been its ability to present major changes of political and ideological direction in an increasingly 'social' discourse. Even more fascinating is the fact that the 'social' discourses are drawn upon as if they were fundamentally continuous with the past – that fudge and compromise past which Thatcherism has so often declared itself dead set against. No doubt there is an important political reason for moderating the rhetoric to suit the occasion, but the ability of the architects of New-Right policies to draw upon the 'social' discourses of a different time and a different political culture in order to advance their own programme, must raise a few questions, not least amongst which are those concerning the significance and integrity of the existing 'social' discourses. In the course of the chapter I want to draw upon four examples, two of a fairly immediate and explicit nature, and two of a more developmental character. Hence, the following discussions are primarily concerned to illuminate these ideological shifts and transformations in the composition of the discourses of 'the social'.

The first example stems from the Conservative government's 1985 White Paper, *Employment: The challenge for the nation* (HMSO 1985a). The issuing of the White Paper coincided with the highest levels of unemployment ever known in post-war Britain. The rapid increases in unemployment had come in the wake of the first Thatcher government's economic policies, in particular, the crucial 1981 budget. But the 1985 White Paper was the first government White Paper dealing specifically with questions of employment and labour market policies since 1944. This was the context, in which, on page 1, the White Paper began to outline its own New Right analysis of the problem of unemployment.

'The world of work is changing fast', it began. The older industrialised countries were finding it especially difficult to cope. 'Behind the statistics lies individual misery', it claimed, the consequences of which 'everyone [was] painfully aware . . . there is a nationwide consensus . . . everyone cares.' But, it went on, caring was not enough. 'There must be nationwide understanding . . . and nationwide action.' Having posed the problem in this way and embraced the care and concern, the national consensus, the misery and frustration, the need for understanding, the White Paper went on to insert its own particular understanding. 'Unemployment reflects our economy's failure to adjust to the circumstances and opportunities of today; to the changing pattern of consumer demand; to new competition from abroad; to innovation and technological development; and to world economic pressures.' Above all, the analysis emphasised responsiveness to the market. The bottom line was that:

> the key contribution of government in a free society is to do all it can to create a climate in which enterprise can flourish, above all by removing obstacles to the working of markets, especially the labour market. . . . In short, the Government must help set the framework for the nation's effort.

And then came the punch-line: 'The words of the 1944 White Paper on Employment Policy still hold good.' The undoubted irony, that a principle drawn from a policy document forty years old and embedded in an essentially social-democratic and Keynesian political economy was being utilised in support of an essentially New Right and monetarist programme by those who had already declared Keynesianism dead, must have delighted the architects of the 1985 policy. The words of the 1944 White Paper read.

> Employment cannot be created by Act of Parliament or by Government Action alone. Government policy will be directed to bringing about conditions favourable to the maintenance of a high level of employment. . . . But the success of the policy . . . will ultimately depend on the understanding and support of the community as a whole and especially upon the efforts of employers and workers in industry; for without a rising standard of industrial efficiency we cannot achieve a high level of employment combined with a rising standard of living.
>
> (HMSO, 1944, p. 3)

Clearly, this particular conception of the range of government activity reflected limits conceived in social democratic ideology. However, the 1944 White Paper's particular declaration came in the context of an attempt to justify the absence of a specific programme of proposed legislation to deal with unemployment once the war was over. Other post-war problems were to be the subject of legislation, but the efficiency and performance of the economy, and hence the levels of employment and standards of living, were thought to be less amenable – though certainly not immune – to government action and legislation. Again, these decisions were founded upon important ideological principles, but the difference is one of degree. Compared with the many problems of the post-war world unemployment seemed least likely to respond to legislation. Government action was not ruled out, rather, as the White Paper put it, 'government action alone' could not do it.

In contrast, the ideological principles staking out the proper limits of government activity in 1985 are somewhat more definitive, more absolute. A government's task is simply to set a framework, not to intervene. Moreover, consistent with the 'negative' visions of freedom embraced by neo-liberal philosophy, this framework is defined in negative terms, 'removing obstacles' to the free play of markets – 'especially the labour market' it adds, suggesting that this is where the real changes must take place. Furthermore, we should note how, once the framework was established, the government intended to take a back seat and allow 'the market' and 'enterprise' to play the active roles. Finally, it is worth noticing how, on occasion, 'the framework', for which the government considered itself primarily responsible, becomes merely a 'climate'; presumably an ideological climate, wherein we simply have to think differently about our objectives and aspirations and their solutions will begin to appear. Where the 1944 White Paper sought to develop a complex social and economic policy for difficult times, its successor simply declares a limit beyond which the state must not go. The 1985 White Paper begins as an economic policy document and ends as ideological exhortation. But what is to be gained by endeavouring to make the two documents appear ideologically compatible?

Before trying to answer this question, I want to draw upon the second example. It also derives from 1985, the Green Paper, *Reform of Social Security* (HMSO 1985b). It was prompted by the mounting rates of dependency upon means-tested benefits due partly to the rising proportion of elderly people in the population, and partly, as I have said, to the unprecedented levels of unemployment. Both factors are in turn compounded by the erosion of the contributory principle and by the relative value of contributory benefits and pensions. Huge numbers of people had become dependent upon Beveridge's 'less desirable' system of last resort – the means test.

The Green Paper began bluntly: 'The British social security system has lost its way.' Even so, it went on to elaborate some of the achieve-

ments of the system; it had helped raise the living standards of some
of the poorest people; it had provided a safety net against urgent need;
and it had improved the position of some of the most vulnerable groups
in the population. If all these claims were true, and if social security
really were this simple, they might serve as a reasonable minimum
definition of the objectives of a social security system. Yet, the paragraph continued, 'those achievements have to be weighed against a
number of other factors.' First and foremost among these 'other factors'
was cost. In the four decades since the end of the Second World War,
the cost of the social security system had risen rapidly and seemed set
to rise steeply during the next four decades. No explanation was provided for these increases; they were not placed in the context of population change and development or related to the comparative cost
of other government programmes. Furthermore, questions of income
redistribution or the issue of transfer payments seemed not to arise.
The Green Paper remained similarly silent on the hidden costs of the
'tax-allowance welfare state'.

Although it was alleged that, 'each new development in social security
since the War has been made for the best of motives', the consequences,
it seems, were complexity and confusion. The resources were not,
apparently, reaching the people who most needed them and the system
as a whole had become difficult to administer and 'at times impossible
for the public to understand'. Just as it had with the employment White
Paper, the government sought to use the social security Green Paper
to turn the difficulties facing the social security system to its own
ideological advantage. Thus, it said, problems had apparently become
so bad that our very understanding, 'of what the social security system
should be seeking to achieve [had become] obscured. Our responsibilities as individuals and collectively through the state have become ill-
defined.' In a sense, therefore, it was not social security that emerged
as the key problem, even its cost now begins to look more like a
symptom than a cause. Rather, the central difficulty looks as if it had
been ideological all along.

Here the Green Paper moves in to propose its own unique ideological
remedy. It declares that we must, above all, endeavour to 'define a
system which is founded on public understanding of the purposes and
workings of social security; which is more relevant to the needs of
today; and which is capable of meeting the demands of the next century'. Later, amidst its outline of the objectives which were to underlie
the 'reform', we were to discover that the 'needs of today' and the
'demands of the next century' were that particular brand of ideological-
ly-charged 'needs' which we have already encountered, namely 'genuine
needs'. Whereas principles of 'need' invariably form part of a normati-

ve/ideological discourse, any emphasis on the supposed 'genuineness' of a particular 'need' adds additional weight to the context in which the 'need' is said to emerge; to the processes by which it is identified and, above all, to the ideological role it is intended to perform. In this case, and consistent with the government's broader objectives, the social security system and the 'genuine needs' which it would henceforth acknowledge, had to be 'consistent with the government's overall objectives for the economy' and 'simpler to understand and easier to administer'. Evidently, 'modern needs' and 'future demands' were only likely to emerge in small, highly conditional and administratively convenient, portions.

In the context of these considerations, the Green Paper set out to refashion the new political environment that social security would have to inhabit. The first principle of the new ideological climate was that 'social security provision should be based on a clear understanding of the relative roles and responsibilities of the individual and the state'. It went on to insist that, 'social security is not a function of the state alone.' And then, drawing upon a phrase that had been common currency in 1942 and the immediate post-war period it stressed that the social security of the future would be based upon 'a partnership between the individual and the state – a system built on twin pillars'. There then followed a rather more forcefully stated version of a number of ideological themes that had first appeared in Beveridge's writing. As the 1985 Green Paper put it:

> Most people not only can but wish to make sensible provision for
> themselves. The organisation of social security should encourage that. It
> should respect the ability of the individual to make his own choices and
> to take responsibility for his own life. But at the same time it must
> recognise the responsibility of government to establish an underlying basis
> of provision on which we as individuals can build and on which we can rely
> in times of need.
>
> (*ibid.* para. 1.7)

In a remark seemingly dedicated to the New Right's liberal-individualist heritage, the next paragraph added, 'State provision has an important role in supporting and sustaining the individual; but it should not discourage self-reliance or stand in the way of individual provision and responsibility.' And then the message is neatly driven home. 'This was a central theme in the 1942 report of Sir William Beveridge.' To endorse the point, the Green Paper cited Beveridge's important claim (see Chapter 7) that, in organising security, the state 'should not stifle incentive, opportunity, responsibility . . . [and] should leave room and encouragement for voluntary action by each individual to provide more' (Beveridge, 1942, para. 9, pp. 6–7).

The 1985 Green Paper's observation is, of course, correct. We have already considered the vital significance of the incentives discourse in the ideological foundations of the Welfare State. The issue of incentives and personal responsibility was strong in the Beveridge Report, but it certainly was not the only one, nor did it always appear the most important. Yet in contrast to Beveridge's eloquent arguments for abolishing want and the multiple deprivations of poverty; for enhancing the meaning of citizenship as a social ideal through the establishment of a wider social policy and the guarantee of full employment, the 1985 Green Paper proposed individualism and a safety net. Beveridge's normative conceptions of 'need' were replaced by ideological conceptions of 'genuineness', and an incipient system of 'welfare rights' by an abstract 'consumerism'.

Continuing in this vein, the Green Paper argued that there had been a great many social changes since Beveridge's time. Noting the spread of home ownership, for instance – a development that the government's own 1980 Housing Act had recently done much to encourage – the Green Paper claimed, 'the ability of most people to make more of their own provision has substantially improved.' So the government's proposals were simply moving with the grain of public opinion; self-help and individualism were more than just an ideology – they appeared as a deeply-rooted aspect of our culture. Instead of establishing a social security system which, it claimed, would discourage thrift and undermine personal responsibility, impose a burden upon the community as a whole and leave an even bigger debt for future generations to finance, the government sought to draw a clear line between public and private responsibilities. Hence, the Green Paper acknowledged the importance of state provision, but sought 'to define its limits'.

Like the employment White Paper discussed earlier, the social security Green Paper is an ideological production. In a sense this is entirely familiar, all policy documents are ideological productions. But there is a marked increase in the intensity with which an explicit ideological commitment is deployed in the New Right's presentation of its proposals (see Alcock, 1988). Moreover, the documents are not just significant for their deployment of ideological commitments for, above all else, the reader is urged to recognise and strongly pressed to share these commitments. As Lonsdale and Byrne argue, 'the present government seems as much concerned with encouraging different values in relation to social security as with changing social security itself' (Lonsdale and Byrne, 1988, p. 163). At the same time, as in employment policies so in social security policies, we are reassured that the proposals are essentially continuous with the past, an endorsement of, rather than a break with, the 'social' principles that were presumed to underpin an essentially positive and progressive welfare ideal. However, as I have already made clear, there is rather less reassurance to be found in the past. Beveridge's idealism and a social democratic discourse are just one side of the story, the disciplinary practices evolving in their wake embody quite another set of principles and philosophies. In this sense, the terms of Esam, Good and Middleton's rejection of the ambitious claims set out in the Government's 1985 Green Paper were quite correct. The reform proposals were, first and foremost, 'a calculated attempt to exploit and intensify' the already divisive and disciplinary character of the social security system (Esam *et al.*, 1985, p. 138).

Before developing these political and ideological dimensions of the complex relationship being established by the New Right with an underlying ideology of 'the social', I must draw upon a third example. In a sense, this third example is more vital, it is more historical and thematic and, in several ways, serves to draw the others together.

'Invisible hands' and free markets: the limits of 'the social'

My third example of the transformations occurring within the discourses of 'the social', involves an examination of a number of the crucial antecedents of the modern New Right. In developing this theme I can begin in 1947, with Quintin Hogg's (later Lord Hailsham) neo-liberal reworking of the political economy of incentives I have already ascribed to the Keynes-Beveridge Welfare State. Somewhat opportunistically adopting the spirit of consensus, the language of incentives and the 'permissive' culture of social democracy, Hogg set out a case for the 'social' purposes of inequality.

> Rich and poor are united in a common brotherhood. . . . The incentive of inequality, if inequality corresponds to skill and energy is one of the main means whereby new wealth can be created. So far from it being the cause of poverty, Conservatives believe it demonstrable historically that the most decisive steps which have been taken in the past towards a higher standard of living for the mass of the people have in fact been taken as a result of this incentive operating in the minds of the few.
> (Hogg, 1947, cited in Conservative Political Centre, 1950, p. 137)

Hogg's discourse of incentives was similar to Beveridge's, but his was connected to a very different political project. Where Beveridge saw incentives as a nominally equal means of helping promote general well-being, collective solidarities and the abolition of poverty and destitution, Hogg's prescription elevated inequality itself into the driving seat of social progress. Beveridge's incentives were frequently founded upon essentially individual or familial desires and aspirations, but Hogg sought to emphasise that these were rooted in the competitive individualism of inequality rather than the 'altruistic' or complementary individualism of Beveridge's social democracy. Hogg's remark was an ambitious post-war effort to draft 'the social' into the service of capitalism; taking it out of the hands of the socialists and 'collectivists' and inserting it back into a comforting historical illusion that capitalism and social progress walked hand in hand. For instance, as Robbins noted, also in 1947:

> I am inclined to hold that the goal of progress lies in a direction different from that of over-all collectivism. . . . I prefer the diffused initiative and quasi-automatism which go, or can be made to go, with private property and the market. I believe that the loose institutions of individualism offer scope for the development of a way of life, more congenial to what most of us desire in our hearts.
>
> (Robbins, 1947, p. 81)

This was rather a bold statement, because it was noticeably out of step with many of the political sentiments of the time, but it was not alone and it connected to a substantial tradition which was not inclined to give up easily (See Scruton, 1980; Turner, 1986). Above all, however, it was Hayek, 'the man who kept the flame of *laissez-faire* individualism burning' (J. Clarke *et al.*, 1987, p. 123), whose work most forcefully asserted the vital importance of competition and the free market as the best available guarantors of societal well-being and 'true' 'social security'. (Indeed, Hayek's work is interesting for its reversion to the older conception of security – the security provided for the rich by private property and the market against the claims of the poor and dispossessed – which I outlined in the previous chapter.) Hayek certainly embraces a principle of common 'social' or 'societal' wealth and well-being, but he is emphatic that this can only be fostered and protected by the careful cultivation of the free market. His conception of government's role, therefore, is not unlike that developed in the 1985 White Paper on employment policy. He was against Beveridge's 'reluctant collectivism' and the 'creeping socialism' of the 1940s and stood for a tradition which insisted upon the apparent contradiction that only when the individual was fully individual could 'the social' become fully 'social' (see Hayek, 1944, pp. 42–3). Above all, only the capitalist free market would provide the increasing prosperity which might make it all possible.

Ditching the Beveridge framework and its ideological assumptions was very much the message of Curran's polemic in 1960. In phrases sometimes disturbingly close to those employed by Crosland four years earlier, he argued:

> Primary poverty has now almost disappeared . . . the Beveridge assumptions have governed our national outlook for a decade and a half. But there is nothing sacred or immutable about them. They postulate a Britain in which the great majority of citizens are too poor to provide for themselves. It is the business of Toryism to thrust that vision into the history books and to thrust the politics of poverty into the dustbin.
>
> (Curran, 1960)

If the politics of poverty were to be jettisoned, neo-liberals were only too keen to replace them with a concocted politics of affluence. In such a new political culture, poverty 'ceased to be a general case, and became a special case'. According to Galbraith, it is this which establishes the peculiarly modern, and marginal, character of modern poverty (Galbraith, 1958, p. 259). In the 'affluent society', 'welfare' came to assume a more and more secular and individualised form: the accumulation of more money, the consumption of more goods, the enjoyment of more leisure, more freedom, more 'experiences' (see Galbraith, 1958, Ch. 23). Ultimately, however, this emerging cult of self-development would generate the pathological, and frequently disciplinary, forms described at length by Lasch (Lasch, 1980).

So, while the Welfare State faced attack from beneath by the work incentives problem, by the 'abuse' question and by the erosion of the collectivist framework of 'needs' and 'rights' on which social security rested, at the same time, a pernicious ideology of affluence contrived to attack it from above. When conservatives and neo-liberals tried to link capitalism to the supposed desires and aspirations of the broad mass of people, they were seeking to detach the 'social' objectives of 'welfarism' from the Welfare State itself. They sought to connect these aspirations to new individualist dreams of domestic life and personal consumption, where 'do-it-yourself' would become less of a hobby and more of a political creed. The Welfare State had to be 'de-socialised' – or perhaps 'anti-socialised' might be the more appropriate term – while capitalism had to be given a 'social' face. Unfortunately, the policy sciences have frequently concentrated on only half of the battle.

Hayek may have been only one of a few to keep the lamp burning for the free market in the 1940s, but rising post-war affluence offered the proponents of the free market and a 'socially' responsible capitalism a little more ideological leeway. Full employment, social mobility, rising material standards of living and increased consumer spending soon began to generate aspirations that were to be quickly capitalised upon. As T. H. Marshall noted, in part, this reassessment of state welfare derived from the very success of the 'full employment' policy and the ensuing increase in the standard of living of the wage-earning classes. In effect, 'a system obsessed with the ideas of poverty and subsistence began to look out of place in a society enjoying the first fruits of a new prosperity' (Marshall, 1985, p. 95).

In 1956, Labour's Anthony Crosland had written that he doubted whether Britain was still a capitalist society (Crosland, 1964, p. 29); the following year found Macmillan claiming that the majority of British people had 'never had it so good', – a message that signalled that they might have had it even better if only private enterprise and the incentive of inequality were given free rein. On the surface, the political idealism of consensus and compromise still prevailed, but in the midst of this elusive regime a rather more markedly political connection was being drawn between capitalism, inequality and welfare under the guise of meritocracy. Even Butler, one of the celebrated figures of 'consensus' politics, sought to develop these meritocratic connections as early as 1954.

> Unless we allow men and women to rise as far as they may, and so allow our society to be served by what I describe as the richness of developed differences, we shall not have the means to earn our national living, let alone to afford a welfare state.
>
> (Butler, 1954, quoted in Eccleshall *et al.*, 1984, p. 107)

These sentiments sound deceptively similar to Beveridge, but are actually closer to Hogg. The Welfare State is posed as the dependant of society, the rather fortunate recipient of an over-large slice of the incomes of hard-working people. For Butler, the motive force of inequality, the freedom to rise 'as far as they may', may seem a small price to pay for a guarantee of welfare for the less able. Yet, of course, put like this, small wonder that most would aspire to the heights rather than the parsimonious guarantees at the base.

But it is not a thorough-going neo-liberal or emergent New-Right critique of state welfarism that I have in mind here. The crucial issue is the attempt to denigrate the welfare of the state and to present free-market individualism as the only true 'social' ideal. Although neo-liberals and politicians of a right-wing persuasion have some difficulty in accepting certain conceptions of 'society' (the 'social' sphere), even down to Margaret Thatcher's denial that society exists, a latent vision of 'social' order remains none the less implicit, even in the most rigid of neo-liberal analyses. For the neo-liberals society, or 'social' order, has a kind of consequential character. Whilst the market, guided by an 'invisible hand', emerges as a result of the myriad transactions undertaken by free individuals, society, or 'social order', emerges only as an accidental consequence of the mass of essentially self-interested actions of free people. 'Invisible hands', in the form of 'natural desires', patriotism – a natural love of one's country and distrust of 'aliens' – heterosexual desire, the bonds of family and friendship, ambition and personal advancement, religious faith and perhaps even 'common decency', are the only collective (barely 'social') bonds allowed. Only here and there is the 'visible' hand of the 'active citizen' or public altruism – itself merely the sign of a deeper personalist ethic – permitted an appearance. Nevertheless, upon these fragile, normative and essentialist foundations neo-liberalism rests an entire 'social' order. The irony is, of course, that the New Right deems this ordering of society more essentially 'social', more 'natural' and, above all, a more effective protector of individual and collective welfare than any Welfare State. Furthermore, according to Friedman, this holds true even though social policies are usually the work of 'men of good intentions and goodwill who wish to reform us' (Friedman, 1962, p. 201).

The important political corollary of such neo-liberal theory is the fact that, in the ideology of the New Right those incentives to personal achievement – inequality itself, patriarchy and imperialism, even biological determinism – all become the paradoxical benefactors of 'the social', the guarantors of true welfare. In more explicitly secular forms, this is precisely the message that neo-liberalism has been advancing since the 1950s. In 1957, for instance, Hollis argued for maintaining the relationship between the privileges of the class system and what he believed to be the 'general good' (Hollis, 1957). In a similar vein, according to Walker, Macmillan's great contribution to the development of a modern Conservative ideology was his insistence that 'unless capitalism could show sufficient social responsibility it could never win mass support' (Walker, quoted in Gamble, 1988, p. 151). Furthermore, in the context of a critique of the failings of the existing Welfare State, Joseph developed a similar line. Connecting the entire range of 'anti-social' discourses which had come to focus upon the shortcomings of state welfare, he argued, in the wake of the 'rediscovery of poverty', that the social security system, far from helping the poorest out of their poverty, was merely condemning them to struggle through it. 'Time and time again', he said, 'we have stressed our belief in competition, incentives and enterprise.' These, then, were to be the real principles of neo-liberal 'social' security. But – and this was the important point – he added that 'a competitive society could be a compassionate society' (Joseph, 1966, p. 7). Capitalism, it seems, could embrace a form of 'social' interest. Ultimately, the success of the neo-liberal, or New Right, political project would depend upon its ability to deepen and broaden these allegedly 'social' dimensions of capitalism.

Joseph returned to these themes in a book he wrote with Jonathan Sumption in 1979 as a polemic against equality. Society, they argued, was a congregation of autonomous individuals, having 'natural' characteristics which must be allowed to flourish. Noticeably, 'men are so constituted that it is natural for them to pursue private rather than public ends', and accordingly, 'the duty of governments is to accommodate themselves to this immutable fact about human nature.' Above all else, it appears that the true function of government is simply to 'avoid the inconveniences which attend the uncontrolled pursuit by private individuals of private ends'. That is to say, governments must not undermine competitiveness or ambition, rather, in Joseph and Sumption's words, merely prevent it from 'taking violent, fraudulent or anti-social forms' (Joseph and Sumption, 1979, pp. 100–1).

These extracts tell us a good deal. On the one hand they confirm that these isolated attributes – individualism, private ambition, competition, etc. – form the parameters of the neo-liberal idea of 'the social'. After all, it is the one true function of neo-liberal government to control the 'anti-social' aspects which these attributes of the free society occasionally display. On the other hand, the minimalist role of government is construed precisely in terms of fostering and encouraging those attributes and tendencies which are already deemed part and parcel of individual (and collective) character.

It transpires that, for Joseph and Sumption, the most 'anti-social' political culture of all, indeed, the 'greatest tyranny possible', is the political culture which, in the name of equality and fraternity, denies and frustrates the talents and ambitions of individuals, 'for no better reason than that the talents are resented by those who do not have them' (Joseph and Sumption, 1979, p. 125). Wrongly postulating liberty and equality as alternatives, Joseph and Sumption reiterate a theme which had achieved some prominence in the early 1950s when conservatives and neo-liberals were first beginning to mount a sustained critique of state welfare. As Lord Denning claimed in *The Times* in 1953, 'welfare [was] breeding selfishness and ingratitude among the people' (Denning, quoted in Golding and Middleton, 1982, p. 228). Easy come, easy go, the misplaced charity of social welfare was corrupting the ethic of self-help and hard work. The 'compulsory altruism' of the taxpayer was no substitute for free enterprise and personal initiative and the 'social' virtues which would 'naturally' flow from this optimal, yet entirely fortuitous, arrangement of public affairs. As Joseph and Sumption were to conclude in their book – perhaps echoing something of the 1944 White Paper on employment – 'fraternity . . . cannot be created by Act of Parliament' (Joseph and Sumption, 1979, p. 121).

For the neo-liberal New Right, this is precisely the point: neither 'welfare' nor 'social justice' can be created by Act of Parliament. All that government *can* do is, in effect, what it *should* do: set the framework within which enterprise can prosper and individualism flourish. In the view of the New Right, this is the limit of 'the social'. It provides the ideological key both to the crucial policy documents issued by the Thatcher government in 1985, which I have already discussed, as well as to the gathering assault upon the ideal of the Welfare State by the advocates of the free market. The critics of state welfare sought to establish a political myth regarding the underlying continuity of their own proposals for the 1980s with the founding principles of the 1940s. Yet, at the same time, they sought to contaminate the broad ambitions of post-war welfarism and undermine the actual institutions and policies of the Welfare State. They were partially successful in both their aims because they incorporated very selective elements of the ideological discourse of the 1940s drawn, as we have seen, from the Beveridge Report and the 1944 employment White Paper. Furthermore, the potent ideological critique of collectivism, which was voiced initially by Hayek, Robbins and Hogg in the 1940s, gathered pace and influence between the 1950s and 1970s. It facilitated the neo-liberals' gradual adoption, on behalf of capitalism and the market, of the progressive 'social' idealism of affluence. In turn, this new idealism began to take its toll upon the Welfare State.

This critique, drawing upon the restricted series of neo-liberal ideological themes already considered, implied that the Welfare State could never be an expression of any real or meaningful conception of 'the social', still less the protector of individual well-being. Rather, 'welfarism' became a means by which the state extended a clumsy grip on society as a whole. The public sector was henceforth redefined by the New Right as the home of control, queues and coercion; of means-tests and state supervision; of ill-fitting National Health spectacles and overcrowded classrooms; of barrack-like council estates with few amenities and high-rise blocks with broken lifts; of buses that were often late, town halls ignorant of choice and impervious to criticism and bureaucracies as paternalistic as anything the Victorian philanthropists might have created. Ultimately, this is a vision of 'welfare Fordism' floundering when confronted with the immense variety of the modern social order. An image of society is constructed wherein the need for welfare no longer marks the attainment, but rather the tarnishing, of an ideal of citizenship, where welfare signals not the strength and vitality of a political order but its virtual collapse. In this light, the imagery of public welfarism referred to the problems of the past not the needs of the present and the future. In stark opposition to this, the authors of the 1985 social security Green Paper declared themselves committed to tackling 'the needs of today . . . and the demands of the future' (HMSO, 1985b, para. 1.4).

In a similar vein, though from a quite different perspective, the following remark by Martin Jacques suggests a great deal about the shifting destiny of 'the social'. In an assessment of the politics of welfare in the late 1980s, he claimed that:

> while the Left remains profoundly wedded to the past, to 1945, to the old social democratic order, to the priorities of Keynes and Beveridge, the Right has glimpsed the future and ran with it. . . . It is the Right which now appears modern, radical, innovative and brimming with ideas about the future.
>
> (Jacques, 1988)

And, we might add, it is now the New Right which, in many respects, is endeavouring to cultivate the more profoundly 'social' vision of the future. The private sector purports to be the real home of 'the social', the arena where opportunities are unfolded and ambitions fulfilled and, thanks to the expansion of mass advertising, the market is the place where 'social' aspirations are first formed. Bauman's work underlines this point, to many people 'politics is boring'. The public sector's 'social' vision 'does not supply the stuff of people's dreams, self-definitions and life-plans'. People are, where possible, buying themselves out, and are unwilling to invest their energies in the regeneration of a collective 'social' vision. Depoliticisation is the result, a process all the more advanced in the most developed Western capitalist societies (Bauman, 1988).

Nevertheless, it is a flawed and incomplete vision of 'the social' which is fashioned in New Right ideology, for it embraces aspirations which are both exclusive and divisive, competitive and coercive. In this sense, the New Right's discourse of 'the social' and its vision of welfare are indeed handed down from 1945. But whilst the principles of 1945, in their positive conception of incentives, their limited advocacy in favour of meeting 'needs' and even their halting progress towards the idea of a 'right' to welfare, articulated a plan for the subsistence of individuals with a strategic vision of the welfare of all, the neo-liberal alternative simply replaced both with a 'framework' for innovation and competition, and a 'climate' for the enterprising and successful.

In this neo-liberal 'framework' there are strict limits to the role of the state, and meeting needs through social security takes second place to economic growth. The practical implications of this new political order were made plain by Patrick Jenkin, Minister for Social Security, in 1981 when he said, 'if you believe economic salvation can only be achieved by rewarding success and the national income is not increasing, then you have no alternative but to make the unsuccessful poorer' (Jenkin, quoted in Donnison, 1981).

For the New Right, therefore, achieving this neo-liberal vision of a minimalist 'social' order called for a major exercise in ideological reconditioning – and herein lies the critical significance of the two 1985 policy statements – indeed of the whole thrust of the New Right programme since 1979. The 'obstacles' to the working of markets, to which the 1985 employment White Paper referred, were 'social' obstacles: employees' rights – the right to work, rights at work (rights to strike, to form trade unions, etc.), acknowledgements, however partial, of workers' needs (minimum wage legislation, social security benefits, health care, assistance with housing costs, pension provisions, etc.) – in sum, the scattered traces of a 'social' policy. The idea of removing such 'obstacles' in order to allow the 'free play' of market forces arose as the logical outcome of a profoundly authoritarian and 'anti-social' philosophy and, as suggested by Jenkin, involved the construction of a markedly 'anti-social' policy.

Even as early as 1980, Stuart Hall had begun to outline the gathering power of this new authoritarianism and its 'anti-social' implications. Noting that, despite constant erosion by governments of both left and right, the principle of the Welfare State remained, 'until recently, tattered but intact', he continued:

> The Welfare State entailed a major, substantive redefinition and expansion of social rights at the core of the 'social contract'. . . . The foundation of 'welfare rights' gave a new definition and content to the concept of 'the citizen'. Nevertheless, we have witnessed . . . a steady undermining of the philosophy of welfare rights . . . a critical area of social rights has become progressively vulnerable, not only to economic erosion and regressive social doctrines, but to what can only be described as ideological subversion.
>
> (Hall, 1980, pp. 5–6)

Central to this process of ideological subversion has been the distortion of the social democratic discourses on 'needs', the abrogation of 'rights' and the dismantling of civil liberties. Many examples might immediately spring to mind: the restrictions placed upon needs and rights through the introduction of the Social Fund in the 1986 Social Security Act, the restrictions placed upon rights of public protest under the 1986 Public Order Act, the rights lost under the 1981 British Nationality Act, the curtailment of maternity rights and successive attempts to restrict a woman's right to choose abortion, the rights lost and the needs disregarded as a result of the gradual emasculation of the wages councils, the democratic rights lost as a result of the establishment of selected urban development corporations and the subsequent abolition of the metropolitan county councils; the introduction, in flagrant disregard of equity, social justice or ability to pay, of the community charge (or poll-tax), the contribution made by Section 28 of the 1988 Local Government Act to the climate of hatred and contempt faced by homosexuals, finally, the 'removal' of the 'right to silence' in Northern Ireland and the broadcasting ban imposed upon Sinn Fein. The list could go on (see Hewitt, 1982; Hillyard and Percy-Smith, 1988; Thornton, 1989).

In fact, reaction to what has been seen as a gradual erosion of civil liberties in the United Kingdom led to the formation of 'Charter 88', a campaign organisation seeking the establishment of a Bill of Rights and a written constitution (see Barnett *et al.*, 1988).

Within the arena of 'welfare', one of the more interesting and significant outcomes of this gradual erosion of rights is the emergence into the limelight of the figure of the 'genuine claimant'. I have already alluded briefly to this character in Chapter 6. When discussion of social security turned to questions of 'abuse' – and it often did in the 1960s and 1970s – the 'genuine claimant' invariably put in an appearance. The 'genuine claimant' was a kind of alter ego to the 'scrounger', a character fabricated to serve an important ideological purpose in debate about social security. Whenever the proponents of greater departmental vigilance in the distribution of benefits were moved to speak, they invariably enlisted the help of the 'genuine claimant'.

The fabrication of the 'genuine claimant'

At the outset, perhaps it is worth stating the obvious: the 'genuine claimant' is no more and no less than a modern counterpart of that paragon of Victorian virtue, the 'deserving poor'. Different socio-political discourses and normative frameworks construct each character but the underlying ideological effects are similar. I mentioned the 'genuine claimant' in Chapter 6 in the course of a discussion of the ideological significance of the notion of 'genuine needs'. Obviously only 'genuine claimants' have 'genuine needs'; the important question is how it is possible to make such distinctions. The adjective 'genuine' somehow compromises and devalues the principle of 'need' whilst raising profound questions about the integrity of claimants. As early as 1952, the National Assistance Board had spotlighted the question of 'genuine need' (see Chapter 6); the same year it alluded to the ideal of the 'genuine claimant'. Underlining the Victorian connection, the Board noted that 'a few undeserving applicants . . . take advantage of the provision made for people in genuine need' (NAB *Annual Report*, 1952, p.15).

The language of 'genuineness' shaded into the politics and ideology of social security more and more clearly between the late 1950s and the mid–1970s. The explicit moralism gradually disappeared; later the 'voluntarism' inferred by the growing emphasis upon 'workshyness' and voluntary unemployment went the same way and a seemingly more rigid distinction between 'fraudulent' and 'genuine' installed itself. At the same time, commentators drew attention to an apparently increasing conflict of interests between the two categories of claimants. It seemed more and more legitimate (even necessary) to delay, inconvenience or even intimidate the 'genuine claimant', provided the 'fraudulent' was apprehended. In this way political commentary and administrative practice constantly overlapped and reinforced one another. It seemed that 'genuineness' might be discerned more or less directly by reference to a fixed standpoint – a stated 'right' to benefit, or a fixed (and allowable) notion of need. Recognising this helps us locate the birth of the 'genuine claimant' more precisely.

When the Labour government passed the Ministry of Social Security Act in 1966, it did so, as a number of commentators have argued, largely to improve the image of social security. The Act was very much an exercise in calling the same things by different names (Kincaid, 1973). The means test was to be known as a 'test of requirements' and 'entitlement' was supposed to give a wholly new and positive gloss to 'need', a 'right to welfare' was being emphasised and the 'genuine' were to be invited to come forward and make their claims (see Field, 1982). Yet these new concepts were, ultimately, no less disciplinary or divisive than their predecessors. Divisions between the 'genuine' and others are created by the very structure and operation of the social security scheme. Subsequently, such divisions are reinforced by the mechanisms designed to police social security operations. Even the first annual report of the new Supplementary Benefits Commission (SBC) reiterated this, albeit in moderate tones. 'There are bound to be some . . . exploiting the social services', it argued, 'but the vast majority for whom the Supplementary Benefit scheme caters are people in difficulty and genuine need' (SBC *Annual Report*, 1966, p. 36).

Only three years later, the Secretary of State for Social Services put a similar point rather more abruptly. As he saw it, the central task facing his department was one of, 'sorting out the genuine applicants, who really need help, from the scroungers' (Ennals, quoted in Page, 1971, p. 102). In this instance, something of the role of the 'genuine' becomes quite clear. On the one hand, they feature prominently whenever more severe methods of policing the benefits system are proposed

– for this was precisely what Ennals intended in 1969. On the other hand, they are promoted whenever a more subtle invasion of the social-democratic discourses on 'need' is contemplated. Nevertheless, there was nothing subtle about Robin Page's claim, in 1971, that 'anyone unversed in the complexities of present-day sociology would not be capable of finding poverty, let alone recognising it' (*ibid.* p. 126).

Robin Page's book, *The Benefits Racket*, a supposed exposé of the corrupt world of social security, put forward a case for a more restrictive social security system, for creating more categories, each subjected to appropriate modes of discipline, into which the poor could be slotted. It appeared in the midst of one of the first 'scrounger' scares of the 1970s and at the same time as Boyson made his attempt, in *Down with the Poor* (Boyson, 1971), to outline the damaging impact of the Welfare State on the moral fibre of the nation and almost a decade before the divisive strategies of the Thatcher regime began to emerge. Page's book is little more than a right-wing tirade against state welfare. In it he argued for more discrimination within the social security system; as he put it, 'certainly the *genuine poor* should receive all the help and support they can get; but if it was realised in 1553 that there were different classes of poor, why do we not recognise that in 1970?' (Page, 1971, p. 60, note that Page was not suggesting that the 'genuine poor' should receive all that they need).

Thus, Page introduced the 'genuine poor' to his readers as alleged evidence of a major flaw at the heart of the social security system. The 'genuine' became the silent 'moral majority', whose supposed attributes constitute a virtually unattainable ideal for anyone forced into dependence upon social security benefits. Most important of all, they function as the silent but perpetual reminder of the supposed shortcomings of all other claimants. In this fashion, the imputed interests of the 'genuine' are even co-opted to strengthen the case for intensifying the claims control process. For instance, as Robert McCrindle MP put it, speaking in the House of Commons in 1980 to endorse the decision to deploy an additional 1,050 social security investigators:

> While warmly welcoming the appointment of additional Social Security inspectors – which is at least as much supported by genuine claimants as by anyone else – will my right honourable friend take this opportunity to repeat that he has given instructions to move gently and slowly with those who are likely to be genuine claimants, before attempting to detect the perpetrators of fraud.
>
> (*Hansard*, 25 March 1980, Col.1157)

Apart from what such a remark – along with the Rayner Survey's invention, the 'potentially genuine claimant' (Rayner Report,

DE/DHSS, 1981, p. 63) – suggests about an implicit shift in the burden of guilt, McCrindle's comment also demonstrates the way in which the social division mobilised by the ideal of 'genuineness' is utilised politically. Similar issues arise within the 1973 Fisher Report. Measures to combat the fraudulent 'might very well lead to delays and frustration for the vast majority of genuine claimants', but they were, nevertheless, 'a price which has to be paid to avoid a greater evil' (HMSO, 1973, p. 10).

This supposed relation between the 'genuine' and the rest was developed in the wake of the 1980 Social Security Acts. The stated objective of the Social Security (No. 1) Act had been to eliminate the discretionary basis of large areas of the supplementary benefits system and replace it with a rigorous system of specific rights and entitlements with regulations itemising each and every 'allowable need' available. Of course, entitlements drafted stringently and administered in a manner designed to deter claims could well come to resemble disentitlements. The more tightly the net was drawn around those who were allowed access to benefits, the more people it excluded. The Social Security (No. 2) Act, 1980, set the tone of the legislation by penalising strikers by removing a sum of money (initially £12) that the government deemed they were receiving in the form of strike pay. The money was deducted whether or not strike pay was actually being received – an 'obstacle' to the operation of the free market was thereby removed. The government followed the Acts by launching a 'campaign against fraud and abuse' during 1980–1. Defending the campaign, the Secretary of State argued that the emphasis of the reformed social security system had been on 'entitlement', adding that 'it seems likely that genuine claimants will be readier to take up their entitlement without feeling tarnished by association with the dishonest' (Patrick Jenkin, House of Commons Statement, Hansard, 6 May 1981, paras 15–16).

Finally, the 'genuine claimant' turned up in a document issued to the fraud investigators of the Department of Health and Social Security, *The Fraud Investigator's Guide*. The Guide was emphatic that 'fraud work' was an integral part of the social security system: 'We have to pay benefit to the right people and avoid paying it to the wrong ones. Neglect of this second task can discredit the scheme and work against the interests of genuine claimants.' It added, 'though your work may mean that a high proportion of the people you deal with are cheats, the department has millions of honest claimants' (DHSS, 1978 revised 1980, paras 8–9). Nevertheless, it was the Rayner Report itself which made the most expressly political connection between 'policing' the benefit system, redefining 'genuine need' and containing public expenditure in its observation that 'if ways could be found to reduce substantially the loss of benefit through fraudulent claims, and some of the gain was redistributed to genuine claimants, all sorts of policy options would unfold for Ministers' (Rayner Report, DE/DHSS, 1981, p. 63).

So the tale of the 'genuine claimant' is undoubtedly a story of the evolution of underlying preoccupations in the history of social security, but it is also a story about welfare, needs and rights being backed into a corner. The more intensively that governments have policed the poverty line the more vehemently have they asserted that they did so in the interests of 'genuine claimants'. Nevertheless, in a political climate increasingly intolerant of the supposed 'burden' of welfare, the more persistent that successive governments became in their efforts to distinguish the 'genuine' from the rest, the more difficult it became to be a 'genuine' claimant. While the new framework of entitlements installed following the 'legalisation of welfare' in 1980 (see Allbeson and Smith, 1983) might, at first glance, have seemed to be introducing firmer 'rights' in return for a rather more circumscribed range of 'needs', no such trade-off occurred in practice. Rather, in the context of a deliberately cultivated atmosphere of 'fraud awareness', under-resourced administration and, apparently, increasing political indifference to problems of poverty, the new framework of entitlements assumed an increasingly restrictive, discriminating and outwardly 'anti-social' character.

As Stevenson has noted, in the transition to more precise determinations of 'entitlement', 'there may be a new kind of injustice, in which the individual finds there is no rule to fit his own case' (Stevenson, 1973, p. 26). Titmuss referred to this kind of inflexibility, where 'needs' are subordinated to closed bureaucratic rules, as the 'pathology of legalism' (Titmuss, 1971). And Stevenson added a rather prophetic note; commenting, in 1973, upon the interaction between a strict focus upon 'entitlement' and a prohibitive political climate for welfare, she argued that the British supplementary benefits scheme had so far avoided the worst excesses of restrictive legalism. But she went on to add that it 'could easily be driven into this position if its administration came under mounting attack' (Stevenson, 1973, p. 27). As the political pressure on the social security system increased towards the end of the decade, her prediction proved all too accurate. In a deepening climate of 'fraud awareness', the politics of disentitlement came of age.

In these ways, an ideology of the 'genuine claimant' retained its political utility. However stringently and inadequately the regulations governing entitlement redrafted the map of modern needs, they facilitated the evolution of a more and more restrictive definition of 'genuineness'. Ultimately, 'genuineness' rather than 'need' became important – that is to say, the circumstances out of which the needs arose and the processes by which needs were determined, assumed a greater significance than the needs themselves. For instance, regulations restricted the level of benefit payable for accommodation, irrespective of the actual cost of accommodation; or, if benefit had been allocated to cover a particular 'need', nothing further would be payable even if the 'need' persisted; or, confusingly, items for which lump-sum payments had been made would be 'deemed to exist' even if they no longer did, and sums of money would be 'deemed to exist' even though they may have already been spent. In the field of housing, homelessness would not constitute a priority need if the homelessness was considered to be 'intentional', and so the list goes on.

However, having detached one concept of 'need' from considerations of social security organisation, the government proceeded to replace it with another. Out went a conception of 'need' rooted in a nominally 'social' and collectivist discourse, and in came one more firmly planted in neo-liberalism. The arguments surfacing in May 1989, following the Secretary of State's attempt to deny the extent and significance of poverty in the United Kingdom, centred precisely upon this point. While at the DHSS, Norman Fowler had consistently argued the case for a more restrictive 'targeting' of benefits onto the 'really needy'. 'Our aim must be to move . . . towards a system that will allow people to keep more of their own money and enable the state to concentrate its help on those who really need it' (Fowler, 1984, quoted in Ward, 1985, p. 3). The obvious implication behind the idea of concentrating help on 'those who really need it' is that there are others who do not need help or need it rather less. Selectivity was the key. In his notorious attack upon the ideology of the British poverty lobby, John Moore developed the neo-liberal case. 'In the 1960s', he argued, 'poverty was not "rediscovered" it was *redefined*' (Moore, 1989). There is an important point to Moore's attack but, in fact, he had it the wrong way around. The so-called 'rediscovery' of poverty in the 1960s involved an extension of a 'social' and collective concept of poverty – admittedly a rather problematic concept – already outlined in the Beveridge Report. If poverty were being redefined, it was Mr Moore and his colleagues and predecessors who were doing the redefining. By squeezing the idea of poverty back into a simple, absolute and quantifiable shell, the New Right was seeking to deny the 'social' character of contemporary needs and to reassert instead the principles of the free market.

In this harsh light, the 'really needy', the 'genuine claimants', were those who could not help themselves in any way. All the rest would have to help themselves (see for instance, Boyson, 1971; Minford, 1987). And following a legislative process which began with the publication of the 1985 Green Paper on Social Security (considered earlier), these ideas began to insinuate themselves more and more deeply into the politics of welfare – amidst calls for a more selective benefit system, a tightening-up on eligibility and, above all, 'better targeting' of benefits. As we have seen, all such proposals had been long-standing political priorities for the neo-liberals. Coinciding with these, the discourse of the 'genuine claimant' provided support to the delusion, which had been the staple diet of right-wing ideologies of welfare since the mid–1940s (see Miller and Wood, 1982), that an over-generous social security system was holding the nation's future prosperity to ransom.

'Anti-social' policies and the disciplinary state

Above all, the New-Right ideology of welfare and its reconstituted discourse of 'the social' and 'social' order has permitted the evolution of a significantly different role for the state. As Gamble emphatically shows, retrenchment in the field of public welfare is not associated with the diminution of state activity but with the development of new forms of state activity (Gamble, 1988). And Hillyard and Percy-Smith have detailed the emergence of the 'coercive state' in Britain, its resort to more and more authoritarian forms of intervention and its increasing tendency to undermine the rights and freedoms of social democracy (Hillyard and Percy-Smith, 1988).

In many respects, the dislocation of 'social' modes of disciplining from the public sector to the market sector, has left the state free to play a more explicitly coercive role in a number of critical areas. Despite the narrow and increasingly myopic visions of welfare afforded within the newly stripped-down and privatised discourse of 'the social', the state has assumed a more and more explicitly coercive series of roles with respect to the management of need and a more and more restrictive protection of rights. This is apparent in many areas of 'social' policy although, for my immediate purposes, many explicit examples can be unearthed in the field of social security.

Perhaps the most striking example of the deterrent character of the new politics of social security was the infamous 'Operation Major', mounted jointly by Thames Valley Police and the DHSS Regional Fraud Squads. A phony benefit office was set up in a school building in Oxford and a large number of claimants living in lodging-houses in the city were invited to attend for interviews. As they entered the Office they were arrested by plain-clothes police officers disguised as claimants. In all, 283 claimants were arrested and confined in 'secured' classrooms for up to ten hours before being charged or released. One hundred people were released without charge, twenty more were subsequently found to be not guilty. Of the remainder who were found guilty, some 137 received custodial sentences, although many had already spent a considerable time incarcerated because they had no fixed address (see Franey, 1982 for a full account of the incident).

These few details provide only the briefest outline of Operation Major, but its significance cuts very deeply into modern ideologies of welfare. Operation Major is significant, above all, for what it said about the needs, rights or social worth of anyone who might have reason to visit a social security office in the 1980s. People who had accompanied friends to the phony office were arrested along with the claimants themselves; claimants who turned up simply to make enquiries were arrested. No one was allowed to leave the office for fear that they might alert others and thereby remove the element of surprise. Operation Major was a form of blanket injustice that spoke volumes about the new coerciveness at the heart of ideologies of social security.

Attempts to instate a uniformly deterrent pressure within the Department of Health and Social Security gathered pace following the official cultivation of what became known as 'an atmosphere of fraud awareness' during the mid–1970s. Increasingly claimants faced suspicion and distrust and later they had to contend with the investigations of the Specialist Claims Control teams in the DHSS and the Regional Benefit Investigation teams in the Department of Employment. The two departments were adamant that their new claims control and investigation teams were not merely trawling through random samples of claimants in order to pressurise them into withdrawing their claims. Nevertheless, the criteria they employed in order to identify the 'suspicious' cases certainly had a rather random look. They included: cases where the claimants concerned had 'a marketable skill or trade' or 'a record of self-employment', cases where claimants had 'a significant money-earning occupation which could nevertheless be followed on a casual or spare-time basis', cases where 'current unemployment has lasted for more than four months'. On the one hand, cases where claimants seemed to have 'a suspiciously high standard of living' were to be drawn to the attention of the claims control teams, but so too were cases where there was current debt. Better still, 'apparent good health and fitness' or, in the case of female claimants, 'signs of a male presence' would be enough to draw the attention of the investigators (SCC Internal Memo, DHSS, 19 January 1981).

Having selected their targets, the investigators subjected them to what was called a 'non-prosecution interview'. Despite express instructions to the effect that investigators were not to make 'deals' with claimants (a guarantee of non-prosecution in return for withdrawing a claim) a growing body of evidence seemed to suggest that this was precisely what was happening (see P. Moore, 1981). Furthermore, the specific objectives of the new techniques, namely general deterrence and cost-effectiveness, strongly suggest that convenience weighed rather more heavily than rights and due process. Following the introduction of similar procedures into the Department of Employment in 1983, David Hencke noted that the new procedures required 'not so much the dogged pursuit of evidence looked for in normal fraud work but a lightness of touch in being able to confront claimants with a few suspicions which will lead the suspect either to declare work or otherwise leave the register' (*Guardian*, 9 August 1983; for a fuller discussion of Specialist Claims Control and the non-prosecution strategy outlined in the revised *Fraud Investigator's Guide*, see Squires, 1984, vol. 2, and Cook, 1989).

Many further instances of the increasingly coercive twist taken by social security policies can be found in the gradual erosion of the contributory principle, long believed to form the heart of the British social security system. Following the 1981 Rayner Report (which I have already discussed), the 'availability-for-work' test was intensified. Subsequently, more detailed interviews and questionnaires administered by staff at job centres were introduced in order to apply pressure by 'testing' claimants' availability for work – or in order to encourage them to sign off. After 1986, following the introduction of the Restart programme, the longer-term unemployed were subjected to similar six-monthly interviews. Failure to attend the interview or responses to questions indicating 'unsatisfactory' attitudes to work could result in the withdrawal of benefits. 1989 saw the reintroduction of a test not dissimilar to the 'genuinely-seeking-work' test of the 1920s. The government became increasingly convinced that large numbers of unemployed people were no longer pursuing employment with appropriate vigour and a White Paper, *Employment in the 1990s* (HMSO 1988), argued the case for an 'availability test' which required that claimants demonstrate that they were 'actively seeking work' – a requirement which both shifts and increases the burden of proof. The new requirement was incorporated in the 1989 Social Security Act, though little guidance was provided as to how a claimant might satisfactorily demonstrate his or her 'active' search for work.

Corresponding to both of the above changes, the period of benefit disqualification for 'voluntary unemployment' – leaving work without good cause, placing 'unreasonable' restrictions upon availability or not 'actively seeking' work – has undergone two significant increases in its duration and a major extension of its scope of application. In 1986 the period of disqualification was increased from six to thirteen weeks and, only eighteen months later, further increased to twenty-six weeks (see

Byrne and Jacobs, 1988). The extension in scope now implies that the disqualification conditions apply with similar rigour to all aspects of the Youth Training Scheme which has, in effect, become compulsory. (For a very useful review of these developments see Wikeley, 1989). The combined effect of these changes strongly suggests that the British model of unemployment insurance has moved considerably closer to the American 'workfare' model (see Digby, 1989, pp. 113–4).

A further important example of the disciplinary state's relative neglect of needs and rights is provided by the introduction, in 1988, of the Social Fund, following the 1986 Social Security Act. The Social Fund was set up in order to remove the complicated administrative burden of single payments and urgent-needs payments from the reformed Income Support scheme; it also sought to contain the growth of social security expenditure which had occurred under these headings. To this end, Social Fund budgets were cash-limited and the bulk of Social Fund expenditure was envisaged to take the form of repayable loans. Despite the rhetoric about 'targeting help on the most needy', the neediest of all – those with existing debts – were specifically excluded from applying. Furthermore, the right to appeal against a local office decision was abolished for claims to the Social Fund; rights therefore, were being eliminated and concepts of need pushed into a tighter and tighter corner.

Finally, even the briefest overview of the social politics of the disciplinary state cannot afford to overlook the significance of the introduction of the community charge, or poll tax and, in particular, its interaction with the benefit system. It is not simply the disingenuous egalitarianism of the poll tax, or the further constraints it imposes upon local democracy and financial accountability which mark out its regressive character. Furthermore, neither the threats to civil liberties implicit in the interchange of personal data nor the punitive powers introduced to ensure compliance, exhaust its coercive potential. Above all, the 'anti-social' character of the whole scheme lies in the powerful reinforcement it gives to patterns of inequality, in the demands it makes upon the resources of many of the poorest people in defiance of the evidence of need and inability to pay, and in the way it compromises individual freedoms by subjecting more and more people – especially those reliant upon state provision – 'to greater bureaucracy and a diminution of rights.' (see Esam and Oppenheim, 1989). In the wake of a more severely 'targeted' and deterrent benefit system and a more and more regressive system of taxation, the community charge is destined only to exacerbate the consequences of the powerful dynamics of inequality operating throughout the new modes of state intervention. But, of course, the incentive of inequality is the key to the New Right's world view, the minimal foundation upon which its threadbare vision of a neo-liberal 'social' order has to rest.

Conclusion I: in praise of Good Samaritans

In the course of a speech she made to the Conservative Political Centre in 1983, Mrs Thatcher used one of her biblical references in order to make the point that prosperity was a precondition of welfare. 'Even the Good Samaritan had to have the money to help', she said, 'otherwise he too would have had to pass on the other side' (Wappshott and Brock, 1983, p. 278). On a later occasion it was St Paul's dictum, 'If a man shall not work he shall not eat' (from his Letter to the Thessalonians), which prompted Mrs Thatcher to observe that, 'abundance rather than poverty has a legitimacy which derives from the very nature of creation' (Thatcher, 1988).

Clearly Mrs Thatcher's intention in using these biblical extracts in her speeches is to suggest that there is a moral, or even a spiritual, foundation for liberalism and capitalism. Early in her speech to the Scottish Assembly, she had said: 'Most Christians would regard it as their personal Christian duty to help their fellow men and women. . . . These duties come not from any secular legislation passed by Parliament, but from being a Christian.' she went on to say that such duties 'stem not from the social but from the spiritual side of our lives' (*ibid.*). To Mrs Thatcher, 'the social', implied a spurious ideal of solidarity and responsibility, whereas the claims of spirituality and individualism are presented as somehow more real and immediate; more concrete.

Like Sir Keith Joseph, cited earlier as saying that 'fraternity cannot be created by Act of Parliament', Mrs Thatcher, and many other advocates of the New Right, are denying that a government should be responsible for social welfare and are seeking to place responsibility on the shoulders of individuals. There is no place, in their scheme of things, for collectivism, for the Welfare State, or for a public sector. According to the capitalist ethic, individual effort, hard work and personal thrift are the best guarantees of welfare and the last resting place of 'the social'. John Moore, rounding upon his detractors in the poverty lobby, expressed the point in rather more secular and emphatic terms than the Prime Minister.

> It is capitalism that has wiped out the stark want of Dickensian Britain. It is capitalism that has caused the steady improvements in living standards throughout this century. And it is capitalism which is the only firm

guarantee of still better living standards for our children and our grandchildren.

(Moore, 1989)

Welfare and happiness will only emerge from the free interaction of responsible individuals. From Mrs Thatcher's standpoint, 'any society which is not founded upon the acceptance of individual responsibility will do nothing but harm' (Thatcher, 1988). The effect of such phrases is to narrow the basis of 'the social' and erase any conception of the *common welfare* almost entirely; there is only individual welfare and an aggregation of individual welfares. As Leadbeater has put it, 'for Thatcherism society is constituted by individuals: it is nothing other than a set of human atoms. . . . Individuals are not intrinsically social, their characters, resources, abilities are not formed in a social setting.' Society is merely the site where people strive for their predetermined individual satisfactions. Furthermore, 'people co-operate for purely instrumental reasons, to achieve their chosen ends more efficiently' (Leadbeater, 1988).

When in the hands of the state, 'the social' is denounced; it is both contrived and artificial; it is a force for evil. The New Right offers people the opportunity to free themselves literally, as Bauman has argued, to buy themselves out from this kind of politics. 'Politics is not where you invest your hopes. Life is elsewhere. Politics is a nuisance. The less of it the better. . . . Thatcherism has promoted freedom as the right not to be bothered by public affairs' (Bauman, 1988, pp. 37–8). And after all, exponents of market liberalism had spent the best part of four decades yearning for the free relations of the market, denigrating the false security afforded by the Welfare State even as, in office, they sought to incapacitate it and undermine its ability to deliver real security. From the neo-liberal viewpoint, simply allowing 'the social' to emerge naturally from the free relations of the market, from individual conscience and the 'organic' institutions of society, would make it appear pure and untrammelled – stripped of its older collectivist inhibitions and coercive power no doubt – and no longer the means by which the state swelled beyond its legitimate bounds. Rather – and this is the crucial point – 'the social' would collapse in upon itself. It would, quite literally, implode into the space of 'the personal'. This would have several consequences.

On the one hand, 'the social' would cease to have any meaning other than that of some aggregate of personal desires. On the other hand, the forces which hitherto had played a significant role in constructing 'the social' would shift their emphasis to the realm of personal desires. I have already discussed the construction of 'the social' but, of course, individuality and personal desire are no less fabricated entities, as my review of the evolution of the 'genuine claimant' has revealed. If so mundane a character as the trapped, barely visible and overwhelmingly *ordinary* dependant of the state can be the recipient of so much ideological effort, how much more ideological effort will all manner of consumers – owner-occupiers, motorists, holiday-makers, etc. – receive from the advertisers who are anxious to depict the exciting lifestyles of the young, affluent, glamorous or famous?

Of course, if capitalism and the market are established after all as the mainspring of progress and welfare – ideals which were often intrinsic to the ideology of 'the social' – then it follows that capitalism and the market will have acquired much of the resonance and legitimacy that the idea of 'the social' once conveyed. Though it is not quite the same ideology of 'the social'; in its earlier statist and collectivist manifestations it stood for a normative and disciplinary mode of order, for planning, for intervention and determinate 'social' objectives. In its new manifestation it stands for the exclusive discipline of the marketplace. Capitalism is 'social' because it appears natural, organic, inevitable, rooted upon basic individual aspirations and desires, steeped in individual preferences – the 'real world' of consumer demand. The paradox is that no sooner is the integrating rationale of 'the social' displaced from the arena of the Welfare State and the public sector, than it shifts to decorate each and every facet of the neo-liberal universe.

When we enter this new universe we emerge into a new 'social' landscape and are confronted daily by its images of personal achievement and its mirages of progress, wealth and well-being – private affluence – but everywhere we turn we are haunted by its opposite – public squalor. The paradox of late capitalist affluence runs deep, however, as Hirsch has acknowledged. 'Contemporary capitalism generates a tension between aspirations widely shared' – the new dreams of 'the social' – and 'opportunities which . . . remain restricted and unequally distributed' – the 'anti-social' consequences – (Hirsch, 1977, p. 110).

Nevertheless, these ambiguous new discourses of 'the social', steeped in the language of the market, emanate from every medium of communication and encircle us. The dissonant chatter of a distorted and fragmenting 'social' discourse rushes out at us from the television screen and entices us from the printed page; in the streets it stares at us from shop windows and billboards demanding our attention; even in the gutter, as litter, it diverts us. In the shopping arcades and supermarkets it has a captive audience and can be more persistent. Explicitly here, implicitly there, these scattered images of a new kind of privatised 'social' discourse tempt us to consume, beseech us to join, persuade us to experience, invite us to become. It is as if we only become 'social' beings in our own most private moments or in our individual relationship to the market; for instance when we are at home, within the 'family', or driving our cars, when checking our bank balances or spending our money, during our leisure time or having sex. Only when pursuing these activities do we correspond most closely to the predominant images of the fabricated modern individual generated by the culture industries and endlessly repeated throughout the advertising media. The image is generally of someone who is white, culture- and gender-specific and invariably Western and middle-class. Such minimalist conceptions of 'the social' are all that remain of a moral order in the neo-liberal universe.

With the right jobs, credit cards, cars and homes, – and the correct attitudes – we are assured that the world is our oyster. Without them, however, it is quite a different story. The sub-plot to the neo-liberal vision is one in which racism and sexism, poverty and powerlessness, violence and isolation are familiar or even routine. The dynamic inequalities, the regressive political economy of incentives and the competitive individualism which define the contours of a modern ideology of 'the social' imply that the increasing opportunities of the few are necessarily bought at the expense of the many.

In the ascendant social democracy of the first half of the twentieth century, collectivist strategies of normalisation, mobilised through 'the social' sought to ensnare almost everyone – admittedly the networks of discipline were more or less coercive depending on rank and social virtue, colour or gender – now, however, the 'socialised' market simply beckons to everyone, but its glittering symbols of success are attainable by rather fewer. In fact, as we have seen, the new dynamics of 'the social' are rather more exclusive and divisive than inclusive (see Golding, 1986). And the state has come to assume a more precisely disciplinary role alongside the market order, in the process exacerbating the division of welfare, heightening inequalities and forcing acceptance of an increasingly individualised version of the future.

Whilst social democracy undoubtedly represented a uniquely disciplinary political culture, in the era of the Welfare State coercion and social division were tempered by principles of a different, more 'social', order. Welfare certainly had significance as a means to economic regeneration and political stability but it sponsored discourses and ideals with a life of their own. Amongst the most powerful were the languages of 'rights' and principles of need. But it is no use pretending that these concepts were the entirety of 'the social', far from it. Even these fragments of a progressive political discourse have their origins in a uniquely normative and disciplinary politics. Yet they were 'social' none the less, they had a place in a political economy of welfare that stretched far beyond the horizons of individual choice and personal preference.

Hijacked by the New Right, the ideology of 'the social' is mostly just that – an ideology. It serves as an ideological veneer for a range of activities which have individuals, families, corporations or economies as their ultimate beneficiaries but eschew any attempt to construct broader 'social' loyalties which acknowledge needs and value rights. In this respect, the new 'private' constructions of 'the social' turn out to be fundamentally 'anti-social' in their broadest and most enduring implications. The capitalist market's 'social' ideals of individualism, consumerism and personal choice are frequently achieved only in the face of the most blatantly 'anti-social' consequences. For instance, the celebration of affluence and economic revival by a succession of government ministers hardly conceals the fact that the numbers on or around the poverty line have grown dramatically in the past decade and that the gap between rich and poor continues to widen; the virulent ideology of owner occupation cannot hide the fact that there are more and more homeless people in towns and cities throughout the country; the developed world's production and consumption seems increasingly irresponsible in the light of its impact upon the Third World and the environment; the unrestricted use of private cars has led to increasing urban congestion and battles over the despoliation of countryside and community. Finally, the ideology of economic growth itself, for long so central to neo-liberal, social democratic and, not least, socialist political agendas, poses fundamental questions about the sustainability of the competitive individualism of the lifestyles of international capitalism (Hirsch, 1977; Ryle, 1988).

Conclusion II: new times – new 'social' movements?

Only in scattered and isolated roles do fragments of our 'social' selves manifest themselves, but they may be the raw material from which a new political culture will emerge, the moral and political resistance, often submerged, ridiculed or overwhelmed, out of which a sustainable democratic future giving prominence to needs, rights, and both collective and individual welfare might evolve. These fragments emerge during the course of conflicts and confrontations which still populate the 'social' spaces of the consumerised society. In this respect another series of transformations, weaving in and around the discourses of 'the social', might be discerned alongside those already considered. Formed in the same contexts, mobilised by the same forces and even embracing many of the new realities, these new 'social' movements are rather more subversive of the dominant political culture and its ideologies of progress. New modes of domination generate their own new forms of subjectivity and of resistance.

Even though, as Laclau and Mouffe have argued, 'there is practically no domain of individual or collective life which escapes capitalist relations' and 'the individual is subordinated to capital through his or her incorporation into a multitude of social relations: culture, free time, illness, education, sex and even death', this does not spell the complete obliteration of new 'social' aspirations extending beyond the realm of the private and personal (Laclau and Mouffe, 1985, p. 161). On the contrary, the violent dispersal of new discourses of individuality and new worlds of subjectivity, style and personal desire are already fuelling new radicalisms. What is being destroyed with the dislocation of the older normative and disciplinary orders of social democracy is the bureaucratic centralism, state collectivism or 'welfare-Fordism', which froze the patriarchy, imperialism, and hierarchy of the nineteenth century into the 'social' principles of the Welfare State. The explosive fragmentation of this conception of 'the social' throughout the consumer culture of market society may serve to liberate politics from the narrow tramlines of the public sector and reconstitute the entire field of lifestyles and well-being as issues of political concern.

> What has been exploded is the idea and the reality itself of a unique space of constitution of the political. What we are witnessing is a politicisation far more radical than any we have known in the past, because it tends to dissolve the distinction between the private and the public . . . [leading to a] proliferation of radically new and different political spaces.
>
> (*ibid*. p. 181)

Much the same political transformations are signposted by the calls for a new democratic politics recently emerging from sections of the political 'Left' in Europe and the United States (see for instance, Keane, 1984 and 1988; Hall, 1988 and 1988b; Hobsbawm, 1988; Hall and Held, 1989) and the re-emergence of a debate centring upon the ideals of a new 'democratic citizenship'. The pursuit of this debate goes beyond the scope of this book though it allows the reiteration of a point made by way of introduction and at the beginning of this chapter. There may be hidden potential within 'the social', or there may be new 'social' visions emerging to take its place.

If the corrosive ideals of neo-liberalism and the contaminating imperialism of the market have consigned an older normative and disciplinary conception of 'the social' to 'the dustbin of history', in the fractious new world of the market, new antagonisms, generating new 'social' movements, may still emerge. Despite the hostile divisions and fragmented loyalties imposed by the market, new solidarities can still form themselves in the midst of the disciplinary society and in the face of the coercive state. Whether as prisoners or claimants, customers or clients, the 'dependants' of the older 'social' modes of public welfare and the 'consumers' of the new are, in many ways and many contexts, able to discover a new sense of political equivalence amongst themselves. Whether confronting prison authorities, reacting against police and state, protesting against social security cuts or the closure of nursery schools or hospitals, or mobilising communities against bulldozers, people have shown both a willingness and an ability to piece together a new 'social' idealism. For instance, in the face of the Aids panic and ideological repression under 'Section 28' a new gay politics has asserted itself. And even the institutions and processes of mass communication – supreme examples of one-dimensional ideological technology, which have done so much to disrupt the political realms of the 'social' age – can, if handled carefully, serve in the reconstruction of a new vision. Live Aid and the 'Free Mandela' concert might begin to suggest something of the possibilities here (see Hebdige, 1989).

Ironically perhaps, even the most retrograde political initiative of recent years, the community charge or poll tax, imposes its own authoritarian construction of equivalent individualism upon the entire adult population. In the computer programmes of the community charge, we all stand as legally responsible and financially obliged, *citizens*. And even the 'active citizens' of Thatcherism, have rights. The New Right's suggestion that the first instinct of the 'active citizen' ought not to be to make demands upon the state may well rebound with a vengeance. It may be that the more active the citizen becomes, the more demands he or she will make. Thus, when Bauman describes Thatcherism as part of an effort to promote the exit of human concerns from politics, he is effectively describing the transformation of a type of politics.

The demands made by the newer 'active citizens' are unlikely to be 'claims'; that is to say, they will be unlikely to be formulated in the older normative discourses of need inherited from the 1940s, but will, if they are to challenge the disciplinary legacy of 'the social', be assertions of a right. The new politics will not centre upon the disciplinary 'social' democracy of the Welfare State but upon the radical democracy of a form of political equivalence boldly enunciated by Marx and Engels in the *Communist Manifesto*: 'the free development of each should be the condition for the free development of all' (Marx and Engels, 1967 edition, p. 105). More contemporaneously, Hall and Held have put it as follows:

the politics of citizenship today must come to terms with, and attempt to strike a new balance between, the individual and the social dimensions of citizenship rights. These two aspects are interdependent and cannot be separated. Neither, on its own, will suffice. On the other hand, there is no necessary contradiction between them.

As Walzer has suggested, this would imply that we should break with the old normative idealism embodied in collectivist and universal concepts of 'the social' and think in terms of the pluralist frameworks of a 'complex equality' (Walzer, 1983). To attain this ideal, 'it is necessary to broaden the domain of the exercise of democratic rights beyond the limited traditional field of citizenship.' The new language of rights must exceed the 'classic political domain' and break into the economy, the society and the domains of the personal and private (see Laclau and Mouffe, 1985, p. 185, and Hall and Held, 1989).

In prefiguring these alternatives to the predominantly 'anti-social' policy which has so far been our political inheritance, my concern has simply been to caution against any sense of despair which might have associated itself with an analysis of the evolution of the disciplinary state. We are not on an inevitable one-way journey to the police state, the prison society or a new 'social' totalitarianism. In fact, much of the original potency may have already drained from an older style of 'social' reformism, which has now been swept aside by a 'universal logic of the market' (Hebdige, 1989). Nevertheless, we should certainly not become complacent about the political authoritarianism of recent times – not least because the 'anti-social' policies it has sponsored have all but destroyed the protective features of an older form of 'the social' entirely. This destruction of an earlier collectivist discourse and its substitution by a limited ideal of competitive individualism (but still clothed in an ideology of 'the social') concerning only the desires of a few, is of no small significance – precisely because of its neglect of the welfare and democratic rights of the many. Even so, the radical energies and aspirations set in motion by the new politics may still be sufficient to confront the 'strong states' and private powers presently engaged in safeguarding the unequal relationships of the 'free economy' – even as the competition for scarce resources intensifies.

References

Abel-Smith, B. (1980) 'The Welfare State: Breaking the post-war consensus', *Political Quarterly*, vol. 51, pp. 17–23.

Alcock, P. (1988), 'A better partnership between state and individual provision: Social security into the 1990s', *Journal of Law and Society* vol. 16, no. 1, pp. 97–111.

Allbeson, J. and Smith, R. (1983) *We Don't Give Clothing Grants Any More: The 1980 supplementary benefit scheme*, Child Poverty Action Group, London.

Anderson, M. (1976), 'Sociological history and the working-class family', *Social History*, vol. 1, no. 3.

Annette, J. (1979) 'Bentham's fear of hobgoblins: Law, political economy and social discipline', in National Deviancy Conference/Conference of Socialist Economists (eds) *Capitalism and the Rule of Law*, Hutchinson, London.

Ashforth, D. (1976) 'The urban Poor Law', in D. Fraser (ed.) *The New Poor Law in the Nineteenth Century*, Macmillan, London.

Atkinson, A. B. (1974) *The Economics of Inequality*, Oxford University Press, Oxford.

Bahmueller, C. F. (1981) *The National Charity Company: Jeremy Bentham's silent revolution*, University of California Press, Berkeley and Los Angeles.

Barker, M. (1981) *The New Racism*, Junction Books, London.

Barker, R. (1984) 'The Fabian state', in B. Pimlott (ed.) *Fabian Essays in Socialist Thought*, Heinemann, for the Fabian Society, London.

Barnett, A. (1982) *Iron Britannia: Why parliament waged its Falklands War*, Allison & Busby, London.

Barnett, A. (1988) 'Charter 88', *New Statesman and Society* December 2.

Barrett, M. and McIntosh, M. (1982) *The Anti-Social Family*, Verso, London.

Barry, N. (1983) 'Review article: The new liberalism', *British Journal of Political Science* vol. 13, pp. 93–123.

Barry, N. (1987a) *The New Right*, Croom Helm, London.

Barry, N. (1987b) 'Understanding the market', in M. Loney *et al.* (eds) *The State or the Market*, Sage, London and New York.

Bauman, Z. (1982) *Memories of Class*, Routledge & Kegan Paul, London and Boston, Mass.

Bauman, Z. (1988) 'Britain's exit from politics', *New Statesman and Society* July 29.

Bell, D. (1960) *The End of Ideology*, Collier-Macmillan, New York.

Berg, M. (1980) *The Machinery Question and the Making of Political Economy: 1785–1848*, Cambridge University Press, Cambridge.

Berman, M. (1986) *All That is Solid Melts into Air*, Verso, London and New York.

Beveridge, W. (1909) *Unemployment: A problem of industry*, Longman, London, reprinted 1930.

Beveridge, W. (1942) (The Beveridge Report) *see under* HMSO.

Beveridge, W. (1944) *Full Employment in a Free Society*, Allen & Unwin, London.

Beveridge, W. (1948) *Voluntary Action*, Allen & Unwin, London.

Blacker, C. P. (1936) *The Social Problem Group*, Oxford University Press, London.

Blaug, M. (1963) 'The myth of the Old Poor Law and the making of the New', *Journal of Economic History*, XXIV.

Booth, C. (1902) *Life and Labour of the People in London*, vol. 1, Macmillan, London.

Booth, W. (1890) *In Darkest England and the Way Out*, Knight, London (introduced by E. Wickberg).

Borchorst, A. and Siim, B. (1987) 'Women and the advanced Welfare State – A new kind of patriarchal power', in A. Showstack-Sassoon (ed.) *Women and the State*, Hutchinson, London.

Bosanquet, B. (1902) *Aspects of the Social Problem*, Macmillan, London.

Bosanquet, B. (1909) 'The Reports of the Poor Law Commission: The Majority Report', *Sociological Review*, vol. 2, pp. 109–26.

Boulding, K. (1967) 'The boundaries of social policy', *Social Work*, vol. 12.

Boyson, R. (ed.) (1971) *Down With The Poor*, Churchill Press, London.

Bridges, L. (1975) 'The Ministry of Internal Security: British urban social policy, 1968–74', *Race and Class*, vol. XVI, no. 4, pp. 375–86.

Brown, J. (1968) 'Charles Booth and the Labour Colonies: 1889–1905', *Economic History Review*, vol. XXI.

Brundage, A. (1978) *The Making of the New Poor Law 1832–39*, Hutchinson, London.

Burman, S. (ed.) (1978) *Fit Work for Women*, Croom Helm, London.

Burton, F. and Carlen, P. (1979) *Official Discourse: Discourse analysis, government publications, ideology and the state*, Routledge & Kegan Paul, London.

Byrne, D. and Jacobs, J. (1988) *Disqualified from Benefit*, Low Pay Unit, London.

Campbell, T. (1983) *The Left and Rights*, Routledge & Kegan Paul, London and Boston, Mass.

Centre for Contemporary Cultural Studies (CCCS) (1982) *The Empire Strikes Back*, Hutchinson, London.

Chance, W. (1895) *The Better Administration of the Poor Laws*, Swann Sonnenschein & Co., London.

Checkland, S. G. and Checkland, E. O. (eds) (1974) *The Poor Law Report of 1834*, Penguin, Harmondsworth.

Churchill, W. S. (1909) 'Notes on malingering', *Churchill Papers*, D.026. 6 June.

Clarke, A. (1983) 'Prejudice, ignorance and panic: Popular politics in a land fit for scroungers', in M. Loney, D. Boswell and J. Clarke (eds) *Social Policy and Social Welfare*, Open University Press, Milton Keynes.

Clarke, J., Cochrane, A. and Smart, C. (1987) *Ideologies of Welfare: From dreams to disillusion*, Hutchinson, London.

Clarke, P. (1978) *Liberals and Social Democrats*, Cambridge University Press, Cambridge.

Clayton, P. (1981) *The Cohabitation Guide*, Wildwood Press, London.

Cohen, S. (1985) 'Anti-Semitism, immigration controls and the Welfare State', *Critical Social Policy*, no. 13, Summer, pp. 73–92.

Colledge, D. and Field, J. (1983) 'To recondition human material: An account of a British labour camp in the 1930s', *History Workshop Journal*, no. 15, pp. 152–66.

Collie, J. (1913) *Malingering and Feigned Sickness*, Edward Arnold, London.

Conservative Political Centre (1950) *Conservatism 1945–50*, London.

Cook, D. (1989) *Rich Law, Poor Law: Different responses to tax and supplementary benefit fraud*, Open University Press, Milton Keynes and Philadelphia.

Cormack, U. M. (1945) 'Developments in casework', in A. F. C. Bourdillon (ed.) *Voluntary Social Services and their Place in the Modern World*, Methuen, London.

Corrigan, P. (1975) 'State formation and moral regulation in the nineteenth century', Ph.D. Thesis, University of Durham.

Cousins, M. and Hussain, A. (1984) *Michel Foucault*, Macmillan, London.

Creighton, C. (1980) 'Family, property and relations of production in Western Europe', *Economy and Society*, vol. 9, no. 2, pp. 129–67.

Crosland, C. A. R. (1964) *The Future of Socialism*, Jonathan Cape, London, first published 1956.

Crossman, R. H. S. (1977) *The Crossman Diaries*, vol. III, Hamish Hamilton and Jonathan Cape, London.

Crowther, M. A. (1978) 'The later years of the workhouse: 1890–1929', in P. Thane (ed.) *The Origins of British Social Policy*, Croom Helm, London.

Crowther, M. A. (1981) *The Workhouse System 1834–1929*, Batsford Academic, London.

Cullen, M. J. (1975) *The Statistical Movement in Early Modern Britain*, Harvester Wheatsheaf, Hemel Hempstead.

Curran, C. (1960) 'Forward from Beveridge', *Crossbow*, Autumn, pp. 25–6.

Cutler, T. Williams, J. and Williams, K. (1987) *Keynes, Beveridge and Beyond*, Routledge & Kegan Paul, London and New York.

DE/DHSS, (1981) *Payment of Benefits to Unemployed People*, London. (The Rayner Report).

DHSS, (1978) *The Fraud Investigator's Guide*, London, (revised 1980).

Davin, A. (1978) 'Imperialism and motherhood', *History Workshop Journal*, no. 5, pp. 9–65.

Davis, J. (1980) 'The London garotting panic of 1862: A moral panic and the creation of a criminal class in mid-Victorian England', in V. Gatrell *et al. Crime and the Law*, Europa Publications, London.

Davis, W. (1971) *Hints to Philanthropists*, Irish University Press, Dublin. First published Bath, 1821.

Deacon, A. (1976) *In Search of the Scrounger: The administration of unemployment insurance in Britain – 1920–1931*, Occasional Papers in Social Administration, no. 60, Bell & Sons, London.

Deacon, A. (1981) 'Unemployment and politics in Britain since 1945', in B. Sinfield and B. Showler (eds) *The Workless State*, Martin Robertson, London.

Deacon, A. and Bradshaw, J. (1983) *Reserved for the Poor: The means test in British social policy*, Basil Blackwell, Oxford.

Dean, H. (1988/9) 'Disciplinary partitioning and the privatisation of social security', *Critical Social Policy*, no. 24, Winter, pp. 74–82.

Deleuze, G. (1980) 'The Rise of the social', Foreword to J. Donzelot *The Policing of Families*, Hutchinson, London.

De Schweinitz, K. (1943) *England's Road to Social Security*, Oxford University Press, Oxford.

Digby, A. (1978) *Pauper Places*, Routledge & Kegan Paul, London and Boston, Mass.

Digby, A. (1989) *British Welfare Policy: Workhouse to workfare*, Faber & Faber, London.

Dixon, D. 'Thatcher's People: The British Nationality Act 1981', *Journal of Law and Society*, vol. 10, no. 2, pp. 161–80.

Donnison, D. (1981) *The Politics of Poverty*, Martin Robertson, Oxford.

Donzelot, J. (1979) 'The poverty of political culture', *Ideology and Consciousness*, no. 5, Spring, pp. 73–86.

Donzelot, J. (1980) *The Policing of Families*, Hutchinson, London.

Dreyfus, H. and Rabinow, P. *Michel Foucault: Beyond structuralism and hermeneutics*, Harvester Wheatsheaf, Hemel Hempstead and University of Chicago, Chicago.

Durbin, E. (1985) *New Jerusalems: The Labour Party and the economics of democratic socialism*, Routledge, London and Boston, Mass.

Eccleshall, R., Geoghegan, V., Jay, R. and Wilford, R. (eds) (1984) *Political Ideologies*, Hutchinson, London.

Edelman, B. (1980) 'The legalisation of the working class', in *Economy and Society*, vol. 9, no. 1, pp. 50–64.

Ehrenreich, B. and English, D. (1977) *For Her Own Good: 150 years of the experts' advice to women*, Anchor Press/Doubleday, New York and Pluto Press, London.

Esam, P. *et al.* (1985) *Who's To Benefit: A radical review of the social security system*, by P. Esam, R. Good and R. Middleton, Verso, London.

Esam, P. and Oppenheim, C. (1989) *A Charge on the Community: The poll tax benefits and the poor*, Child Poverty Action Group and Local Government Information Unit, London.

Evans, R. (1982) *The Fabrication of Virtue: English prison architecture 1750–1840*, Cambridge University Press, Cambridge.

Fawcett, H. (1871) *Pauperism: Its causes and remedies*, Cambridge University Press, London.

Fido, J. (1977) 'The Charity Organisation Society and social casework in London', in A. P. Donajgrodski (ed.) *Social Control in Nineteenth Century Britain*, Croom Helm, London.

Field, F. (1975) 'Social security: Are we getting value for money?' *Royal Society of Health Journal*, vol. 95, no. 4.

Field, F. (1982) *Poverty and Politics*, Heinemann, London.

Field, F. and Grieve, M. (1971) *Abuse and the Abused*, CPAG Evidence to the Fisher Inquiry, Child Poverty Action Group, London.

Finer Report (1974) *see under* HMSO.

Fisher Report (1973) *see under* HMSO.

Foucault, M. (1967) *Madness and Civilisation*, Tavistock/Random House, London.

Foucault, M. (1970) *The Order of Things*, Tavistock, London.

Foucault, M. (1977) *Discipline and Punish*, Allen Lane, Penguin Books, London.

Foucault, M. (1978) *The History of Sexuality*, vol. 1, Allen Lane, Penguin Books, London.

Foucault, M. (1980) 'On governmentality', *Ideology and Consciousness*, no. 6.

Franey, (1982) *Poor Law: The mass arrest of homeless claimants in Oxford*, Child Poverty Action Group/CHAR, London.

Fraser, A. (1978) 'The legal theory we need now', *Socialist Review*, no. 40–1.

Fraser, D. (1973) *The Evolution of the British Welfare State*, Macmillan, London.

Fraser, D. (ed.) (1976) *The New Poor Law in the Nineteenth Century*, Macmillan, London.

Friedman, M. (1960) *Capitalism and Freedom*, University of Chicago Press, Chicago.

Friedman, M. and Friedman, R. (1980) *Free to Choose*, Secker & Warburg, London.

Frisby, D. and Sayer, D. (1986) *Society*, Tavistock and Ellis Horwood, London and New York.

Galbraith, J. K. (1958) *The Affluent Society*, Penguin, Harmondsworth.

Gamble, A. (1988) *The Free Economy and the Strong State*, Macmillan, London.

Garland, D. (1985) *Punishment and Welfare*, Gower Publishing, Aldershot and Brookfield, Vermont.

Gatrell, V. and Hadden, T. (1972) 'Criminal statistics and their interpretation', in Wrigley, E. A. (ed.) *Nineteenth Century Society: Essays in the use of quantitative methods for the study of social data*, Cambridge University Press, Cambridge.

Gatrell, V. *et al*, (1980) *Crime and the Law*, by V. Gatrell, B. Lenman and G. Parker, Europa Publications, London.

George, V. (1968) *Social Security: Beveridge and after*, Routledge & Kegan Paul, London.

George, V. and Wilding, P. *Ideology and Social Welfare*, Routledge & Kegan Paul, London.

Gerando, J. M. Baron de (1833) *The Visitor of the Poor, Designed to aid in the formation and working of provident and other kindred societies*, translated and introduced by J. Tuckerman, Simpkin & Marshall, London and Boston.

Giddens, A. (1982) 'Class division, class conflict and citizenship rights', in A. Giddens (ed.) *Profiles and Critiques in Social Theory*, Macmillan, London.

Gilbert, B. B. (1966) *The Evolution of National Insurance in Britain*, Michael Joseph, London.

Gillis, J. (1981) *Youth and History*, Academic Press, London and New York.

Golding, P. (1982) 'It's the poor what gets the blame', *New Society*, April 1, vol. 60, no. 1011, pp. 12–13.

Golding, P. (ed.) (1986) *Excluding the Poor*, Child Poverty Action Group, London.

Golding, P. and Middleton, S. (1982) *Images of Welfare*, Martin Robertson, Oxford.

Gordon, C. (ed.) (1980) *Michel Foucault: Power/Knowledge*, Harvester Wheatsheaf, Hemel Hempstead.

Gordon, P. and Klug, F. *New Right, New Racism*, Searchlight Publications, London.

Gosden, P. (1973) *Self-Help: Voluntary associations in the nineteenth century*, Batsford Academic, London.

Graff, H. J. (1977) 'Pauperism, misery and vice: Illiteracy and criminality in the nineteenth century', *Journal of Social History*, vol. 11, no. 2.

Gramsci, A. (1971) *Selections from the Prison Notebooks*, Lawrence & Wishart, London.

Gray, R. Q. (1977) 'Bourgeois hegemony in Victorian Britain', in J. Bloomfield (ed.) *Class, Hegemony and Party*, Lawrence & Wishart, London.

Green, D. (1987) *The New Right: The counter-revolution in political, economic and social thought*, Harvester Wheatsheaf, Hemel Hempstead.

Green, P. (1981) *The Pursuit of Inequality*, Martin Robertson, Oxford and Pantheon Books, New York.

HMSO (1909) *Report of the Royal Commission on the Poor Laws and the Relief of Distress*, Cd. 4499, Majority Report.

HMSO (1942) *Social Insurance and Allied Services*, (The Beveridge Report) Cd. 6404.

HMSO (1944) Ministry of Reconstruction, *Employment Policy*, Cmd. 6527.

HMSO (1948–65) National Assistance Board, *Annual Reports*.

HMSO (1966) Supplementary Benefits Commission, *Annual Report*.

HMSO (1973) *Report of the Committee on Abuse of Social Security Benefits*, (The Fisher Report), Cmnd. 5228.

HMSO (1974) *Report of the Committee on One-Parent Families*, (The Finer Report), Cmnd. 5629.

HMSO (1985a) Department of Employment, *Employment: The Challenge for the Nation*, Cmnd. 9474.

HMSO (1985b) Department of Health and Social Security, *Reform of Social Security*, Cmnd. 9517.

HMSO (1988) Department of Employment, *Employment for the 1990s*, Cm. 540.

Hall, S. (1980) *Drifting into a Law and Order Society*, Cobden Trust, London.

Hall, S. (1988a) *The Hard Road To Renewal*, Verso, London.

Hall, S. (1988b) 'Brave new world', *Marxism Today*, October, pp. 24–9.

Hall, S. *et al.* (1978) *Policing the Crisis: Mugging, the state and law and order*, by S. Hall, C. Critcher, T. Jefferson, J. Clarke and B. Roberts, Macmillan, London and New York.

Hall, S. and Schwarz, B. (1985) 'State & society: 1880–1930', in M. Langan and B. Schwarz (eds) *Crises in the British State: 1880–1930*, Hutchinson/Centre for Contemporary Cultural Studies, London.

Hall, S. and Held, D. (1989) 'Left and Rights', *Marxism Today*, June.

Harris, J. (1972) *Unemployment and Politics*, Oxford University Press, Oxford.

Harris, J. (1977) *William Beveridge: A biography*, Oxford University Press, Oxford.

Harvey, A. (1960) *Casualties of the Welfare State*, Fabian Tract Number 321, Fabian Society, London.

Hastings & Jay (1965) *The Problem of the Problem Family*, Fabian Research Pamphlet.

Hay, D. (1975) 'Property, authority and the criminal law', in D. Hay, P. Linebaugh, J. Rule, E. P. Thompson, and C. Winslow, *Albion's Fatal Tree*, Penguin, Harmondsworth.

Hayek, F. (1944) *The Road to Serfdom*, Routledge & Kegan Paul, London.

Hayek, F. (1976) *The Mirage of Social Justice*, Routledge & Kegan Paul, London.

Healy, P. (1981) 'Liable lore', *New Society*, April, p. 61.

Hearn, J. (1978) *Domination, Legitimation and Resistance: The incorporation of the nineteenth-century English working class*, Greenwood Press, New York.

Hebdige, D. (1989) 'After the masses', *Marxism Today*, January.

Held, D. (1984) 'Power and legitimacy in contemporary Britain', in G. McLennan *et al.* (eds) *State and Society in Contemporary Britain*, Polity Press, Oxford.

Hemming, R. (1984) *Poverty and Incentives: The economics of social security*, Oxford University Press, Oxford and New York.

Hewitt, P. (1982) *The Abuse of Power*, Martin Robertson, Oxford.

Hillyard, P. and Percy-Smith, J. (1988) *The Coercive State*, Fontana, London.

Hirsch, F. (1977) *The Social Limits to Growth*, Routledge & Kegan Paul, London.

Hirst, P. (1981) 'The genesis of the social', in *Politics and Power*, no. 3, Routledge & Kegan Paul, London.

Hobsbawm, E. J. (1988) *Politics for a Rational Left*, Verso, London.

Hogg, Q. (1947) *The Case for Conservatism*, Penguin, Harmondsworth.

Holman, R. (1974) 'Social workers and the "inadequates" ', *New Society*, 5 September, pp. 608–10.

Holman, R. (1978) *Poverty: Explanations of social deprivation*, Martin Robertson, Oxford.

Hollis, C. (1957) *Death of a Gentleman*, London.

Hollis, P. (1973) *Class and Class Conflict in Nineteenth Century England: 1815–1850*, Routledge & Kegan Paul, London.

Hurd, D. (1988) 'Citizenship in the Tory democracy', *New Statesman and Society*, April 29.

Ignatieff, M. (1978) *A Just Measure of Pain: The penitentiary in the Industrial Revolution*, Macmillan, London and Pantheon Books, New York.

Jacques, M. (1988) 'New times', *Marxism Today*, October, p. 3.

Jessop, B. (1982) *The Capitalist State*, Macmillan, London.

Jones, C. (1977) *Immigration and Social Policy*, Tavistock, London.

Jones, C. (1983) *State Social Work and the Working Class*, Macmillan, London.

Jones, C. and Novak. T. (1979) 'The State and social policy' in P. Gorrigan (ed.) *Capitalism, State Formation and Marxist Theory*, Quartet Books, London.

Jones, K. and Williamson, K. (1979) 'The birth of the schoolroom', *Ideology and Consciousness*, no. 6, pp. 59–110.

Jordan, B. (1987) *Rethinking Welfare*, Basil Blackwell, Oxford and New York.

Joseph, K. (1966) *Social Security: The new priorities*, Conservative Political Centre, London.

Joseph, K. and Sumption, J. (1979) *Equality*, John Murray, London.

Kay, G. and Mott, J. (1982) *Political Order and The Law of Labour*, Macmillan, London and New York.

Keane, J. (1984) *Public Life and Late Capitalism*, Cambridge University Press, Cambridge.

Keane, J. (1988) *Democracy and Civil Society*, Verso, London.

Keating, P. (1976) *Into Unknown England*, Fontana/Collins, London.

Kincaid, J. (1973) *Poverty and Equality in Britain*, Penguin, Harmondsworth and New York.

Knight, B. J. and West, D. J. (1977) 'Criminality and welfare dependency in two generations', *Medicine, Science and Law*, vol. 17, no. 1.

Kolakowski, L. (1978) *Main Currents of Marxism*, 3 vols, Oxford University Press, Oxford.

Laclau, E. and Mouffe, C. (1985) *Hegemony and Socialist Strategy*, Verso, London.

Langan, M. (1985) 'Reorganising the labour market: 1880–1914', in M. Langan and B. Schwarz (eds) *Crises in the British State*, Hutchinson, London.

Lasch, C. (1980) *The Culture of Narcissism*, Abacus, London.

Laslett, P. (1974) *The World We have Lost*, Methuen, London.

Le Grand, J. (1982) *The Strategy of Equality*, Allen & Unwin, London.

Lea, J. (1979) 'Discipline and capitalist development', in National Deviancy Conference/Conference of Socialist Economists (eds) *Capitalism and the Rule of Law*, Hutchinson, London.

Leadbeater, C. (1988) 'Power to the person', *Marxism Today*, October, pp. 14–20.

Leadbeater, C. (1989) 'Back to the future', *Marxism Today*, May, pp. 12–18.

Lee, P. and Raban, C. (1988) *Welfare Theory and Social Policy*, Sage, London and Beverley Hills.

Lenin, V. I. (1968) 'Marxism and Revisionism' in V. I. Lenin, *Selected Works*, Progress Publications, Moscow.

Lewis, J. (1955) *The Growth and Nature of the Right*, Columbia University Press, New York.

Lewis, J. (1980) *The Politics of Motherhood*, Croom Helm, London and McGill Queens, Montreal.

Lis, C. and Soly, H. (1979) *Poverty and Capitalism in Pre-Industrial Europe*, Harvester Wheatsheaf, Hemel Hempstead.

Llewellyn-Smith, H. (1910) 'Economic security and unemployment insurance', *Economic Journal*, XX.

Loch, C. S. (1883) *How to help in cases of Distress*, Charity Organisation Society, London.

Loch, C. S. (1910) *Charity and Social Life*, Macmillan, London.

Loney, M. (1983) *Community against Government: The British community development project, 1968–78*, Heinemann, London.

Loney, M., Bocock, R., Clarke, J., Cochrane, A., Graham P., and Wilson, M. (eds) (1987) *The State or the Market*, Sage, London and New York.

Longford, F. A. P., 7th Earl of (1964) *Crime: A challenge to us all*, Labour Party Study Group, London.

Lonsdale, S. and Byrne, D. (1988) 'Social security: From state insurance to private uncertainty', *Yearbook of Social Policy*, 1987–88, Longmans Green, London.

Luckhaus, L. (1980) 'Towards an explanation of the welfare scrounger', MA

Thesis, Sheffield University, Centre for Criminological and Socio-Legal Studies.

McCord, N. (1976) 'The Poor Law and philanthropy', in D. Fraser (ed.) *The New Poor Law in the Nineteenth Century*, Macmillan, London.

MacDonald, A. (1893) *Abnormal Man*, Bureau of Education, Circular no. 4, Government Printing Office, Washington DC.

McLellan, D. (1975) *Marx*, Fontana, London.

Majority Report (1909): Report of the Royal Commission on the Poor Laws and the Relief of Distress, 3 vols, HMSO, Cd. 4499.

Malthus, T. R. (1970) *An Essay on the Principle of Population*, Penguin Harmondsworth, first published 1798.

Mann, K. (1986) 'The making of a claiming class: The neglect of agency in analyses of the Welfare State', *Critical Social Policy*, no. 15, pp. 62–74.

Mann, M. (1987) 'Ruling class strategies and citizenship', *Sociology*, vol. 21, no. 3, pp. 339–54.

Marshall, T. H. (1963) 'Citizenship and social class', in T. H. Marshall (ed.) *Sociology at the Crossroads*, Heinemann, London.

Marshall, T. H. (1981) 'Value problems of welfare capitalism', in T. H. Marshall (ed.), *The Right to Welfare*, Heinemann, London.

Marshall, T. H. (1985) *Social Policy*, 5th edition, A. M. Rees (ed.), Hutchinson, London and New Hampshire.

Marx, K. (1976) *Capital*, vol. I, Penguin, Harmondsworth.

Marx, K. and Engels, F. (1967) *The Communist Manifesto*, Penguin, Harmondsworth, first published 1848.

Meacher, M. (1974) *Scrounging on the Welfare: The scandal of the four-week rule*, Arrow Books, London.

Medick, H. (1976) 'The proto-industrial family economy: The structural function of household and family during the transition from peasant Society to industrial capitalism', *Social History*, vol. 1, no. 3.

Meiksins-Wood, E. (1986) *The Retreat from Class Politics*, Verso, London.

Melossi, D. (1979) 'Institutions of social control and capitalist organisation of work', in National Deviancy Conference/Conference of Socialist Economists (eds) *Capitalism and the Rule of Law*, Hutchinson, London.

Miles, R. (1987) 'Recent Marxist theories of nationalism and the issue of racism', *British Journal of Sociology*, vol. 38, no. 1, pp. 24–43.

Miller, R. and Wood, J. B. (1982) *What Price Unemployment?* Hobart Paper 92, Institute of Economic Affairs, Lancing, West Sussex.

Minford, P. (1987) 'The role of social services: A view from the New Right', in M. Loney *et al.* (eds) *The State or The Market*, Sage, London and Beverley Hills, 1987.

Minority Report (1909) of the Royal Commission on the Poor Laws and the Relief of Distress, Part 2, 'The Public Organisation of the Labour Market', London.

Minson, J. (1985 *Genealogies of Morals: Nietzsche, Foucault and the eccentricity of ethics*, Macmillan, London.

Mishra, R. (1969) 'A history of the Poor Law relieving officer: 1834–1948', Ph.D. Thesis, University of London.

Mishra, R. (1982) *Society and Social Policy*, Macmillan, London, revised edition, first published 1977.

Moore, J. (1989) 'The end of the line for poverty', speech to the Conservative Political Centre, May 11, Conservative Political Centre, London.

Moore, R. and Wallace, T. (1975) *Slamming the Door: The administration of immigration control*, Martin Robertson, London.

Moore, P. (1981) 'Scroungermania at the DHSS', *New Society*, January 21, vol. 55, no. 949, pp. 138–90.

Morris, M. and Patton, P. (1979) *Michel Foucault: Power, truth, strategy*, Feral Publications, Sydney.

Mouffe, C. (1988) 'The civics lesson', *New Statesman and Society*, October 7.

Mowat, C. (1961) *The Charity Organisation Society, 1869–1913: Its ideas and work*, Methuen, London.

Myrdal, G. (1960) *Beyond the Welfare State*, Duckworth, London and Yale University Press, New Haven, CT.

National Assistance Board, *see under* HMSO.

Nisbet, R. (1967) *The Sociological Tradition*, Heinemann, London.

Novak, T. (1975) 'Poverty and the State', Ph. D. Thesis, University of Durham.

Novak, T. (1988) *Poverty and the State*, Open University Press, London and Philadelphia.

O'Brien, P. (1982) *The Promise of Punishment: Prisons in nineteenth century France*, Princeton University Press, Princeton, NJ.

O'Neill, J. (1986) 'The disciplinary society: From Weber to Foucault', in *British Journal of Sociology*, vol. XXXVII. no. 1, pp. 42–60.

Page, R. (1971) *The Benefits Racket*, Stacey, London.

Parker, H. (1982) *The Moral Hazard of Social Benefits*, Research Monograph 37, Institute of Economic Affairs, London.

Parker, R. A. (1974) 'Social administration in search of generality', *New Society*, June 6, vol. 28, no. 609, pp. 566–8.

Parry, N. and Parry J. (1979) 'Social work, professionalism and the state', in N. and J. Parry, M. Rustin and C. Satyamurti (eds) *Social Work, Welfare and the State*, Edward Arnold, London.

Pasquino P. (1978) 'Theatrum Politicum. The Genealogy of Capital – Police and the state of prosperity', *Ideology and Consciousness*, no. 4, pp. 41–54.

Pasquino, P. (1980) 'Criminology: The birth of a special savoir', *Ideology and Consciousness*, No. 7, pp. 17–32.

Pasquino, P. (1981) 'Introduction to Lorenz von Stein', *Economy and Society*, vol. 10, no. 1, pp. 1–6.

Peacock, A. T. (1961) *The Welfare Society*, Unservile State Papers no. 2, Unservile State Group, London.

Pearson, G. (1983) *Hooligan: A history of respectable fears*, Macmillan, London.

Philp, A. and Timms, N. (1962) *The Problem of the 'Problem Family'*, Family Service Units, London.

Pinker, R. *The Idea of Welfare*, Heinemann, London.

Piven, F. F. and Cloward, R. A. (1972) *Regulating the Poor*, Tavistock, London and New York.

Plant, R. (1974) *Community and Ideology*, Routledge & Kegan Paul, London.

Popay, J. (1977) 'Fiddlers on the hoof; Moral panics and social security scroungers', Dissertation for MA, University of Essex, Sociology Department.

Poster, M. (1984) *Foucault, Marxism and History*, Polity Press, Oxford and Basil Blackwell, New York.

Powell, E. (1972) *Still to Decide*, Elliot Right Way Books, London.

Procacci, G. (1978) 'Social economy and the government of poverty', *Ideology and Consciousness*, no. 4.

Przeworski, A. (1980) 'Social democracy as a historical phenomenon', *New Left Review*, no. 122, pp. 27–58.

Przeworski, A. (1985) *Capitalism and Social Democracy*, Cambridge University Press, Cambridge.

Raban, J. (1989) *God, Man and Mrs Thatcher*, Chatto & Windus, London.

Rayner Report (1981) *see under* DE/DHSS.

Reeves, F. (1983) *British Racial Discourse*, Cambridge University Press, Cambridge.

Rentoul, J. (1987) *The Rich get Richer*, Unwin Hyman, London.

Richmond, M. (1917) *Social Diagnosis*, Free Press, Collier-Macmillan, New York.

Ritt, L. (1959) 'The Victorian conscience in action: The national association for the promotion of social science', Ph.D. Thesis, Columbia University.

Robbins, L. (1947) *The Economic Problem of War and Peace*, Macmillan, London.

Robson, W. A. (1976) *Welfare State and Welfare Society*, Allen & Unwin, London.

Room, G. (1979) *The Sociology of Welfare*, Basil Blackwell, Oxford.

Rose, M. E. (1976) 'Settlement, removal and the New Poor Law', in D. Fraser (ed.) *The New Poor Law in the Nineteenth Century*, Macmillan, London.

Rose, N. (1979) 'The psychological complex: Mental measurement and social administration', in *Ideology and Consciousness*, no. 5, pp. 5–68.

Rose, M. E. (1981) 'The crisis of poor relief in England: 1860–1890', in W. J. Mommsen (ed.) *The Emergence of the Welfare State in Britain and Germany*, Croom Helm, London.

Rose, N. (1985) *The Psychological Complex: Psychology, politics and society in England 1869–1939*, Routledge & Kegan Paul, London and Boston, Mass.

Ryle, M. (1988) *Ecology and Socialism*, Radius, London.

Salter, F. R. (1926) *Early Tracts on Poor Relief*, Methuen & Co., London.

Saville, J. (1965) 'Labour and Income Distribution', Socialist Register, pp. 147–62.

Scruton, R. (1980) *The Meaning of Conservativism*, Penguin, Harmondsworth.

Scull, A. T. (1977) *Decarceration: Community treatment and the deviant – a radical view*, Prentice Hall, Englewood Cliffs, NJ.

Searle, G. R. (1971) *The Quest for National Efficiency*, Basil Blackwell, Oxford.

Searle, G. R. (1976) *Eugenics and Politics in Britain: 1900–1914*, Basil Blackwell, Oxford.

Sellin, T. (1949) *Pioneering in Penology*, University of Pennsylvania Press, Philadelphia.

Shorter, E. (1981) *The Making of the Modern Family*, Fontana/Collins, London and Basic Books, New York.

Silver, A. (1970) 'The demand for order in civil society', in P. Bordua (ed.) *The Police: Six sociological essays*, Wiley, London.

Sivanandan, A. (1976) 'Race, class and the state: The black experience in Britain', *Race and Class*, vol. XVII, no. 4, pp. 347–67.

Slack, K. (1966) *Social Administration and the Citizen*, Michael Joseph, London.

Smart, B. (1983) *Foucault, Marxism and Critique*, Routledge & Kegan Paul, London and Boston, Mass.

Smelser, N. J. (1968) 'Sociological history: The Industrial Revolution and the

British working-class family', in N. J. Smelser (ed.) *Essays in Sociological Explanation*, Prentice-Hall, New York.

Squires, P. (1981) 'Internal security and social insecurity', *Working Papers in European Criminology*, no. 3, European Group for the Study of Deviance and Social Control, Derry, Northern Ireland.

Squires, P. (1984) '*Studies in the criminalisation of poverty: Pauperism, pathology and policing*', Ph.D. Thesis, 2 vols, University of Bristol.

Statistical Society of London (1833) *Annual Report*.

Stedman-Jones, G. (1971) *Outcast London*, Oxford University Press, Oxford.

Stevenson, O. (1973) *Claimant or Client*, Allen & Unwin, London.

Strachey, J. (1907) *The Manufacture of Paupers*, John Murray, London.

Supplementary Benefits Commission, *see under* HMSO.

Symons, J. C. (1849) *Tactics for the Times: As regards the condition and treatment of the dangerous classes*, John Oliver, London.

Tawney, R. H. (1938) *Equality*, Allen & Unwin, London, revised edition.

Taylor-Gooby, P. (1981) 'The empiricist tradition in social administration', *Critical Social Policy*, vol. 1, no. 2, pp.6–21.

Taylor-Gooby, P. (1983) 'The distributional compulsion and the moral order of the Welfare State', in A. Ellis and K. Kumar (eds) *Dilemmas of Liberal Democracies*, Tavistock, London and New York.

Tebbit, N. (1988) *The New Consensus*, Radical Society Pamphlet no. 1, The Radical Society, London.

Thane, P. (1978) *The Origins of British Social Policy*, Croom Helm, London.

Thane, P. (1982) *The Foundations of the Welfare State*, Longman, London and New York.

Thatcher, M. (1985) 'Facing the new challenge', Speech to the Women's Royal Voluntary Service Annual Conference, reproduced in C. Ungerson (ed.) *Women and Social Policy*, Macmillan, London.

Thatcher, M. (1988) Address to the General Assembly of the Church of Scotland (reprinted in J. Raban (1989) *God, Man and Mrs Thatcher*, Chatto & Windus, London).

Therborn, G. (1977) 'The Rule of capital and the rise of democracy', *New Left Review*, no. 103.

Thoenes, P. (1966) *The Elite in the Welfare State*, Faber & Faber, London.

Thompson, E. P. (1963) *The Making of the English Working Class*, Penguin, Harmondsworth.

Thompson, E. P. (1975) *Whigs and Hunters: The origin of the Black Act*, Penguin, Harmondsworth.

Thompson, E. P. (1978) *The Poverty of Theory*, Merlin, London.

Thornton, P. (1989) *Decade of Decline: Civil liberties in the Thatcher years*, National Council for Civil Liberties, London.

Titmuss, R. (1955) 'War and social policy', in R. Titmuss, *Essays on 'the Welfare State'*, Allen & Unwin, London, second edition 1963.

Titmuss, R. (1958) *Essays on 'the Welfare State'* , Unwin University Books, London.

Titmuss, R. (1959) 'The irresponsible society', in R. Titmuss (1987a).

Titmuss, R. (1962) *Income Distribution and Social Change*, Allen & Unwin, London.

Titmuss, R. (1964) 'The limits of the Welfare State', *New Left Review*, no. 27, pp. 28–37.

Titmuss, R. (1970) *The Gift Relationship: from human blood to social policy*, Allen & Unwin, London.

Titmuss. R. (1971) 'Welfare rights, law and discretion', in Titmuss (1987a).

Titmuss, R. (1974) *Social Policy: An introduction*, Allen & Unwin, London.

Titmuss, R. (1987a) *The Philosophy of Welfare*, edited B. Abel-Smith and K. Titmuss, Allen & Unwin, London.

Titmuss, R. (1987b) 'Welfare State and welfare society', in R. Titmuss (1987a).

Tomlinson, J. (1981) *Problems of British Economic Policy: 1870–1945*, Methuen, London and New York.

Townsend, P. (1961) *The Last Refuge*, Routledge & Kegan Paul, London.

Townsend, P. (1975) *Sociology and Social Policy*, Penguin, Harmondsworth.

Tuckerman, J. (1833) 'Introduction' Gerando *Visitor of the Poor*, Simpkin & Marshall, London.

Turner, B. (1986) *Citizenship and Capitalism: The debate over reformism*, Allen & Unwin, London and Boston, Mass.

Von Leyden, W. (1976) 'On justifying inequality', in A. Blowers and K. Thompson (eds) *Inequalities, Conflict and Change*, Open University Press, Milton Keynes.

Walzer, M. (1983) *Spheres of Justice: A defence of pluralism and equality*, Robertson, Oxford.

Wappshott, N. and Brock, G. (1983), *Thatcher*, Macdonald, London.

Ward, S. (1985) 'The political background' in S. Ward (ed.) *DHSS in Crisis*, Child Poverty Action Group, London.

Watson, D. (1980) *Caring for Strangers*, Routledge & Kegan Paul, London and Boston, Mass.

Weale, A. (1983) *Political Theory and Social Policy*, Macmillan, London.

Webb, B. (1979) *My Apprenticeship*, reprinted by Cambridge University press for the London School of Economics (first published 1948).

Webb, S. and Webb, B. (1909) *The Minority Report of the Poor Law Commission*, 2 vols, Longmans, London.

Webb, S. and Webb, B. (1910), *English Poor Law Policy*, Longmans Green & Co., London.

Webb, S. and Webb, B (1926), *The Decline of Capitalist Civilisation*, Longmans Green & Co., London.

Webb, S. and Webb, B (1927) *English Poor Law History*, vol. 1 'The Old Poor Law', Longmans Green & Co., London.

Webb, S. and Webb, B. (1929) *English Poor Law History*, vol. 2 'The last hundred years', Longmans Green & Co., London.

Weisser, M. (1979) *Crime and Punishment in Early Modern Europe*, Harvester Wheatsheaf, Hemel Hempstead.

Wikeley, N. (1989) 'Unemployment benefit, the state and the labour market', *Journal of Law and Society*, vol. 16, no. 3, pp. 291–309

Williams, F. (1987) 'Racism and the discipline of social policy', *Critical Social Policy*, no. 20, Autumn, pp. 4–29.

Williams, F. (1989) *Social Policy: A critical introduction*, Polity Press, Basil Blackwell, Oxford and New York.

Williams, J. and Williams, K. (1987) *A Beveridge Reader*, Allen & Unwin, London.

Williams, K. (1981) *From Pauperism to Poverty*, Routledge & Kegan Paul, London and Boston, Mass.

Wootton, B. (1959), *Social Science and Social Pathology*, Routledge & Kegan Paul, London.

Yeo, S. (1979) 'Working class association, private capital, welfare and the state in the late nineteenth and early twentieth centuries', in N. Parry and J. Parry (eds) *Social Work, Welfare and the State*, Edward Arnold, London.

Young A.F. and Ashton, E.T. (1956) *British Social Work in the Nineteenth Century*, Routledge and Kegan Paul, London.

Young, J. (1981) 'Thinking seriously about crime: Some models of criminology', in M. Fitzgerald, G.McLennan and J. Pawson (eds) *Crime and Society*, Routledge & Kegan Paul, London.

Index